In Performance

EDITED BY
CAROL MARTIN

In Performance is a book series devoted to national and global theater of the twenty-first century. Scholarly essays providing the theatrical, cultural, and political contexts for the plays and performance texts introduce each volume. The texts are written both by established and emerging writers, translated by accomplished translators and aimed at people who want to put new works on stage, read diverse dramatic and performance literature, and study diverse theater practices, contexts, and histories in light of globalization.

In Performance has been supported by translation and editing grants from the following organizations:

The Book Institute, Krakow
TEDA Project, Istanbul
The Memorial Fund for Jewish Culture, New York
Polish Cultural Institute, New York
Zbigniew Raszewski Theatrical Institute, Warsaw
Adam Mickiewicz Institute, Warsaw
Goethe-Institut, New York
Austrian Cultural Forum, New York

OBLIVION

and Other Plays from Post-Revolutionary Iran

EDITED BY
NAHID AHMADIAN
AND ALI-REZA MIRSAJADI

TRANSLATED BY
NAHID AHMADIAN,
ALI-REZA MIRSAJADI,
AND HESAM SHARIFIAN

LONDON NEW YORK CALCUTTA

Seagull Books, 2025

ISBN 978 1 8030 9 522 6

British Library Cataloging-in-Publication Data
A catalog record for this book is available from the British Library

Book designed by Bishan Samaddar, Seagull Books, Calcutta, India

CONTENTS

FIGURE 1. The City Theatre, Tehran, 2019. *Photograph by Nahid Ahmadian*.

INTRODUCTION

NAHID AHMADIAN and ALI-REZA MIRSAJADI

> "Fearless of the rise and fall of the price of history on the
> other side of the wall,
> I will write your history—
> But in my own language!"
>
> —Hamid Amjad, *Oblivion*

In the final moments of Hamid Amjad's monumental play *Oblivion*, Jiang and his sister Huang console one another as they mourn the loss of their parents. Set in the early years of Imperial China around the third century BCE, the play explores the fraught relationship between historical narratives and power. Before his death, the pair's father was a respected warrior and historian, chronicling the shifting politics of his land, a history that he acknowledged was born from violence and militarism. When an act of betrayal turns his historical opus into ashes, the patriarch takes his own life, and Jiang and Huang must chart a path forward amid the chaos and sorrow. Huang turns to her brother, imploring him to write a new book detailing the history of their people. Jiang attests, "I am that history, myself. / Not because I have rewritten and reviewed it, / Not because I know it by heart, / But because I have lived it, / I was burnt by it and born with it!" When first performed for audiences at a staged reading at Tehran's Shams

Hall in 2011, Jiang's assertion of lived experience spoke to the ways tumultuous Iranian history resonates across time and space and is embedded within the collective memory of the Iranian people.

Like *Oblivion*, each of the plays in this anthology is invested in the contemporary lives of Iranians, even when their settings and characters allude to other nations and historical moments. Written by playwrights who have come to prominence in different developmental eras of Iranian theater, these five plays represent a unique fusion of the style and structures of Western drama and Persian cultural aesthetics and indigenous performance. While Iranian indigenous theater and performance date back millennia, the Western-style plays in this anthology (written between 1995 and 2019) represent a brief span of that history. The historical and cultural context for these plays and the particular hybrid form of theater that they represent necessitates both an overview of Persian indigenous performance practices and an account of the changes in Iranian theater as it incorporated Western dramatic forms.[1] Considering these five plays in relation to one another, we interrogate the special poetics of contemporary Iranian theater and performance, with its signature style of linguistic and thematic ambiguity, its melding of the past and present, and its deep engagement with social realities.

---

1 The country known today as Iran was called Persia throughout much of its history until the name was officially changed by Reza Shah Pahlavi in 1935. In this text, we use "Persian" to describe the cultural and historical legacies of the country that predate the name change. We use "Iranian" to describe the people, culture, and politics of twenty- and twenty-first-century Iran.

Histories of Iranian theater have often found it difficult to locate the precise origins of Iran's theatrical tradition. Bahram Beyzaie—a preeminent Iranian playwright, filmmaker, and historian whose play, *The Sacrifice of Senemar*, is included in this anthology—was among the first to write a scholarly text on the nation's vibrant performance tradition in his influential *Namāyesh dar Irān* [Theater in Iran], published in 1965.[2] Beyzaie traces the roots of Iranian theater to ancient Persian performance traditions that date back millennia. In *The History of Theater in Iran*, Willem Floor locates the origins of Persian performance even earlier in the dialogues of the *Avesta* (*c.* 1000 BCE), asserting that "the first recorded dramatic performance in Iran was noted by Xenophon in around 400 BCE" (2005: 20). Floor acknowledges that "Western-style drama was indeed introduced in Iran in the nineteenth century," but Iranian folk theater and performance have much more ancient roots, although this is "not necessarily of the kind that Westerners identify as theater," particularly given its focus on

2 Although Beyzaie's book is among the best-known and most commonly cited historical texts on Iranian theater, other historians have also engaged with this subject. The first complete history of Iranian theater was Abolghasem Janati Ata'i's *The Origin of Performance in Iran* (1954), a genealogical study of the indigenous forms of Iranian theater that traced its roots and influences to the broader Persian-speaking world, Mesopotamia, and India. Majid Rezvani's *Theater and Dance in Iran* (1962) was another study of the origin of these artforms in ancient Persia, offering occasional analyses of different forms of performances in the Middle East. As of this writing, nearly 250 works of Iranian theater scholarship—including histories, bibliographies, transcripts, interviews, biographies, and dissertations—have been published (primarily in Persian, English, and French), some of which have made significant contributions to this scholarship. For more information on Iranian theater historiography, see Nahid Ahmadian (2022).

"improvisation emphasizing the limited role that written text played" (2005: 13–14).

This tendency towards oral and physical performance traditions not governed by dramatic texts is deeply ingrained in Iranian culture because its historical legacies intersect with the wider Muslim and MENA world. Although Iran has a formidable literature—such as Ferdowsi's monumental historical-mythological tome, the *Shahnameh*,[3] and the poetry of Omar Khayyam, Rumi, and Hafiz—its performance practices have largely grown out of oral storytelling that bridges memorization and recitation with improvisation and a deeply engaged relationship with audiences. One of the earliest known styles of Persian performance is *naqqāli*, a tradition of minstrel storytelling dating to the court of Median King Astyages (r. 564–550 BCE) (Floor 2005: 82). In medieval Persia, itinerant bards and minstrels sang the stories of gods and deceased heroes to audiences, who would often congregate at bazaars, town squares, and later teahouses to watch performances. While *naqqāli* has persisted through the ages, it has also evolved into other performance forms like *pardeh-khāni* (or *soorat-khāni*), which incorporates the use of a large, embroidered tapestry backdrop, upon which is depicted the most famous scenes from the story being told.[4]

---

3 The *Shahnameh*, the master epic of Persian literature, was written by Abol-Qasem Ferdowsi, the eleventh-century Iranian poet and literary scholar. Recounting the legendary lives and adventures of Iranian kings, heroes, and mythical creatures, the book conveys Iran's pre-Islamic mythology and history in some 50,000 couplets. *The Persian Book of Kings*, as it is translated by Dick Davis, has been a monument of global classical literature and a source of inspiration for many since its composition.

4 According to Beyzaie, *naqqāli* has also generated other performance forms such as *sokhan-vari* (rhapsody), *hamleh-khāni* (a form of *naqqāli* with religious themes

Naqqāl and *pardeh-khān* performers rely on a deeply expressive voice and exaggerated movement to captivate audiences, embodying many characters through the telling of a single story. Tales from the *Shahnameh* feature heavily in *naqqāli*, whereas *pardeh-khāni* traditionally centers on religious stories, especially those related to the Ashura narratives, which focus on the events surrounding the martyrdom of Hussein, the third Shi'a Imam in 680 CE.[5] Like *pardeh-khāni*, *rowzeh-khāni* is an experience of shared physicalized mourning of the passions of Imam Hussein and other Shi'a figures, during which spectators are implicitly encouraged to cry, wail, and beat their chests while seated, listening to the narration by the *rowzeh-khān* (the storyteller). This outward performance of grief is a means of transforming the historical narrative into a communal reenactment of grief and an expression of sorrow among the audience.

Persian texts dating back to the fifth century BCE allude to puppets, although historians are unclear as to when distinctly Persian forms of puppetry developed (Floor 2005: 62). These include, most prominently, *kheimeh-shab-bāzi*, Iran's marionette tradition, which Omar Khayyam (1048–1131) wrote about in his *Rubaiyat*. A typical

---

and stories), and *rowzeh-khāni*, which is discussed in this introduction. See Bahram Beyzaie (1965) and Peter Chelkowski (1989).

5 According to the Ashura narratives, Hussein was murdered in a bloody massacre in the desert of Karbala (about sixty miles outside Baghdad), alongside seventy-two of his relatives (sons, brothers, cousins, and companions) as he fought for his right to the esteemed position of the Caliphate. Hussein's death is believed to have occurred on the Ashura, or "tenth," day of Muharram, which has since become the month of commemorative mourning for Shi'ite practitioners. His death and the battle that preceded it figure heavily in Ashura mourning rituals that take place during the month of Muharram, including *pardeh-khāni*, *rowzeh-khāni*, and *ta'ziyeh*.

FIGURE 2. A storyteller in *naqqāli* using a tapestry to tell the tale of an historic battle, 2016. *Courtesy of Tiwall.com.*

kheimeh-shab-bāzi troupe consists of three performers: a puppeteer, a musician, and a narrator who functions as the interlocutor. The puppeteer performs all the puppet roles, and a reed held in their mouth lends a squeaky, buzzing tone to some of the characters' voices. The narrator and puppeteer play off one another in their dialogue and improvised banter, and the narrator typically accompanies the performance on the *tombak* (a hollow drum) while the musician plays the *kamāncheh* (a stringed instrument like the violin). Of Iran's puppetry traditions, *kheimeh-shab-bāzi* is the most developed and detailed in its customs, whereas glove puppetry (*lo'bat-bāzi*) and shadow puppetry (*khayāl-bāzi* or *sāyeh-bāzi*) have been practiced for centuries in a variety of different fashions. Persian puppetry is typically unscripted, relying on the improvisation of its performers and their

FIGURE 3. Performers of *kheimeh-shab-bāzi*, early nineteenth century. *Photograph courtesy of Kheimeh Shab Bazi Museum, Tehran.*

knowledge of a trove of passed-down stories and character archetypes still common today.

Taqlid, Iran's comedic performance tradition, is often compared to the Italian *Commedia dell'arte*. Like its European cousin, *taqlid* relies on stock characters and scenarios, and the actors improvise dialogue and incorporate physical comedy, which fuel the performance. Although the Persian comedic tradition has its roots in pre-Islamic times, references to *taqlid* first became particularly abundant in historical texts from the Safavid period (1501–1736), when performers were invited to entertain at the royal courts (Floor 2005: 33). Traveling troupes typically performed in teahouses or in residential courtyards, where they would place wooden slabs over pools and fountains to construct an elevated stage (known as *takhteh-howzi* or *ru-howzi*, which roughly translates to "planks over the pool"). Historically, music and dance have been significant features of *taqlid* performance, as has the use of blackface for the central clown-servant characters.[6]

---

6 As of this writing, blackface performance (known as *siyāh-bāzi*) is still common in Iran, particularly through the character of Haji Firuz, a beloved Black clown character who rings in the Persian Nowruz (New Year). During this time of year, blackface performance becomes commonplace throughout schools, television programs, and on the streets, as men put on the character's traditional red ensemble (complete with tambourine) and paint their faces, leading communities in song and celebration. There is some debate among Iranians as to the origins and poetics of Persian blackface performance and whether it should remain a common practice. Some Iranians have begun to critique and push back against the ubiquity of blackface in Nowruz festivities and *taqlid*. In *The Color Black: Enslavement and Erasure in Iran* (2024), Beeta Baghoolizadeh traces the history of *siyāh-bāzi* within the nation's slave trade and performances by Black minstrels in the Qajar courts, arguing that Iranian media and culture has worked to simultaneously erase its history of slavery while also equating enslavement with blackness. On the other side of this debate are artists and scholars like Beyzaie, whose 2016 *taqlid*-influenced play *Tarabnameh* was produced at Stanford University using blackface performers. Beyzaie justified this choice by citing ancient Persian historical precedents that predated Iran's history of African slavery, noting that in this culture, the color black was associated with "power, youth, freshness, and fertility" ("Tarabnameh: Part 2, Discussion"). Situating the roots of ancient Persian deities and rituals in their people's agricultural life, he reports evidence of blackface performance in the *nowruzi-khāni* (Nowruz storytelling) tradition, dating back to pre-Islamic times. In these performances, two actors would mask their faces with white and black goat furs, seemingly symbolic of the blackened face of the spring deity, and proceed to brawl over a woman. The white-masked actor represented old age and the black-masked performer symbolized youth and fertility; the latter would defeat the white performer and win over the woman. Referring to Anna Kransowolska's piece, *Some Key Figures of Iranian Calendar Mythology*, Angelita Reyes also finds evidence of "ritual enactments of

Like *taqlid*, *ta'ziyeh* is performed by an ensemble of virtuosic actors, although its narratives are predominantly pulled from tragic moments in Shi'a history surrounding the events of Ashura during the Islamic month of mourning, Muharram. While *rowzeh-khāni* narrates these stories through sung recitation by a single storyteller, *ta'ziyeh* brings the parables to life through the embodiment of its characters by multiple actors and the use of mimesis. Historians are unsure of the exact origins of *ta'ziyeh*. Some believe it to have emerged from the intersection of Muharram ritual processions (where people parade through the streets chanting, crying, drumming, and carrying banners) and the more narrative-focused ritual of *rowzeh-khāni* (Mottahedeh 2005: 26). Others date *ta'ziyeh* back to the distinctly Persian rituals surrounding the death of Siyavash, a mythological Persian prince who was killed in a foreign land for a crime that he did not commit, as detailed in the *Shahnameh* (Sahamizadeh 2022: 9).

While many of the *ta'ziyeh* performances one might witness today across Iran resemble one another, they existed in a much more varied rustic form prior to the sixteenth century. With the founding of the Safavid dynasty and its rulers' intent upon creating a collective national identity for Persia by establishing the state religion of Shi'a Islam, *ta'ziyeh* became more formalized in its structure and started receiving governmental support. *Ta'ziyeh* reached the height of its popularity during the Qajar dynasty (1794–1925), and the monarch Naser al-Din Shah even constructed the majestic Tekiyeh Dowlat in the style of London's Royal Albert Hall in 1868 to house these performances. *Ta'ziyeh* has a significant place among Persian indigenous performance

---

cosmic renewals [that] had role players 'dressed in rags and with *blackened face* [. . .] red cap and suit,'" an image reminiscent of Haji Firuz (2019: 538).

FIGURE 4. Actors reenacting the Battle of Karbala in a *ta'ziyeh* performance outside a mosque, 2014. *Photograph Courtesy of Surf Iran.*

traditions, one that has been particularly legible from the vantage of Western theater, given its common use of scripted texts, multiple actors, and theatrical staging.[7] Substantial scholarship has been written

7 The *ta'ziyeh* of the Western imagination was first introduced during the Shiraz Arts Festival, which was overseen by Queen Farah Pahlavi and held from 1967 to 1977 to promote global exchange through performances by Iranian and international artists in the fields of theater, music, and dance. As a part of the 1967 and 1970 festivals, the television actor and director Parviz Sayyad was hired to stage *ta'ziyeh* performances, which were styled as a spectacle and featured various inauthentic and Western-inspired characteristics such as a children's choir (Afshar 2019: 30). Although these performances fascinated the international guests of the festival (including such theatrical luminaries as Peter Brook, Jerzy Grotowski, Tadeusz Kantor, and Robert Wilson), they presented and disseminated a version of *ta'ziyeh* that was significantly removed from its traditional practice across Iran. For the 1976 festival, an international symposium on *ta'ziyeh* was organized, and theater director Mohammad Ghaffari produced and directed seven different *ta'ziyeh* pieces in two villages outside of Shiraz. Ghaffari grew up watching *ta'ziyeh*

on *ta'ziyeh* in the West where it is often regarded as the primary form of theatrical performance emerging from the Islamic faith. This notion, however, ignores the wide range of performance practices in Iran and the Greater Middle East, which have grown and developed since before and throughout the time of Islamic rule.

THE DEVELOPMENT OF EUROPEAN DRAMA IN IRAN

Many of Iran's indigenous performance traditions experienced a heyday between the Safavid and Qajar dynasties, during which time the Persian empire found a unified national consciousness, established Shi'a Islam as its state religion, and experienced significant economic and cultural growth. This period was also a time of great cultural exchange, as Persia became a site of fascination for European travelers, and Persian emissaries returned home from trips abroad, sharing accounts of Europe's architecture, music, literature, and theater. Because of these interactions, the Persian rulers decided to prioritize the importation and understanding of European culture, as a step to integrate Iran with the global project of modernity.

---

and did significant research and outreach in preparation for the project, and the resulting productions were much more closely aligned with traditional *ta'ziyeh* than the earlier versions at the Shiraz Festival. Still, the framing of these pieces through an international festival (with 10,000 spectators crowded into the villages to attend) once again communicated a version of *ta'ziyeh* to global audiences that was quite removed from its traditional indigenous practice. Over the next three decades, scholarship on *ta'ziyeh* grew in popularity in the West, eclipsing all other forms of theater in Iran and generating a specific understanding of *ta'ziyeh* performance and its intent that was distanced from its context in both Shi'a religious practice and Iranian theatrical tradition. For more information on *ta'ziyeh*, see Jamshid Malekpour (2004); Winter 2005 special edition on *ta'ziyeh* in *TDR: The Drama Review*; and Peter Chelkowski (2010).

That mission gained momentum in the nineteenth century, which began a time of great theatrical transformation in Iran, led by Naser al-din Shah's translation project and the Dar al-Fonun.[8] With the emergence of Persian translations of Moliere and Shakespeare plays in particular, Persianate playwrights started crafting dramatic texts in this European mode. Although theater makers, performers, and writers had flourished in Iran for millennia, replicating European-style dramatic literature was a new development. In this context, Fat'h-Ali Akhundzadeh (1812–78) is generally recognized as the first Persian playwright, and he wrote satirical plays originally in Azeri Turkish, which were then translated into Persian. The nineteenth century also brought a new class of European-educated Iranians, such as Mirza Malkom Khan (1833–1903), who studied in both Persia and France and whose satirical political plays reflect familiarity with European dramatic traditions. Many of the plays written by Akhundzadeh and Malkom Khan were meant to function primarily as dramatic literature—texts to be read and not necessarily performed. Iranian theater scholar Farindokht Zahedi believes that the earliest performances of Western-style theater

8 The Dar al-Fonun was Persia's first secular high school, established in 1851 by Amir Kabir, the prime minister and chief commander of the military for Naser al-din Shah. Mostly serving the sons of aristocrats, this polytechnic school taught "classes in foreign languages, political science, engineering, agriculture, mineralogy, medicine, veterinary medicine, military sciences, and band music" (Ganjeh 2017: 95). Although the school was invested in disseminating European culture to the Persian elite, it had a particular investment in its relationship to France: the official language of the school was French, most of the instructors were French nationals, and upon construction of a theater at Dar al-Fonun in 1882, it was christened with an inaugural production of Moliere's *The Misanthrope*. In all, the school greatly contributed to the growth of Persian–European relations and cultural exchange in the late nineteenth century.

in Iran were courtesy of Armenian and Zoroastrian acting troupes, who performed translated versions of European plays primarily for the Persian royal court (2006: 139). Although some of these performances are documented, it is unclear in what capacity and style they were staged. It is also documented that some *taqlid* performers acted in these European plays for Persian royalty, and they fused their comedic stylings and improvisatory approach to language with the narratives of the likes of Moliere and Shakespeare. As European-style theater grew in popularity throughout the first half of the twentieth century, many performers of the indigenous traditions worked to incorporate it within their existing practice. At the same time, Iranian playwrights similarly sought out ways to bring indigenous performance practices into their texts, beginning a hybrid theater tradition that continues to this day and is evidenced by *The Sacrifice of Senemar* and *Oblivion* collected in this anthology.

In the first half of the twentieth century, the Constitutional Revolution (1906–11) proved to be a paradigm shift. In that moment, politically driven Western-style agit-prop theater proliferated in Iranian cities. Saeed Talajooy writes that during the first two decades of the twentieth century, Iranian playwrights "cared more for constructing their sociopolitical or cultural critiques than for the qualities of their works as performance pieces. Nevertheless, these performances, particularly those held in parks, functioned as vehicles for conveying modern ideas to the minds of average Iranians" (2015: 377). Various amateur theater companies were born in the aftermath of this revolution, including the Te'ātr-e Melli (The National Theater), Sherkat-e Farhang (The Culture Company) and Komedi-e Iran (The Iranian Comedy). When Reza Shah Pahlavi took over the throne in 1925, his attempts to modernize Iran in the model of Western nations resulted in the diminishment of *ta'ziyeh* as a prominent theatrical practice, as the new king sought to distance Iran's global image from its religious practices, which he imagined to be a misrepresentation of the nation's identity (Beyzaie 1965: 150). Political dissent in the theater was also banned, which put pressure on playwrights like Ali Nasr to produce work that explored themes aligned with the political agenda of the government. Talajooy explains that "the period between 1918 and 1941 is [. . .] characterized by the rise of musical performances, professional theater companies, emphasis on décor, costume and directorial standards, the establishment of the first actor training institutes and the first appearance of Muslim women on mixed public stages," while playwriting became a secondary pursuit (2015: 388).

It was not until the abdication of Reza Shah Pahlavi in 1941 and the consequent loosening of restrictions on the nation's political speech that a distinctly Iranian "modern" theatrical performance tradition became prevalent. Iranian playwrights of this era merged Persian aesthetics and performance traditions with the European dramatic forms seen on the country's stages, fueling a distinctly political theatrical movement. They wrote provocative plays and many of the nation's theater companies aligned themselves with leftist groups and/or the Tudeh Party (Iran's communist party). According to Mohammad Faique, at the start of the 1950s, "about a hundred different plays had been staged within the course of a few years" (1999: 106). However, M. R. Ghanoonparvar explains that in the aftermath of the 1953 coup d'état that overthrew Prime Minister Mohammad Mossadegh and reinstated the Pahlavi dynasty under Reza Shah's son, "martial law and strict censorship were imposed, and Persian dramatists focused their attention of necessity on artistic aspects of drama and production techniques [. . .] few critically significant plays were written in Persia [at this time], at first because of political confusion and then because of censorship" (2014 [1995]).

This focus on artistic merit created a newfound emphasis on stagecraft, acting, directing, and design. Iranian plays written during the first half of the twentieth century resembled the dramatic models of *ta'ziyeh* with what Talajooy calls "heroic religiosity and heightened depravity [that] reinforced religious ideals" and "in that it created a communal space where heightened models of human behavior were contrasted. The difference [from *ta'ziyeh*] was in the distance created between the actors and the audience and its concern with topical issues" (2015: 378–79). The declamatory style of *ta'ziyeh* did not fit well with the European plays being staged, and the Iranian performances of these canonical texts paled in comparison to those of touring companies. This led to a new European style of actor training in Iran, and the Tehran Acting School was constructed in 1939. Vahram Papazian (1888–1968), an Armenian theater director who had worked extensively in Russia, Turkey, and Armenia, was invited to lead the school. Throughout the 1940s, theatrical training institutions grew in Iran, and many of these early instructors learned stagecraft, design, acting, and directing in Moscow and Germany. Perhaps the most influential acting teacher was 'Abd al-Hussein Nushin, who established the Farhang Theater in 1944, staging plays like Ben Jonson's *Volpone* and Maurice Maeterlinck's *The Blue Bird*. Nushin trained in Moscow and Paris, and he is credited with bringing Stanislavskian acting methods to Iran. His famous acting classes placed an emphasis on speech and voice training using the *Shahnameh* as a performance text. In 1952, Nushin became the first Iranian to publish a book on acting.

The Tehran Acting School and other training programs of the time were given added weight with the official support of the new Pahlavi government in the mid-1950s, at which point they transitioned into university degree programs. Between 1956 and 1958, the University of Tehran began offering theater courses, and to lead them, it hired three American professors—Frank Davidson, George Quinby, and Francis S. Belcher—instead of Iranian practitioner-teachers like Nushin and Papazian. The professors taught acting, stage design, make-up, costume design, playwriting, theory, script analysis, and the history and development of the American theater (Emami 1987: 148–50). Their actor training emphasized the Stanislavski method, and the department productions were mostly realistic. Meanwhile, Iran's first great generation of stage directors—Hamid Samandarian, Ali Rafie, and the female director Pari Saberi—were studying the theatrical avant-garde in Europe with some of the foremost artistic innovators of the period. They credited their influences as Max Reinhardt, Bertolt Brecht, Jacques Lecoq, and the work of Western absurdists like Samuel Beckett, Eugene Ionesco, Arthur Adamoc, Jean Genet, Max Frisch, Harold Pinter, Edward Albee, and Fernando Arrabal, all of whom were translated into Persian and became very influential on playwriting and staging practices in the 1960s as Iranian state censorship increased. In 1969, Samandarian and Saberi founded the School of Theater within the University of Tehran, and many of Iran's theater makers today are still trained in the methods originally pioneered by these luminaries.

The influence of the Shiraz Arts Festival (1967–1977) on theatrical work was particularly significant, and global theatrical visionaries such as Peter Brook, Robert Wilson, Jerzy Grotowski, Shuji Terayama, Peter Schumann, and Andre Gregory were invited to Shiraz to perform and occasionally collaborate with Iranian actors and theater artists. During the 1970s, the Iranian government also started establishing regular festivals that were meant to celebrate and support the country's

FIGURE 5. Performance of *Hymnen* by Karlheinz Stockhausen, Persepolis, 1972. *Photograph courtesy of Stockhausen-Stiftung für Musik.*

indigenous performance traditions. This was further supported after the 1979 Revolution, with the new government's attempts to suppress the practice of Western culture in Iran, a policy that began with the state's Cultural Revolution in 1981. During this period, numerous festivals for indigenous theater flourished (especially after the Iran–Iraq War) as a means to advance and advocate for local traditions.[9] While the melding of indigenous performance practices with Western dramatic forms had already begun in the 1960s as a reaction to the rapid Westernization of Iran, the growing interest in indigenous performance during the post-war years ushered in a greater cultural investment in these forms. In addition to playwright-directors who

9 Some of these festivals include the Ritual and Traditional Theater Festival, the Mobarak Puppetry Festival, and the Ta'ziyeh Festival.

began this work in the pre-revolutionary period—such as Bahram Beyzaie, Esma'il Khalaj, and Mahmood Ostad-Mohammad—new multi-hyphenate practitioners, including Mohammad Rahmanian and Atila Pesyani, emerged in the post-Revolutionary era. They developed a hybridized performance aesthetic that fused European avant-garde practices with indigenous performance traditions. This approach continues today through the work of directors like Behrooz Gharibpour, Zahra Sabri, and Reza Gooran.

THEATER IN POST-REVOLUTIONARY IRAN

The 1979 Revolution in Iran was as much a cultural revolution as it was sociopolitical.[10] Within two years of its establishment, the new state-installed Islamic codes of conduct worked to change the cultural landscape of Iran from a secular modern society to one based on Islamic mandates, a shift that was far from straightforward. From the first phase of the Cultural Revolution (1980–83) through the Iran–Iraq War (1980–88) and into the postwar period (1989–97), the country's

---

10 Also known as the Islamic Revolution, this historical turning point brought an end to the Pahlavi monarchy on February 11, 1979. Within a year, an Islamic Republic was established, built on doctrines appropriated by Shi'a clerics. Despite relative prosperity and rapid modernization during the Pahlavi era, revolutionaries from across the political spectrum—from liberals to communists, leftists to Islamists—viewed the shah's reforms to be alienating Iranian culture and instead serving the Western bloc, especially the United States. The new regime advanced a religious autocracy in place of the secular Western values promoted by the Pahlavi monarchy. Following the Revolution, Ayatollah Khomeini suppressed rival factions and launched the Cultural Revolution to eradicate secularism in favor of a homogeneous society based on the doctrines of Shi'a Islam. This drastically altered the cultural, political, and social landscape of Iran, ushering in a new era in the country's contemporary history.

superstructures—such as education, legislation, and so on—underwent significant change to adapt to life under new ideological standards. Abbes Kholqi suggests that fundamentalism grounded in the ideals of the Islamic Revolution was the key factor in these sociocultural restructurings (2007: 34). As one of the cultural sites, Iranian theater underwent a profound transformation. Aiming to replace all forms of Western art and culture with ones that advanced Islamic doctrines, the new state began to reshape artistic productions. According to Ghanoonparvar, the new government had become aware of "the power of performing arts in reshaping public opinion and instigating its value system in the country" (2001: 98). Therefore, within a few years of the Revolution, Iranian stages shifted from producing a diverse range of theater—populated with plays by professional practitioners with varying views, methodologies, and political orientations—to *te'ātr-e arzeshi* or "theater of values," populated mostly with plays written and produced by untrained amateurs advancing Islamic and revolutionary ideals.

Although this refashioning of the theatrical scene was effective in eradicating pre-revolutionary modes of cultural production and served to advance the state's legitimacy, it also resulted in outcomes that the government did not intend. The promotion of Islamic theater eliminated anti-theatrical prejudices among conservative Iranians and gave rise to alternative and underground theater movements that navigated and negotiated the imposed restrictions through new forms and narrative approaches to create a socially vital theater scene in Iran. Also, as Farhad Khosrokhani and Oliver Roy suggest, given the lack of other leisure activities and places to socialize, the theater scene became an important cultural hub for Iranian youth to gather, participate, and assert their presence: "through their massive attendance at theater performances, Iranians have participated in the revival of Iranian drama, and voice their demands for progressive change" (quoted in Anjo 2013: 83).

During the Iran–Iraq War (1980–88), theatrical productions in Iran slowed down owing to the national focus on war efforts, the effects of the Cultural Revolution on theatrical practitioners, and the widespread move towards Islamicization. Iran's theatrical culture started growing again in the post-war years, and during the presidency of Mohammad Khatami (1997–2005), the state relaxed some of its policies around theatrical productions and increased attention toward the arts. Although governmental oversight increased during Mahmoud Ahmadinejad's presidency (2005–13), by 2010, economic pressures propelled the Iranian government to divert state funding from the arts and allow for commercially produced enterprises to greatly expand, resulting in the privatized state of Iranian theatre today. Although theater in Iran must still be approved for public consumption by the state's Ministry of Culture and Islamic Guidance, founded after the 1979 Revolution, this privatization has resulted in a much greater number of productions across Iran, independent from the state's financial support (see Bassiri 2020).

Theatrical performance in Iran today is an amalgamation of constantly changing forms and narrative styles. It is in conversation with the Stanislavskian traditions pioneered by Nushin and Iran's American professors, the mid-century avant-garde aesthetics of Samandarian and Saberi's training, the hybridized indigenous-Western work of playwrights like Beyzaie, Abbas Na'lbandian, and Bijan Mofid, and the constant influx of cutting-edge theatrical styles from across the globe. Many of Iran's popular stage directors spent time studying or training abroad, and this education has undergirded the pedagogy of Iran's undergraduate and graduate-level theatrical training, which has exploded in Iran since the 1990s. With the Iranian government's decision in 2010 to permit privately produced and staged theater, the nation's theatrical scene grew significantly in comparison with the early post-revolutionary years. Kaveh Bassiri explains: "Whereas in 2007 and 2012 Tehran saw stagings of ninety and 193 plays, respectively, in 2017 the number of plays produced reached 738. In the summer months of 2019 alone, theatergoers could choose from more than 200 plays" (2020: 362).[11] Some of these plays were staged in grand auditoriums and concert halls, others in medium-sized blackbox theaters, and many in cramped converted spaces such as basements, apartment lofts, backyards, and so on. Audiences also surged over this period. At Iranshahr, one of Tehran's most prominent theatrical venues, annual audiences grew from 92,000 in 2013 to 986,000 by 2019 (Bassiri 2020: 364). This growth in theatrical productivity and engagement coincided with increased diversity in performance styles and aesthetics, resulting in significant experimentation in theatrical form, language, and design.

The heyday of privatization slowed down as political unrest became more widespread in Iran, fueled in part by economic hardships

11 The accumulation of power and resources in Tehran and the relative neglect of other cities has created a cultural dichotomy that is reflected in the scholarship on Iranian theater. Historical texts often frame this in binary terms—"theater of Tehran" versus "theater of the provinces," which groups together all theater produced outside the capital. This has created a theatrical archive that is Tehran-based and overlooks developments elsewhere in Iran. The theater of Tehran has thus come to serve as a metonym for Iranian theater as a whole. Nonetheless, the capital's theatrical output has long had a profound impact on work staged in "the provinces," often setting the tone and direction for both mainstream and avant-garde movements nationwide.

following the return of historical sanctions when the US withdrew from the Joint Comprehensive Plan of Action in 2018.[12] The following year, Iran was among the first countries impacted by the Covid-19 pandemic, resulting in widespread shutdowns across the country. These disruptions, coupled with widespread political unrest, plunged Iranian theater into one of the most trying periods in its history. Despite theater practitioners' attempts to reshape their art by shifting to digital modes and media, the lack of governmental support left theater in a critical condition. One relatively successful example of the transition to online performance was the Tiwall Online Theater launched by the Tiwall website, a private social network that provided a platform for art and entertainment events during the pandemic. With the gradual reopening of Iran's theaters in 2021, there was hope that the country's artistic scene would return to its vitality of the pre-pandemic moment. This, however, did not come to pass, owing to political unrest and nationwide protests, which were already on the scene as early as 2017 but escalated in November 2019, culminating in the 2022 "Woman, Life, Freedom" movement. Triggered by the killing of Mahsa Amini by the morality police while she was in their custody, this protest movement ushered in one of the most turbulent periods in Iranian history since the 1979 Revolution. People from diverse

12 The Joint Comprehensive Plan of Action (JCPOA), commonly known as the Iran Nuclear Deal, was signed in 2015 by then US president Barrack Obama along with leaders of the UN Security Council member states and the European Union. The agreement aimed to ease longstanding sanctions on Iran in exchange for restrictions on the development of its nuclear program. Although the deal was originally intended to last for fifteen years, the United States under president Donald Trump officially withdrew from the JCPOA on May 8, 2018, imposing even harsher sanctions on Iran.

backgrounds took to the streets in violent confrontations with the regime to demand basic human rights, freedom of choice, and a return to a secular lifestyle. As we write this introduction, the country is going through a transformative period, and the theater remains a central site of resistance and perseverance. Despite the unprecedented practice of surveillance and the fragility of the nation's economy, Iranian theater practitioners continue writing, staging, and protesting, even via underground performances when official productions are not an option.

The process for receiving the Iranian state's official approval for theatrical performance has been complex since the 1979 Revolution. Even earlier, the Iranian government had a complicated relationship with the nation's theater artists who sought to use the stage for social and political critique. As the Western dramatic tradition grew in popularity during the Pahlavi era, Iranian theater artists sought new ways to create incisive work while evading state censorship. One of these methods relied on the deeply embedded Persian tradition of ambiguity, or *ihām*.[13] Under the Ministry of Culture and Islamic

13 Pulling from the writing of twelfth-century Persian poet and philologist Rashid-al-Din Vatvat, Seeger A. Bonebakker (1966) identifies *ihām* to be a specific type of wordplay in which a single word can have multiple meanings, related in part to amphibology. In this tradition, one meaning is obvious (*qarib*) while the other is hidden (*gharib*), putting the onus for understanding on the reader. The famous Iranian poet Hafez (*c.*1325–90) was particularly adept in his use of *ihām*, harnessing ambiguity to explore romantic and political themes that defied cultural norms while evading persecution. This ambiguity has become popular throughout Iranian art, literature, and performance (see Mir-Hosseini 2001). For some, *ihām* is an act of rebellion and subversion, allowing artists to navigate censorship and other limitations on free speech by speaking truth to power under the protective veil of ambiguity. For others, as Shamsur Rahman Faruqi (1997) explains, *ihām* is simply part of "the pleasure of poetry." In both iterations, however, *ihām* acts as "a means for 'meaning-creation.'"

Guidance, *ihām* became an essential tool for navigating the pressure of government oversight of artistic expression. The ministry's theatre wing decides which productions are granted state approval for public staging; throughout the 1990s, these plays were also given a performance space and some financial support. This monitoring process is termed *nezārat* ("observance" or "surveillance"), and the state sees itself in an advisory position to provide feedback on artistic choices.

The ministry's *nezārat* process consists of multiple steps spanning the production's conception through to the final performance. Although the particulars of this process have evolved over time, especially given the impact of privatization on Iran's theatrical scene, some elements remain constant. The first phase involves each production submitting a detailed application, through which the ministry decides whether to approve the production and, if approved, whether it merits placement in one of the country's most prestigious performance venues. The largest such venues, which are controlled by the state, are particularly sensitive to social and political critiques in the plays they stage. The wealth of private theaters allows for more diverse, alternative, and incisive work to be performed, but these spaces are driven by profits from ticket sales. Plays that are unlikely to recoup costs and make money are less likely to receive support from private theater owners. In this way, the newly capitalist enterprise of Iran's private theaters becomes a system of censorship in itself—one in which profit margins, rather than political ideology, determine which stories are told and which are silenced. Owing to this pressure for financial viability, a form of mainstream comedic theater called *te'ātr-e āzād* (free theater) has become particularly popular, prioritizing entertainment through bawdy humor and low comedy. Some within the theater community have taken to calling it *te'ātr-e ebtezāl* (vulgar theater), arguing that its dominance amounts to a new kind of censorship by monopolizing Iran's already limited theatrical resources.

The second phase of *nezārat* takes place during rehearsals and performances of plays, when ministry officials monitor approved productions to ensure that the staging aligns with government values. They may demand changes to the text, action, or design if they deem content as subversive or incompatible with state values. While directors can contest and negotiate, the ministry has the final say in the productions' public performances. With the privatization of Iranian theater in the 2010s and the subsequent surge in productions across diverse venues, the government's capacity to evenly monitor the wealth of Iran's theatrical activity has diminished. As a rule of thumb, the *nezārat* process is more rigorous for high-profile theatre professionals with greater influence on Iranian audiences and discourse. Censorship also depends on individual officials' personal tastes and attitudes, due to the ambiguity in state guidelines and in the role of audience reception in shaping interpretation.

The development of Iranian post-revolutionary theater reveals a fluid and evolving art form with shifting themes, diverse subject matter, and different styles shaped by changing political contexts. Despite complications arising from government intervention, Iranian theater continues to navigate shifting paradigms, experimenting with new modes of artistic expression. Theater remains one of the primary conduits for cultural engagement in Iran and a crucial lens to explore the dynamics of contemporary Iranian cultural identity. Today, Persian theater is constantly learning, excavating, reconfiguring, and innovating to pave the way toward a more global and impactful theater.

STRUCTURE

The five plays collected in this anthology showcase a range of post-revolutionary Iranian playwrights and theatrical styles. Written between 1995 and 2019, they have all emerged from Iran's twentieth-century dramatic tradition, which blends European theatrical form with indigenous Persian performance and poetry. Thematically, they explore history and memory, gender and motherhood, nationhood and borders—issues that resonate with contemporary Iranian audiences. The most established playwright in this anthology is Bahram Beyzaie, a prominent theater artist since before the 1979 Revolution and a key contributor to the artistic renaissance that continues to influence Iranian theater and cinema. Mohammad Charmshir began writing in the 1980s, during the Iran–Iraq War, when there were fewer opportunities to publish or produce plays due to wartime precarity and state restrictions.[14] Hamid Amjad and Iran's most prolific female playwright, Naghmeh Samini, started working in the 1990s, with their work flourishing during the reform era under the presidency of Mohammad Khatami. The final playwright in this anthology, Sepideh Khosrowjah, began writing in the 1990s and has been particularly influential as a diasporic artist, living in the United States since after the 1979 Revolution.

The first two plays in this anthology—Bahram Beyzaie's *The Sacrifice of Senemar* (1998) and Hamid Amjad's *Oblivion* (2013)—

---

14 The appointment of Ali Montazeri to the chairmanship of the Center for Performing Arts at the Ministry of Culture and Islamic Guidance in 1987 led to a modest rise in theatrical activity, but licensing requirements for productions still posed challenges. His dismissal in 1992 ushered in a new period of strict control and regression that gradually eased in 1997 with the onset of the reform era under President Khatami.

interrogate the relationship between history and storytelling, using indigenous Persian performance traditions to navigate the complexity of representing the past through the present. Traditions such as *naqqāli* and *ta'ziyeh* similarly use embodied performance to enact cultural identity through retellings of Iran's historic and mythic past. Beyzaie's and Amjad's plays approach the supposed reliability of historical narratives with skepticism, acknowledging the roles power and interpretation play in the construction of historical metanarratives. As Amjad writes in *Oblivion*, "History does not have a beginning! / It is an extended scene before us." Both plays blend indigenous Persian performance and European dramatic writing, are largely in verse, and bridge Persian poetry with the multilayered narratives and heightened language evident in classical Western theater.

The Sacrifice of Senemar (2001) tells the story of Senemar, a popular Persian-Roman architect, who was commissioned by the Lakhmid Arab Emir Na'man I (r. 390–418 CE) to build the most luxurious palace in the desert to welcome the visiting Persian king. Though jealous and suspicious, the emir promises Senemar his daughter in marriage and a life of luxury if he completes the palace in less than a year. When the palace is finally finished and Senemar asks for his reward, the emir refuses. Fearing that the architect's future creations may outshine Na'man's castle, the Emir throws Semenar from the palace roof. Before dying, Senemar prophesies that Na'man's dynasty will end when his grandson is crushed under an elephant's feet during the rule of the king's grandson. Beyzaie uses elements of *naqqāli* and *ta'ziyeh* as framing devices, demonstrating how this localized history and performance might serve as a platform for interrogating the relationship between power and historical narratives.

Oblivion (2013) recounts the story of a family living under the rule of the first Chinese emperor, referred to as the Khagan, around 200 BCE. The family patriarch, a respected warrior and historian, returns from war victorious but deeply disillusioned by the Khagan's brutality in suppressing the native tribes. He begins writing a history of the region's civil wars. Meanwhile, he takes custody of Fusai, the son of a fallen comrade, and raises him alongside his own son and daughter. Over the years, taking advantage of the country's political turmoil, Fusai betrays his adoptive family and ascends to the position of prime minister. He burns his adoptive father's history book and breaks the heart of the family's daughter. Overwhelmed by grief, the parents take their own lives, believing their efforts have been destroyed and will be forgotten. In the aftermath, the siblings, however, start rewriting their father's book and ultimately witness Fusai's demise.

In *Oblivion*, Amjad explores power, borders, and historical writing through the interpolation of ancient Chinese history and Persian indigenous performance. In addition to *naqqāli* and *ta'ziyeh*, Amjad makes significant use of *khayāl-bāzi,* Iran's tradition of shadow theater. Scholars have traced the origins of Persian shadow play back to the eleventh century, and historian Shiva Massoudi suggests it may have emerged from cultural exchanges along the Silk Road, with Persia stationed between Egypt and China, both cultures famous for their shadow theater (2009: 261). *Oblivion* places itself at the crossroads of the Middle East and the Far East. In a particularly compelling twist on Iran's shadow-theater tradition, it stages the interplay of live actors and shadows throughout its storytelling. Amjad blends shadow puppetry with the Persian minstrelsy tradition of *naqqāli,* fusing these performance forms with the dialogic style of European-influenced dramatic literature to create a truly hybrid theatrical practice.

The next three plays in this anthology engage in critical conversations around gender roles and women's rights, reflecting a hallmark of post-Revolutionary Iranian art and culture, which regularly explores contemporary social issues. The plays depart from Beyzaie's and Amjad's focus on history while still interrogating the relationships between power, nationhood, and borders. These plays—Mohammad Charmshir's *The Dance of Mares* (2003), Naghmeh Samini's *The Child* (2019), and Sepideh Khosrowjah's *Bird of Dawn* (1995)—exemplify a playwriting practiced throughout Iran today, emerging largely from the Western dramatic tradition mixed with Persian poeticism.

The Dance of Mares is among the many celebrated adaptations in the Iranian theatrical canon, reimagining Federico García Lorca's *Yerma* through a disjointed, dreamlike structure set outside a specific time or place. It follows Yerma's yearning to bear a child, weaving in scenes of bullfighting and a critique of patriarchal traditions of her village. Despite having been married to Juan for several years, Yerma remains childless. The other women in her village share their stories of oppression, unsatisfied desire, and unfulfilled longings. After rumors emerge about their affair, Yerma's lover Victor decides to leave the village but is soon found stabbed to death in the street. Yerma's close friend Maria loses her infant child and joins Yerma on a pilgrimage to a mountain hermitage. Upon returning, Maria kills herself and is buried outside the cemetery. Yerma later exhumes her body and buries her properly in the cemetery—then returns home and kills her husband.

The play explores how power and gender are used to control and distort women's lives. Charmshir's characteristically lyrical yet colloquial free verse offers a poetic voice distinct from the classical tones found in Beyzaie's work. Famous for his adaptations, Charmshir blends

Brechtian episodic scenes with Lorca's raw poetic phrasing to create a fluid dramatic structure. Spanning fifty-nine scenes of monologue and dialogue, the play familiarizes the foreign setting for local audiences. Like the other plays in this anthology, *The Dance of Mares* uses global material to address contemporary, local issues such as oppressive patriarchal systems and restrictive gender norms. Charmshir juxtaposes poetic twists to scenes of bullfighting and domestic life to create a liminal world where dreams and reality converge, capturing the tension between his characters' inner desires and the external constraints placed on them by society.

The Child and *Bird of Dawn*, both written by female playwrights, are rooted in the present day and reflect contemporary realities through references to global conflicts and popular culture. Addressing themes such as gender roles, immigration, and life in the diaspora, these plays speak directly to the lived experiences of their audiences. Naghmeh Samini's *The Child* is set in an interrogation room on the border of an unnamed country, where an immigration officer is interviewing three refugee women—an Izadi Kurd, an Afghan, and a Libyan—all of whom go by the name of Mina. With the help of an Iranian interpreter, the officer attempts to determine which Mina is the mother of a newborn baby in the encampment. Over the course of several months, each woman denies giving birth to the child, asserting that one of the other Minas is the mother. During the interrogation, they tell the officer stories of hardships they endured in fleeing their home countries. Positioned between the officer and the women, the interpreter becomes a silent but pivotal figure—mostly seen as a shadow—who subtly alters translations to aid the women. In the final scene, the officer and interpreter meet several months after the interrogation to process paperwork granting the interpreter custody of the child. By this point, the officer knows the child's true parentage, but they both agree that it is better for the interpreter not to know which of the three Minas is the birth mother.

The Child dramatizes the global refugee crisis by depicting how language can function as a barrier, further disorienting the lives of displaced individuals. With their unreliable narratives, which are further complicated by the interpreter's translation, the women challenge the credibility of a single narrative being "true." Furthermore, by obscuring the identity of the nation in which the Minas are seeking refuge, Samini's play speaks to both local and global contexts, underscoring a broader call for national accountability in offering refuge and care to those in need.

The final play in this anthology, Sepideh Khosrowjah's *Bird of Dawn*, takes its name from a famous Iranian song that advocates for freedom through reflections on Persian history. Set in a Los Angeles laundromat at daybreak, the play follows three Iranian immigrant women who share their life stories. Ms. Arjumand, an elderly widow, has come to wash her late husband's clothes for the first time since his death many years ago. She strikes up a conversation with Sima, a woman in her thirties who lives a lonely life after divorcing her husband who was cheating on her with her close friend. Camille, a young woman in her early twenties, joins them after a fight with her boyfriend. Frustrated and despondent, she repeatedly calls him but gets no reply. As the morning unfolds, the women develop a warm bond. When Camille's boyfriend finally calls back, she decides to stay a little longer with Sima and Ms. Arjumand before returning to him, affirming the newfound sense of connection among them. This intimate engagement in a female-coded space goes beyond immigration to embrace the notion of community and cultural belonging. In contrast to *The Child*,

Bird of Dawn focuses on the assimilation and evolution of diasporic identities after resettlement, highlighting the personal transformations that occur within immigrant communities.

Each of the five plays in this anthology explores timely social issues as well as larger existential questions by blending Western dramatic tradition with Persian performance and poetry to create a hybrid theatrical form that engages with Iran's past and present. Interestingly, none of the plays are explicitly set in Iran, and only three of the five plays feature Iranian characters—a reflection of a notable trend in post-revolutionary Iranian theater, which often uses metaphor and ambiguity, the hallmark of Persian poetry, to address social issues without direct political didacticism that might prove contentious for playwrights. Through their interrogations of power and identity, these plays advocate for the agency of the historically dispossessed—refugees, women, immigrants, or foreign others—presenting narratives of resilience, empowerment, and community. Together, they encourage audiences to challenge oppressive systems and to write their own histories and futures. As Amjad writes in *Oblivion*, "History is the inventory of choices, / And he who does not choose in life, / Might as well have never lived it."

WORKS CITED

AFSHAR, Mahasti. 2019. "Festival of Arts: Shiraz-Persepolis, 1967–1977." *Iran Namag* 4(2): 4–64.

AHMADIAN, Nahid. 2022. "The Development of Theatre in Post-Revolutionary Iran from 1979 to 1997." PhD dissertation, University of Maryland.

ANJO, Liliane. 2013. "Contemporary Iranian Theater: The Emergence of an Autonomous Space," in Annabelle Sreberny and Massoumeh Torfeh (eds),

Cultural Revolution in Iran: Contemporary Popular Culture in the Islamic Republic. New York: I. B. Tauris.

BASSIRI, Kaveh. 2020. "Privatization and the Changing Landscape of Iranian Theater." *International Journal of Middle East Studies* 52: 362–69.

BEYZAIE, Bahram. 1965. *Namāyesh dar Irān*. Tehran: Roshangarān va Motale'āt Zanān Publication.

BONEBAKKER, Seeger A. 1966. *Some Early Definitions of the Tawriya and Ṣafadi's Faḍḍ al-Xitām ʿan at-Tawriya wa-'l-Istixdām*. The Hague and Paris: Mouton.

CHELKOWSKI, Peter. 1989. "Narrative Painting and Painting Recitation in Qajar Iran." *Muqarnas* 6: 98–111.

CHELKOWSKI, Peter. 2010. *Eternal Performance: Ta'ziyeh and Other Shiite Rituals*. London: Seagull Books.

EMAMI, Iraj. 1987. "The Evolution of Traditional Theatre and the Development of Modern Theatre in Iran". PhD dissertation, University of Edinburgh.

FARUQI, S. R. 1997. *Gosh-e dīvār tak to jā nāle / us meñ gul ko bhī kān hote haiñ* (Frances W. Pritchett trans.). https://franpritchett.com/00garden/03c/0336/-0336_02.html (last accessed on 17 July 2016).

FLOOR, Willem. 2005. *The History of Theater in Iran*. Washington, DC: Mage Publishers.

GANJEH, Azadeh. 2017. "Performing *Hamlet* in Modern Iran (1900–2012)." PhD dissertation, University of Bern.

GHANOONPARVAR, M. R. 2001. "Persian Plays and the Iranian Theater," in Sherifa Zuhur (ed.), *Colors of Enchantment: Theater, Dance, Music, and the Visual Arts of the Middle East*. Cairo: American University in Cairo Press.

GHANOONPARVAR, M. R. 2014 [1995]. "Drama," in *Encyclopædia Iranica*, VOL 7, FASC. 5, pp. 529–35. http://www.iranicaonline.org/articles/drama (last accessed November 29, 2011).

KHOLQI, Abbes. 2007. "Barasi-ye Barnāmehrizi va Farāyand-e Tolid dar Te'ātr-e Emruz-e Irān" [A Study of Planning and Production Process in Contemporary Iranian Theater]. Master's thesis, Tarbiyat Modares University.

MALEKPOUR, Jamshid. 2004. *The Islamic Drama*. London: Routledge.

MASSOUDI, Shiva. 2009. "Kheimeh Shab Bazi: Iranian Traditional Marionette Theater." *Asian Theatre Journal* 26(2): 260–80.

MIR-HOSSEINI, Ziba. 2001. "Iranian Cinema: Art, Society, and the State." *Middle East Report* 219 (Summer): 26–29.

MOTTAHEDEH, Negar. 2005. "Ta'ziyeh: A Twist of History in Everyday Life," in Kamran Scot Aghaie (ed.), *The Women of Karbala*. Austin: University of Texas Press.

REYES, Angelita D. 2019. "Performativity and Representation in Transnational Blackface: Mammy (USA), Zwarte Piet (Netherlands), and Haji Firuz (Iran)" *Atlantic Studies* 16(4): 521–50.

SAHAMIZADEH, Nazanin. 2022. "Introduction" to Aubrey Mellor and Cheryl Robson (eds), *New Iranian Plays*. London: Aurora Metro Books.

TALAJOOY, Saeed. 2015. "A History of Iranian Drama (1850–1941)," in Ali-Asghar Seyed-Gohrab (ed.), *A History of Persian Literature, Volume 11: Literature of the Early Twentieth Century; From the Constitutional Period to Reza Shah*. New York: I. B. Tauris.

ZAHEDI, Farindokht. 2006. *Henrik Ibsen and Iranian Modern Drama: Reception and Influence*. Oslo: Oslo Academic Press.

THE SACRIFICE OF SENEMAR

Bahram Beyzaie

Translated by
Nahid Ahmadian

Original title: *Majles-e Qorbāni-ye Senemār*
Written in 1998
First performed in 2015 at Qashqa'i Hall, Tehran, directed by Shima Javadpour
Published in Persian by Roshangaran va Motale'at Zanan Publication, 2001

CHARACTERS

Senemar

Na'man

The Girl

The First Man, The Second Man, The Third Man (they play the roles of castle workers, guardian servants, bricklayers, beggars, Sheikhs, heads of the tribes, spongers, warriors and the like)

Stagehands, dressed in black (for moving props, helping actors change clothes, playing musical instruments, and producing sounds)

EDITORS' INTRODUCTION

Bahram Beyzaie (b. 1938) is the most celebrated Iranian playwright, filmmaker, script writer, and theater director since the 1960s. The author of more than fifty plays and fourteen screenplays, many of which have won national awards and international acclaim, Beyzaie has directed most of his films and some of his plays in Iran and abroad. He is also the author of many scholarly works on the history of Iranian theater and literature, such as *Hezār Afsān Kojāst?* [Where Is the *One-Thousand-and-One-Nights*?] (2012) and *Namāyesh dar Irān* [A Study on Iranian Theater] (1965). In his plays, Beyzaie demythologizes the deference for and sanctification of sacrificial heroes, exploring instead the notion of common humanity and rearticulating Persian cultural identity through such a lens. His plays have been translated into English, German, French, and Arabic. From the 1970s to the 1990s, Beyzaie faced governmental resistance to his work, and he was banned from filmmaking and directing his own plays. This prompted him to leave the country, and at several points he lived in Sweden, France, and finally the United States. He now lives in California with his wife, the actress Mojdeh Shamsai, and teaches at Stanford University. Some of his award-winning films and plays include *Basho Gharibe-ye Koochak* [Basho the Little Stranger] (1986), *Sag-koshi* [Killing Mad Dogs] (2001), *Marg-e Yazdgerd* [Death of Yazdgerd] (1981), *Shab-e Hezār-o Yekom* [The One Thousand and First Night] (2003), *Nodbeh* [Elegy] (1977), *Siyāvash-khāni* [The Passion of Siyavash] (1993), and *Tarabnāmeh* (2016).

The Sacrifice of Senemar is based on a story by Nizami Ganjavi, the twelfth-century Persian poet, who wrote about the figure of Senemar in his *Haft Peykar*, or *Bahrāmnāmeh*. In translating Beyzaie's play, special attention has been paid to his precise use of classical Persian poetic styles and forms. The epic and lyrical quality of the language in this translation approximates the play to classical Persian poetry, as Beyzaie intended, and the aphoristic elements in particular are reminiscent of the Persian ghazal. The multilayered narrative of Beyzaie's play moves freely between the past and present, at times blurring the line between the two. The play begins at the moment of Senemar's death, then recounts the events leading to the Persian-Roman architect's downfall in a play-within-a-play led by Senemar's ghost. Senemar jumps back and forth between speaking in past and present tense, exemplifying a style of theatrical narration that allows these timelines to coexist. Since the action of the play spans many years, the passage of time is narrated by the actors, who describe the construction of the castle and the development of its interior design. This approach to language—one in which actions, internal dialogue, and changes in setting are directly articulated by the characters—is part of Beyzaie's nod to *ta'ziyeh*. In that tradition, language and stage action are highly symbolic and exaggerated. Like in *ta'ziyeh*, gestures in this play are overemphasized, character archetypes are coded through the use of color and simple costumes, and the chorus plays multiple roles and changes clothes onstage. These elements bridge *ta'ziyeh* with Brechtian epic theatre, which was also influential to Beyzaie's writing. For instance, *Senemar* features three Brechtian "common men" who transition through various roles, representing different classes of society from sheikhs to castle guards to laborers and desert dwellers, and they allegorically represent human characteristics, akin to European medieval morality plays. With its melding of distinct theatrical forms, nods to Persian performance, culture, and history, and its special attention to elevated poetic language, *The Sacrifice of Senemar* is deeply representative of Beyzaie's dramatic oeuvre and the particular hybridized style of Iranian theater.

FIGURE 6. The Construction of the Fort of Kharnaq (1494–95), by Kamal-ud-din Bihzad (1450–1535), displayed in the British Library.

THE SACRIFICE OF SENEMAR

Bahram Beyzaie

On the right-hand side of the stage, there is a double door made of thick wood. It is huge and decorated with doornails. This is the door to the castle; the dim light on it gets brighter as the play progresses. In the background, facing the horizon, is a scaffolding. The stage floor is covered with sand. Somewhere to the left of the stage is a grounded boat. Scattered here and there are one or two ladders and a few wheelbarrows. In the wheelbarrows are bricks, chalk, and clay—as much as needed for makeup work; they should not be seen before they are applied. Pieces of azure, ochre, purple, black, brown, and gray cloth are used to cover the men's shoulders and heads or fashioned into headgear. They should not be visible before they are used. By the end of the play, the cloths are all gone with the scaffolding except for a ladder which will carry Senemar's body offstage.

Absolute darkness. Sounds of stones and straws struck against each other. Primitive music—something between moaning and cheering, which is interrupted at the climax by the cries of several men shouting together in horror. With that, lights come up on the body of Senemar, laid downstage right. The stage is lit up shortly before he breathes his last and drops his trembling hand, which had reached out to something in the air. The First Man, dressed in the dusty outfit of the camel riders, comes hurriedly from upstage. The Second Man, dressed in sailors' clothes, runs on panting from stage left. The Third Man, who was crouched stage left and had put his hands to his head in fright, now stands on his shaky legs and gradually finds the courage to look at the body. He has the spade, helmet, and the belt of the guards, but he is covered in mud.

THE FIRST MAN (*just arrived*). Who is this fallen on the ground?
This broken-neck, bruised-face, this broken-back?

FIGURE 7. *The Sacrifice of Senemar*. Directed by Shima Javadpour at the Entezami Theatre at the Iranian Artists Forum, Tehran, 2018. *Photograph by Shahriar Akbarieh.*

THE SECOND MAN (*just arrived*). Call him the smashed-bone, the lifeless, the-sigh-in-throat!

THE FIRST MAN. Who are you—and who is going to bemoan your loss? Who to avenge? What tribe do you come from?

THE SECOND MAN. How do you call yourself—a name you are known by?

How should I know who you are?

THE FIRST MAN. What did your mother, or your father call you?

THE THIRD MAN (*with eyes fixed on the body*). Senemar!

THE FIRST MAN (*frowns*). What? The one who built this castle?

THE SECOND MAN (*in wonder—gives a closer look*). How could it be him and I not recognize?

THE FIRST MAN (*denies*). No—do not believe it; he was so revered!

THE SECOND MAN (*curious*). And why is he fallen, crushed and humbled?

THE FIRST MAN (*looks up at the castle*). And how come we did not fall?

THE THIRD MAN. He was the one who built this edifice so high;
higher than forty men standing on each other's shoulders;
not *us*!

THE FIRST MAN (*denying*). Do not tell me he fell from what he himself built!

THE THIRD MAN. Indeed, they threw him down from what he raised.
A castle the desert deserved;
and the eyes gaze at, to locate its summit in the sky.
The four elements hand-in-hand
gave rise to such an astounding edifice from which they threw him down!

THE FIRST MAN (*still unbelieving, to the body*). You the wretched, fell down from what you raised;
what then did you build it for?

THE THIRD MAN (*angry*). Why blame him when they throw you down by force?

THE SECOND MAN (*startled*). What—you said they threw him down?

THE THIRD MAN. I would have not said it had I not seen it with my own eyes!—there, from atop
the highest roof; higher than forty men standing on each other's shoulders!

THE FIRST MAN (*furious*). You saw them pushing him down—and yet did not see why?

THE THIRD MAN (*confused, still staring at the body with trembling lips, disgusted*). They did it to say the higher you build, the harder you fall!

(*Grows angrier*) And all he attempted was to his demise!

This was to teach humility! And to say you are but equal to ashes!

And to say, demand no more; nor reach out for more!

THE FIRST MAN (*reprehensive*). If you saw, then you know who did it!

THE THIRD MAN. We cannot but name him with respect;

Na'man the son of Amr al-Qeis, the very one who commissioned this castle!

THE FIRST MAN (*denying*). Oh, you are mocking us, and this burdens me!

THE SECOND MAN. Did you err, or did I hear it wrong?

(*Unbelieving and impatient*) Na'man, the wise man of the desert?

THE THIRD MAN. To me too, he was the wise man of this desert until he commissioned the castle!

And when I saw him pushing Senemar,

I asked, "Where is sanity?"

THE FIRST MAN (*washed out*). Lucky those who did not build,

or built but short,

for when they fell, they neither broke their arms, nor lost their lives!

How blessed is shortsightedness!

It's best to not rise above the ashes

to save from suffering such a downfall!

THE THIRD MAN. Now, who is mocking?

Had no one built, the world would have never begun—

trapped in its infancy.

A wreckage!

THE SECOND MAN. Ay—a person's worth is in the things they make!
And what they make is in their image!

THE THIRD MAN. True; the castle is the image of Senemar,
and death the image of Na'man!

The body rises slowly.

SENEMAR. I, Senemar, rise to tell you how I fell.
I, who was closer to the sky than the earth when I fell.
And at that unbelieving moment—midway between the heavens and the earth—
when the space was opening agape beneath me
and the worlds drifting apart—
between the two worlds, I was counting the bricks
which I laid with my bare hands, one on top of another;
and each one of them, dumbfounded and frightened
asking countless times—
"Why, why, why?"
And my response
was but the sound of my smashing bones!
Together, Na'man and I suffered a great downfall.
His was a name revered, and he demanded a castle to that name.
And I built what ruined me;
a worthy castle for this desert
as high as forty men standing on each other's shoulders!
A castle that spread his name around the world;
but in disgrace!
Since he threw me—and his reputation—down from above.

THE FIRST MAN. Do you see that too?

THE THIRD MAN. Is it out of misery that he is roaming over his body?[1]
SENEMAR. Of what guilt were you convicted, Senemar?
THE SECOND MAN. I heard that. It was my question too!
SENEMAR. Such a long distance you traveled to meet your death!
And your endless patience was shortened
by your broken bones!
Were you rewarded, Senemar?

Na'man comes out from the castle hurriedly.

NA'MAN. Restore my reputation
and the name that fell from above!
Stop—where are you blowing my name, you wind?
Turn into a tornado and spin around,
and cry as much as you want over this evil deed;
but do not go afar; or you will tarnish my name in the world;
I wish the castle was not this high;
I wish he had not raised it as high as my arrogance!
If only it was as humble as the ashes!
So that we would laugh together once he fell from it.
I would then hold his hand and he would rise,
I would sweep the dust from his clothes
and he would again speak of a castle
—as high as forty men standing on each other's shoulders—
which stood for mankind's pride;

---

1 In a surreal move, Senemar's ghost rises from his body and tells the story of his fall. Other characters see him and join in recreating the chain of events that have led to his demise. Directors may choose to place a corpse on the stage throughout the play, or the actor playing Senemar may simply stand up and begin delivering his lines.

and resembled his dream! And my dream, even more than his!
I wish I could clear my name;
since he was the maker of this castle and I, the maker of his death!

THE FIRST MAN. Shall I weep or smile?
This is Na'man, the son of Amr al-Qeis,
who speaks deliriously!

THE SECOND MAN. Speak, Na'man, and speak more!
Your words are worthless as the wind!
It is your deeds that matter.

SENEMAR. In my dream, I built a castle
as high as forty men standing on each other's shoulders;
I was flying over it;
I saw a veiled man—dressed in black—
shooting arrows at me from its roof.
An archer fast and furious was releasing the arrows
which would come buzzing
As I stood entrapped in my horror.
And once it hit my heart and I fell,
I woke up; and Na'man's messenger—riding an Arabian horse—
asked if I was the Persian architect with Roman reputation
who had the idea of a castle in his head?
I said that I was; he said, "Read this then!"

THE THIRD MAN (*draws the letter from his pocket*). How could a messenger know the content of his letter?
If he is carrying the message of life or death?
Of building or destroying?
It looked like he had dreamed about the letter before I took it to him.

NA'MAN (*opens a letter*). I have been the sultan of the desert for years,
counting the innumerable sands—

and today I have more gold than the sands of this desert!
I have decided to live in a city
and build a roof over this kingdom of mine.
I—the sultan of oases—
I have seen nothing but the ruins of kings prior!
Show me a palace in this sandy land, not demolished by the sun
or swept away by the winds.
I—whom they call the sage of the desert—
could weave tents from camel hair;
but not a city—I cannot labor with clay and adobe!
(*Folds the letter*) Bring an architect!
Who is this man from Persia who lives in Rome?
Summon him! Here is gold, and there, the desert—where is his artistry?
Ask him to come and execute it here!

SENEMAR (*opens the letter*). It was in the letter.
"Erect an edifice in the crossroads of winds, on the fleeting sands,
Exposed to the floods, on the path of flowing waters!"

NA'MAN. This is the plan— (*sits down and draws on the ground*)
surround the desert with a wall
and a dome beneath which I could see the heavens
like I see from my tent;
and the day and night—ay—heedless of us,
pass the gate of dawn and dusk!
If you can build this, well done;
if not, do not call yourself an architect!

THE THIRD MAN (*returns the letter to his pocket*). I said:
"Do not wonder how and speak not of disbelief!
This is the story. Winter is coming,

the King of Persia is visiting the desert.
And Na'man wants to rise from the dust and deserve such an esteemed guest.
Ay, he means to be a worthy head over his walking body!"

SENEMAR (*walks confusedly*). Then why did I not hear the sound of my bones breaking?
Why did I not question how to build a palace
on the flowing sand?

NA'MAN (*opens a letter*). The letter says they will stay for the winter.
I should make myself worthy of this friendship!
We are no less than Persia.
They are the grandest of the world and proud of that;
we shouldn't let them see us as inferiors!
I heard they have palaces standing on the shoulders of stone men;
and constellations are visible from their roofs.
Lest they say our table is the desert and our nourishment mingled with sand!
Lest they say we know nothing but muddy water!
Lest they say our blankets are but pebbles and our dreams are dust-ridden!
Lest they say our state is fleeting like our sand!
Lest they say we lean against the wind!

SENEMAR. I said, "My father is from Persia and my mother from the Persian Rome, Anatolia.
I have seen Persian gardens, the dream of every Roman!
And their seven-stair palaces;
they are reminiscent of the celestial spheres.
What should I build that could ever surpass this?
Bring an architect from Persia, the best of them,
To build you a palace better than their own."

NA'MAN. I said, no. The Persian king has already seen plenty of Persian houses—it's enough for him!
Let's do new work—ay.
Be that he steps in a Roman house amidst Arabian ruins; with Persian domes;
So, if he demands the desert, there it is;
if he wishes the sky and stars, there are the heavens and there the zodiac;
and once he tires of the desert, here is the castle,
from which he could watch the world
and count the stars of the celestial heavens, scattered like the sands of the desert!
I said, "Then leave the Persian and bring a Roman—
one who knows the manners of Persia and Rome both!
Ay, someone who could erect an edifice that has the methods of both,
and can build a home deserving of the glory of the kings!
What is this name that I hear? Senemar, the architect—
a man with Persian and Roman blood in him.
Tell him, "Come! and let's amaze the King of Persia with our artistry!"

SENEMAR. The only option on the sea of sands is to build a palace that might float like a ship!
At best I can save myself from drowning in the sea of sand!
I said, "Architects build houses only on solid ground,
not on slippery ground,
not on floating sands,
not on mire!
They are skinks on the sea of sand."
I said, "I will do what no architect has done before!
On the sea of sand,

Na'man's people are all sailors of their tents
who paddle across the sand waves with their spears.
Was it not my dream to build a castle in the manner of Persians?"

NA'MAN. Tell me, Senemar, what are you thinking to do—
Embarrass me before the Persian king?
Time flies and it's early spring;
in the blink of an eye, winter comes, and the guests will be here.
Speak—speak and I am all ears!

THE FIRST MAN. What he said, we heard too;
I was trotting along on my camel!

THE SECOND MAN. I was hoisting my sails and slicing through the waves of the river!

THE THIRD MAN. I was his interpreter, listening and translating!

THE SECOND MAN. Yes, we too heard what he said.
There was no one in this desert who did not hear him.

SENEMAR. I said, "I need brick workers, thousands of them, and mold makers,
and kilns to fire clay!
And surveyors and hatchetmen and sawmen
and those who would wind the woods,
and with nails and ropes, make scaffolds and lumber,
and levers and trebuchet and winches!"

NA'MAN. Oh—but all of them?

SENEMAR. I said, "Construction sieves and trowel and shovels—
thousands and thousands of them—
and wheelbarrows and levels!
All the sifters, hodmen and carpenters!
The planners and plasterers!"

NA'MAN. Tell me, is my gold then gone with the wind? No?

FIGURE 8. *The Sacrifice of Senemar.* Directed by Shima Javadpour at the Entezami Theatre at the Iranian Artists Forum, Tehran, 2018. *Photograph by Shahriar Akbarieh.*

SENEMAR. This is the plan (*kneels and sketches on the ground*).
On the six sides of the castle are six gates and doors facing six landscapes;
one faces the river and the boats, one the desert and the caravans,
one the devilish whirlwinds of the cedar forest,
one the palm grove,
one the bazaar and oases,
and one faces the galloping wild horses of the desert.

NA'MAN. Amidst all this, you are taking away our desert. Are you not, Senemar?
The desert that is so close to our hearts!

SENEMAR. You cannot have the desert and the castle both!
Yes, the castle is what the desert is not!
An interlaced wide space, encircled
with several windcatchers[2] and porches and verandas;
with arch and dais and multi-doored patios;
a castle as high as forty men standing on each other's shoulders!

NA'MAN. You are going too fast Senemar!
Is this a dream or are you really going to build it?

SENEMAR. Give me forty cedar trees, each forty zera[3] in height
to make forty columns for the castle!

---

2 The *bādgir*, or windcatcher, is a traditional cooling system found in Middle Eastern architecture. Typically consisting of a tall tower it channels wind into a building to provide natural ventilation in hot climates. Windcatchers come in various designs and forms and have been used since the Achaemenid period (500 BCE).

3 A unit of length from one's elbow to the tip of their middle finger. This length varies depending on age and gender, approximating between 450 mm to 550 mm. 40 *zera*'is almost 20 meters (65 feet).

NA'MAN. You are asking for the impossible!

SENEMAR. If the cedars are a thousand years old,
give me forty more
to make the columns of your roof!

NA'MAN. You'll make the Arab elders quite angry with me!
You said forty?

SENEMAR. And another forty for joining them under the roof!
And another forty for joining them to the ground!
And another forty for joining them in the middle!
Yet another forty for rafters and stairs!
And forty more for the foundation we will ground the castle in!

NA'MAN. Are you plotting for Na'man's gold?

SENEMAR. We need sawmen and plenty of saws!
The cedar tree shall not fall until you cut it down,
and unless they roll it and pull the tree by rope, it will not move!

NA'MAN. You are moving my cedar forest!

SENEMAR. And I am shaping them into a castle, Na'man!
Construction means real work and rolled-up sleeves;
one cannot create without putting their hands to work!
Adobe means clay; no workwear remains unstained!
No hand, clean!
Until you reach your hand into the mud, you cannot build a castle!

NA'MAN. And these brick layers, do they not want my gold?

SENEMAR. You asked for the castle, not I!
I was at home, dreaming in my sleep!
It was you who summoned me to make your dream come true!

THE THIRD MAN. I was listening and saying to myself he was going too fast!
"This Na'man is a righteous man but not when gold is involved!"

NA'MAN. Gold is for decorating the columns and gifting to the guests!

SENEMAR. Do you have anything else in your possession?

NA'MAN. Nothing at all!

SENEMAR. I will take a little of this "nothing" to feed many!

THE FIRST MAN. So much impudence in the face of Na'man?
All who heard this story said he was riding a wild camel!

THE THIRD MAN. Call it unbridled!
This was uncharacteristic of the Persians and Romans both!
Who both speak but in irony;
such straightforwardness was of his very own character!

NA'MAN. I truly have nothing, Senemar—did you not hear?
Neither do I have the power to force them as the way of kings,
nor can I make incredible promises—like the Canaanites' prophets—
to deceive them!
So take it or leave it; nothing!
And you know well that when all I have is nothing,
I truly mean not a thing!

SENEMAR. But I do. I have a humbler castle for each of them!

NA'MAN. You are not speaking the truth!

SENEMAR. What other choice do I have but to tell the truth?

NA'MAN (*furious*). Are you mocking me?

THE THIRD MAN. I thought, "This is the fury of a person, his lies unveiled."

THE SECOND MAN. Have you ever been in a tattered ship?
The one that unwits the sailor?
I see now that he was on an unruly boat,
piercing the hull with an ax!

SENEMAR. Come, all, if you look forward to the castle
that Na'man plans to build.

Come! Here is the adobe. Look—I am sketching the plan of a house on it
Whatever your profession is, use it to build your houses.
Whoever cuts down a cedar for the castle
will get the branches for his own roof!

NA'MAN (*groaning*). You are donating my cedar branches!

SENEMAR. The castle falls without columns!

NA'MAN. Ay me, I am in trouble!

SENEMAR. You wanted to equal the heights of Persia and Rome,
the two worlds you imagine as superiors—
teach yourself to behave like them first!
Have foresight and think;
Erect pillars under your roof!
The true pillars are those who build!

NA'MAN. I shall remember his imprudence. He ignores me!

SENEMAR. Anyone who makes a hundred bricks for the castle
shall take ten to his own house and ten to his storage.

NA'MAN (*grumbling*). You are giving away my adobe bricks for free!

SENEMAR. The bricks that you will not have unless they mold?
You are resolute and generous like kings!
So hear—anyone who builds a door for the castle will get a window for himself!

NA'MAN (*grumbling*). I wish I had not asked for the castle!

SENEMAR. Masters of wood and ceramics
shall get dates and goat milk and chestnut bread,
and every ten days, roasted camel will be served among them.

NA'MAN (*grumbling*). You give away my dates, my goat milk, my chestnut bread,
my camels!

SENEMAR. Give them away and they will sacrifice their lives for you!

THE FIRST MAN. I stepped in as a brick worker!

THE SECOND MAN. And I as a sawman!

THE FIRST MAN. I said, "What is this occupation we have?
I am tired of riding camels!"

THE SECOND MAN. And I, of sailing!
I was crafting wooden skein!

THE FIRST MAN. I was firing adobe in the kiln!

THE THIRD MAN. I was feeding the brick workers with water and nourishments.

THE FIRST MAN. I drank goat milk and ate chestnut bread at last!

THE SECOND MAN. Dates every day and roasted camel regularly!

THE FIRST MAN. I was making truss for the pillars;
And stairs to reach the roof!

THE SECOND MAN. I climbed tall scaffolds to make the dome of the castle!

NA'MAN. This castle cost me more than I expected.
I had never seen Arabs so greedy in devouring free food!
Were they starving and I did not know?
Why should I reach into my gold pouch
when each time, hands reach out to grab my coins!
No—no—no. I am paying for my stupidity!
No—you are wasting my resources, Senemar;
do you really need to feed them?

SENEMAR. Can a starving man be agile?
One who carries heavy loads and knows no fatigue?
No, Na'man—if you steal from their food, they will steal from your work!
You seven, who can read maps and write,
keep in my vicinity like the planets orbiting around the sun,
so I assign each of you a task!

NA'MAN. You make yourself popular by giving away *my* resources;
I bemoan, and you are happy!
SENEMAR. I am happy because the walls are erected
and the pillars are standing firm and strong;
and the doors, they are what I desired.
And the seven domes are azure on the outside
and a rainbow from within!
And if you bemoan this, shut it down!
Forget the castle—and I know the road back to Rome!
NA'MAN. No, the reputation of this castle unraised
Has gone to the ends of the world!
What I see robs me of my dreams.
My soul needs this court more than anything.
Summon my scribe to write to Ethiopia.
Call as many job seekers as possible.
With sleeves rolled up and ready for work!
And we have not yet spoken of your reward!
Speak in your Roman manner, I will not argue—
what reward do you want for your service?
SENEMAR. I speak out of my Persian manner.
What am I supposed to say since I am summoned by an Arab king?
It suffices that this edifice is what you desire!
NA'MAN. Do not tease me, Senemar, and do not make me laugh!
No wages or compensation? I will not believe it!
Even the gods of al-Hirah do not perform their divinity wageless;
all those invocations, sacrifices and offerings,
yet nobody has seen them building castles!
How can you build it while unpaid?

SENEMAR. Look at this wasteland, sultan; I fear futility.

NA'MAN. Come on, leave formalities, Senemar!
I swear on the tribal gods,
I will reward you beyond your dreams; if truly
you erect on this desert, what you showed me on the sand!
I am not bragging—No! I, too, am building this castle for a reward,
and for a king who gives back twice as much as he is gifted.
What are *you* building for?

SENEMAR. I told you. I am building it for its own sake!

NA'MAN. No, do not make me owe it to you, Senemar,
Tell me all about it and leave formalities!
I swear to the supreme gods, you will have my best camel!
My best horse with its saddle and stirrups!
No, these are not enough; seventy of my best goats from my goat trip, with their bells!
I will be giving and generous;
even my oldest daughter, reputed for her beauty among Arabs, shall be yours!
Yes, my daughter with a dowry!

THE THIRD MAN. I would be a fool if I believed this;
Each day he demanded something new.
One could neither accept nor reject!
I was the interpreter between the two when they could not communicate,
and I witnessed, very closely,
how Senemar would make one brick and break another.

Senemar smashes two bricks together.

NA'MAN (*angry*). I used to walk a straight path in the desert
from this side to the other with no trouble!

Why should I make a detour around the castle?
The wind would caress my face when I closed my eyes;
but now I close them and fumble into walls!
Still, what a handsome castle!
It is identical to what I have seen in Persian images;
it's better than all I have heard about Roman palaces!
How could such a huge palace rise from humble ashes
but with artistry?

SENEMAR. We checked the flowing sand with division walls!
And made a foundation with cedar trees and mortar!

NA'MAN (*cries*). Damn the wall; I want the flowing sand.

SENEMAR. We branched a stream from the Euphrates to pass through the castle!

NA'MAN (*shouting and distrustful*). What am I supposed to do when it flows and ebbs?
And with the flooding river?

SENEMAR. We surrounded the castle with cedar and palm trees to make a wall against the tempest!

NA'MAN. That tempest is now in me!

SENEMAR. The world was old, we renovated it!

NA'MAN. I want the world like the first day it was created!

THE FIRST MAN. I still remember—your fears!
The day we all fled from Na'man's wrath.
I jumped into the Tigris, and many fled to the desert!
The day he appeared with arrows and bow, spear and sword,
roaring on his horse,
it was as if a djinn imprisoned for a thousand years had fled from a cave!

Na'man is on a puppet horse with an arrow and a bow. His horse trots, and his face is veiled. All the three men flee; they either fall, or climb up the scaffold.

SENEMAR (*scared*). Why have you veiled your face, Na'man, and why are you in black?
By God, you look like the archer I saw in my dream!

NA'MAN. Where shall I shoot this arrow to take my anger to?

SENEMAR. Shoot it at the ghouls and djinns hidden in the sandstorm who make trouble for us!

NA'MAN. Trouble? No, by the supreme gods
I am the person who made this trouble for myself,
not the ghouls or djinns!

THE THIRD MAN. Unveil yourself! Are you Na'man's friend or foe?
You are shooting at those who serve him!

THE SECOND MAN. Help! A titan! Save us, Na'man, from this shooter!

THE FIRST MAN. By God, this is Na'man's horse and a fiend is riding it!

NA'MAN. Why should I give you my best camel? No!
They know this castle by Senemar's name not Na'man's!
Why should I give you seventy of my best goats?
Those who make this palace, they thank you not me!
Why should I give you my best horse saddled and sound?
So that you ride it around the castle loud and proud of what *you* did?
Why should I reward you with my eldest daughter
—who is reputed for her beauty among Arabs—
so that she holds her husband and not her father in high esteem?
And prefer a foreigner to her family?

THE FIRST MAN. And that girl—may she be protected from the evil eye—is truly exemplary among Arabs!

Poets write odes to her eyes;
some under real names, some under pseudonyms!
And caravans shorten their journey by recalling her long hair,
In songs and in silence!

THE SECOND MAN. You forgot to mention the sailors—
And the recitation of verse between the wind and the sail; the waves and the boats!

THE FIRST MAN. Hmm—the sound of the camels' bells is one of a thousand songs that the desert sings for her beauty.

THE SECOND MAN. Her graceful walking makes men break their fast and make the sheiks forget their prayers!
It is as if she has risen from Leily's ashes!

THE THIRD MAN. You are insane! Which one is more handsome, the castle or the girl?

Na'man, weeping and tearing at his clothes, walks in a circle and pours sand on himself.

NA'MAN. You changed my cedars to pillars!
You buried my sand under the bricks!
You covered my sky with the roof,
and my galaxy and the Milky Way!
You made my winds—the gentle and the wild winds—
flee from behind the four walls.
You left for me but a small view
of the Euphrates, the cedar forest and the wild desert!
Why am I sacrificing my desert?
Why should I open and close a door?

SENEMAR. It was you who desired a castle
and you would penalize me if I did not abide!

You think I did not hear the threatening whispers
and the confusing cries of complaint?
It was you who wanted to expand his tent to become as spacious as the desert
and bring the world under your roof,
and pin down the nails such that no wind could move!
It was you who spoke of sharp blades and Arab zealotry!
You who would brag and boast and bluster
and imagine that the world was blaming you!
It was you who wanted to be worthy of a world better than your good self!
What is this malice, then? Choose this or that;
you cannot be a wild man of the desert and live in a castle too!

The three men cover themselves with a dark cloth.

NA'MAN. Last night, I dreamed about my father Amr al-Qeis!
He asked, "Where is the desert
we used to travel through on our enduring tireless camels?"
I pointed!
But the desert disappeared with a blow of the wind,
and the camels were only images on the walls of the castle!
He asked, "Where is the cedar forest
To frighten us with its demons?"
I pointed with my finger!
But the forest disappeared with a blow of the wind,
and the tall cedars, in the manner of ghouls and djinns,
were the guards of the castle!
My father Amr al-Qeis disappeared with a blow of a wind,
and I imagined he cursed me!

SENEMAR. I said I am willing to withdraw if you demand it, Na'man!
We will do as you wish;
I will forget all about the castle at your command!

NA'MAN. I said yes and no! By God, I go to sleep every night with the thoughts of destroying it,
and wake up in the morning with the desire to build it!
To discontinue?—But how?
Will you be able to return my cedar forest?
Can we return the soil we ransacked from the mountain to make bricks?
Are you going to return
the dates you gave, which they ate,
and the camels you roasted, which they devoured?

SENEMAR. Oh Na'man, by God, this is not about raising the castle
but raising yourself!
We are but our own makers!
I have not seen a great man achieve greatness
but with toil and trouble!
Name the castle after yourself, not Senemar, if that's what's bothering you!
How did such a dry desert of thatch and thorn
—the pathway of fantastical djinns and frightening ghosts—
become so dear to you
that you drove your father out of the grave to convince me?
You are inconsistent, Na'man!
You cannot decide whether you want to develop or not;
you do not know if you want the world to be natural or nurtured;
you want to have a castle without building it;
do you wish to preserve the desert as it is?

You are asking for the impossible!
Or—if I am not mistaken—you are afraid of reaching into your pouch;
you do not want development paid out of your pocket?
With no change, effort, and investment?
How could anything develop by itself?
Others toil and you avoid.
Invest some gold out of your pouch!

THE SECOND MAN. I remember. This was the cry I heard too!

THE FIRST MAN (*peeved*). And who did not?

THE THIRD MAN. The work was not progressing,
They would make one brick and break another!
One day he was ordered to build
and the day after he was commissioned to destroy!

SENEMAR (*furious*). What are all these excuses?
I did not ask for your daughter!
Nor for your best horse, your goat trip, or your best camel!
I made this for the sake of making it, and that suffices me!

NA'MAN. What ill song is this and from what throat does it come?
You lowborn Persian,
you unchaste Roman,
you dismiss the reward of the sultan of the al-Hirah—the reward the world is after?

SENEMAR. I have received no compensation but distress;
and by God, I am afraid of the reward you are promising!
Let's put an end to this!
I do not want you to return my wasted life
or my wasted hopes on this!
I said, "I will return, Na'man;

if you do not want my artistry,
I will take my art elsewhere."

NA'MAN. I will break the legs of the horse that takes you away from me!
I will tear the throat of the camel
that hides you in between its humps!
Leave?—And let people ask, "Where is the castle that has amazed the world by its reputation?
Where is the castle wherein Persia and Rome have become one image?"
And let my father Amr al-Qeis blame me from his grave
for I did not respect such an adept artisan?
I regret that I offended Senemar
And aggravated the Persian king for the castle I promised but did not build?

SENEMAR. I will not listen, Na'man, I will not!
Tomorrow you will not be what you are today!
Give me back my horse;
the swift black steed I came with!
Or sell it to me if you must;
or any horse that is not blind or crippled!

NA'MAN. Hit him—quick!—break the legs of his horse!

Three men attack Senemar and cover him while he is shouting.

NA'MAN. Tie his feet—the stronger knots the better!—
but not in a way to disable him from climbing the bulwark!
Or—God forbid—to make him fall from the ladder! Did you tie him up?
Now you can mount the tower and the scaffold, Senemar,
but you cannot ride a horse or a camel!

FIGURE 9. *The Sacrifice of Senemar.* Directed by Shima Javadpour at the Entezami Theatre at the Iranian Artists Forum, Tehran, 2018. *Photograph by Maryam Aslani.*

You have no choice. Do you understand?
Clearly I do not mind breaking both your legs,
If you take one step to escape!

SENEMAR. I demanded freedom and this imprisoned me further!
Who shall believe they tie up people in al-Hirah
in return for their art?

THE FIRST MAN. Caravans, traveling from one oasis to another,
were singing the songs of the bricklayers!

THE SECOND MAN. The song of the bricklayers became the chant of the sailors
voyaging on the Euphrates from one city to another!

THE THIRD MAN (*sings*). To all the sand of the desert— (*the other two join him*)
all that the wind carries,
say blow as hard as you can for the castle is upright,
and the thunderstorm can never reach its height!

SENEMAR. By God, you are tormenting me!
You do not let me go, you do not allow me to complete the castle,
and you leave me with no hope!
I remember one night—in concealment and under the torch lights—
you brought your harem to observe the castle.
I was busy with my work.
You, who were complaining an hour ago,
were now pompous and proudly bragging.
And I—as is my nature—was hiding,
for I was ashamed of its defects.
In a fraction of a moment, I saw her;
had these peeking eyes come to see the castle or me?
This jewel of an Arab
had come to visit the castle,
while a hundred castles must have gone to visit her.
And she was there to visit me.
Was it she who was enchanted by the castle?
Or was the castle enchanted by her?
You had introduced her to me briefly,
to afflict pain on me
so that I lose sight of leaving.
Or has she come willingly—
curious perhaps about the foreigner
whose name was entangled with hers?

And this look that burned me, was it accidental?
By God, you are tormenting me!
Why am I dusting the castle every night waiting for her to visit?
Why does the heat of the sand remind me of the fire in my heart?
Why does the crescent moon appear like a dagger in my heart?
Why do I see the torn clouds, like my body and soul?
By God, you have inflicted nightmares upon me!
The stars are more than I can count
and the sands more than I can string into a necklace for her.
If only I could engrave that magic on the wall—no!
Why should I engrave the image of her eyes on the wall?
That would bring it to the attention of the King of Persia!
He will fall in love and will ask for her.
I said no—I shall sleep no more;
I will busy myself with the castle for a while.
You will either reward me with her or let me go!

NA'MAN. I erred—alas—I mentioned her name!
This Persian of Rome is truly in love and deluded.
He already considers that beauty his wife
and takes pride in her as the reward for this rare work!
Still, I am not sure if I want to marry her to this man between two races
or gift her to the King of Persia—there is more benefit in that!

Clamor; the sounds of jolly men or announcements. Three men veil their heads and faces in black headgears. They wear shining breastplates with daggers fixed to their waists. Arm in arm, they make a wall that hides Na'man's daughter.

THE FIRST MAN. We are castrated slaves, the confidants and the guards of Na'man's daughter—

who, despite her young age, has great men at her service.
We have brought you a few questions from her!

SENEMAR. Deeply honored; and I greet that beautiful gem!

THE SECOND MAN. She asks, "May you be safe, master; how many stars are in the sky?
And how many grains of sand in the desert?"

SENEMAR. My father was once speaking of the Zoroastrian priests' *Pandnāmeh.*[4]
All these grains of sand are the zeros to a number
that no one can count or read!
And by God—I never wrote your name on any sand;
lest the wind may sweep it!
And the stars are the guards of the veiled moon,
if only I could catch a glimpse of her moonlit face!

THE THIRD MAN. She asks, "May you be safe, master; what does your name mean?"
She queries this because of a dream she had!

SENEMAR. My father would say (*referring to the book of names*) the *simorgh*[5] of the sun!
My father knew the story of the *simorgh*,
who flew all around the world to find a summit most high
so that he could fly higher than that!

---

4 Zoroastrian book of manners.

5 *Simorgh* is a legendary bird in Persian mythology and literature. It literally means thirty birds. Of the two most famous simorghs, one appears in the eleventh-century Persian epic the *Shahnameh* by Abolqasem Ferdowsi, and the other appears in the thirteenth-century Persian book of poems *The Conference of Birds* by Attar of Neyshabur.

FIGURE 10. *The Sacrifice of Senemar*. Directed by Shima Javadpour at the Entezami Theatre at the Iranian Artists Forum, Tehran, 2018. *Photograph by Shahriar Akbarieh.*

THE GIRL (*restless*). She says, "Oh, but you spoke of my dream and my heart melted!"[6]

SENEMAR. So did my heart from the melody of this voice!

THE FIRST MAN (*to the other two men*). We did not hear this conversation!

THE SECOND MAN. She asks, "What was your reward for such great craftsmanship?"

SENEMAR. By God, I have seen no reward better than the sunrise and the sunset;
when my heart is close to those I am far from!
Gold? No! What am I to gain by it?
Youth? Love? Or reputation?
My reward is to see the castle upright,
the edifice which was but a fantasy yesterday
and is full of love if you come again to visit it.
An edifice which—like my dreams—
changes colors throughout the day;
And an arrow from this rainbow of colors has struck my heart,
telling me that there is no better color than the black of your eyes!

THE THIRD MAN. She asks, "May you be safe, master; this is the desert for winds
and we are in the crossroads of this wuthering land;
what do you think of these seasonal winds?"

SENEMAR. I am not of the kind—no!
If you come to Rome or Persia, you will honor me beyond words!
And if you are devoted to your home here, I will forget everything and stay with you!

---

6 This is the only time the girl speaks during this scene in her encounter with Senemar. For the rest of this scene, her words are relayed to Senemar by the guards.

THE FIRST MAN. And yet another question—

THE SECOND MAN. If you please!

THE THIRD MAN. She asks, "You and I are of two separate religions!
What do you think of our gods?"

SENEMAR. I know but one deity in the world;
and please know that I worship her with every bone in my body!

NA'MAN. What wrong did I commit—oh my girl,
she fell in love with him. Why did I mention his name?
I feel the Arab honor boiling in my blood.
I wish I had buried her alive when she was born!
Such a beauty envied by the houris of paradise;
if only the old Arab manners were still practiced,
I would have married her myself![7]

A clamor of voices arises as the three men resume their former roles.

THE FIRST MAN. Do you regret what you gifted?

THE SECOND MAN. And perhaps soon you'll regret that you regretted it!

THE THIRD MAN. I have also heard excuses for the wrongs of time.
Self-deceiving and pretentious excuses!

NA'MAN. You never knew about my sufferings. No, you did not!
And if you shall not—or never do—
whom shall I open my heart to?

---

7 In the pre-Islamic Arab world, known as Jāhiliyeh, the practice of burying baby girls upon their birth was common among many Arab cultures, who believed that daughters brought shame to their tribe and family. Condemned in the Quran (the Surah "An-Nahl" [The Bee], verses 58 and 59, and Surah Takvir, verse 9), the practice was banned as Islam was established. A variety of marriages were practiced in the ancient times, including those between fathers and their daughters, which the Quran declared *harām* (forbidden by Islamic law) in the Surah "An-Nisa" [The Women], verse 23.

My adversaries line up with diatribes against me,
as do the girl's suitors. Yet you knew nothing!

SENEMAR. I did know, but I never wished for it.

NA'MAN. No, you did not see that they buzzed in my ear!

SENEMAR. I could imagine, though I never saw.
I could hear all the same, even though I never eavesdropped.

NA'MAN. They were Arab bricklayers
who never made anything but fantasy.

The three men, who have been hammering a wheelbarrow, cover their head and rise.

THE FIRST MAN. Na'man has cast us away and approached Senemar!
Was there no architect in al-Hirah
that you should summon this damn fellow from nowhere?

THE SECOND MAN. You revered a foreigner and humiliated the Arab!

THE THIRD MAN. You chose a Roman man with Persian blood,
which means Arabs are nothing to you!

NA'MAN. What are you talking about?
I commissioned an architect who knew the job.
I did not choose him for his Persian or Roman blood!

THE FIRST MAN. What did he do that an Arab would not?
Laying bricks on bricks is a job anyone could do!

THE SECOND MAN. Are you not ashamed to hear that Arabs were unable to build such an edifice?

THE THIRD MAN. Does it not embarrass you to offer your best camels, horses,
and seventy of your best goats to a foreigner?

THE SECOND MAN. And worst of all, your daughter,
who is a beauty among Arabs?

THE THIRD MAN. No sultan ever honored a foreigner
at the expense of humiliating his people the way you did.
NA'MAN. I responded, Senemar, and I turned my back to them!
Not for you,
but because they were not speaking the truth,
and they were selling me the artistry they never had;
yes, they were using it as a club to hit me on the head!
THE FIRST MAN. Did you ever try us?
Did you ever hear us say that we could not build a castle?
THE SECOND MAN. Why shouldn't the King of Persia see you as a villain
when you see us as villains—
and not your tribesmen?
THE THIRD MAN. Everyone knows that the King of Persia—whose glory baffles you—
has not demanded a palace.
It is you who wants to impress the Persian king with a palace!
NA'MAN. Yes—people come in groups to visit the castle already.
The caravans make a detour to come this way,
and damsels accept the proposals of those suitors
who promise to take them to visit the castle!
Already a bazaar is set up nearby
offering goat milk and chestnut bread to the pilgrims.
They lease tents for different prices.
The more expensive ones are camel hair, and the cheaper ones, goat!
The poets rhyme their panegyrics line by line,
inspired by each brick of the castle.
Come and observe the images on the wall.
The fish is swimming in the sea;
or perhaps, it is the sea that floats among the fish!

And the bird is flying in the sky;
still, one could imagine the sky as a bird flying over us!
By God, the King of Persia is coming
not to visit one of his vassals but to see a king of his own rank!

THE FIRST MAN. You are soaring too high, Na'man.
All these qualities in a Roman?
Do you not observe the Arab hands in the mud?

NA'MAN. I do, and that is a blessing! And you should note.
The sluggards are now agile!
Those who would measure the desert merely by the look of it
now precisely survey the scale of wind!
They speak of plumb lines and compasses
and of mixing a variety of mortars for the walls!
And they speak of a castle which is to stand for a thousand years!
We have revived the manners of the kings of Babylon and Assyria!
Bricklayers from various tribes,
with idols of clay, wood, or stone
—who swear by different gods—
have buried axes and are busy building.
Where are you, Senemar? How many days until winter?
Will you promise to finish in time?

THE FIRST MAN. The castle must have been ours!

THE SECOND MAN. Your best camel, your best horse,
your seventy best goat herds
and your daughter—the eldest—exemplary among Arabs for her beauty!

NA'MAN. Truly? Speak no more, you can build nothing grander than hovels and huts,
each of them as ugly as a toad!

Observe the castle;
which of you has ever built a wall taller than his own height?
Which of you has made a shack that could withstand the wind?
Which of you has built a roof over his family's head that has lasted?
Your slums—made out of reeds—let the wind in,
and your buildings—still under construction—are in a dilapidated state!
Yes, you are Arab and arrogant—why should you want a roof when you have the sky?
And why the need for a bedchamber when your pillow is but the desert?
Yes, you ride your horses of bigotry, stuck in the sand!
And now that someone is riding his horse at the pace of a gallop,
you mean to break him down.
Why all these excuses?
Is it because he is a foreigner?
Because he is not one of us?
Who relies not on our bigotry
but on his own knowledge and expertise?

THE FIRST MAN. Who has ever seen an Arab sultan
arguing with his own people
for the sake of a Roman—who is far from the best?

THE SECOND MAN. He knows—and so we are neglected!

THE THIRD MAN. He knows—all his knowledge mocks our ignorance!

THE FIRST MAN. He disgraces us with this castle
By showing what we have never done!

NA'MAN. I know what agitates you.
Everyone knows how to lay one brick on top of another!

What you lacked was the idea of what one can do with bricks!
He had the image of the castle in his mind,
an image that we did not have until he made it come alive!

THE FIRST MAN. Na'man, you speak Persian with the King of Persia;
we have listened to the stories of Persian *gusans*[8] too!
You assume we have not heard the names of Rostam, Zal, and Esfandiyar?[9]

THE SECOND MAN. You are intimidated by their greatness
and you thought we were incapable of building such an edifice!

THE FIRST MAN. You responded to their grandeur with Roman splendor!

THE SECOND MAN. You made Arabs beg of Romans!

THE THIRD MAN. What does an Arab, the pillar of his own tent,
have to do with Persian domes,
which Rome, by the way, has plenty of.

---

8 *Gusāns* were performing artists in Parthian courts (247 BCE to 224 CE), skilled in the arts of music, dance, and storytelling.

9 These three men are legendary figures from Persian mythology whose stories are recounted by Ferdowsi in his master epic, the *Shahnameh*. Rostam, a heroic warrior and the son of Zal and Rudabeh, is best known for his Seven Labors (*Haft Khān*)—a series of trials undertaken to rescue his king—reminiscent of Hercules' adventures. His father Zal is a renowned Persian warrior and king from Sistān, most famous for the story of his miraculous survival as an infant. Born with poliosis (white hair), Zal was abandoned by his father near Mount Damavand, only to be rescued and raised by the mythical bird Simorgh. Esfandiyar is an invincible hero-prince who met his death at the hands of Rostam. Like Achilles, he was nearly invincible—having been dipped in holy water—but his closed eyes remained vulnerable, making him fatally susceptible to Rostam's poisonous arrows.

FIGURE 11. *The Sacrifice of Senemar*. Directed by Shima Javadpour at the Entezami Theatre at the Iranian Artists Forum, Tehran, 2018. *Photograph by Shahriar Akbarieh.*

THE SECOND MAN. And their wind breakers made of checkered lattices!
And those *mils*[10] they make between two caravansaries![11]

THE FIRST MAN. Comfort us with your placation!

---

10 Lighthouse-like edifices built between two cities to guide travelers and messengers through darkness or fog.

11 Caravansaries were roadside inns made for travelers to rest and recover on their journeys. Located near major ancient thoroughfares like the Silk Road, they provided shelter and functioned as commercial hubs for traders. Caravansaries in Iran date back to the Achaemenid period (500 BCE).

NA'MAN. By the supreme gods, he will not stay, but you will!
So do not mess with him. Let him finish and go!

THE FIRST MAN. Yes, he will go and build the same castle for someone else!

THE SECOND MAN. And perhaps better than this one!

THE THIRD MAN. It is we who will remain for you, and completely disgraced!

NA'MAN. What? Better than this castle?
Or even its twin, for someone else?
You said better than this?

THE FIRST MAN. One who builds this, why should he not be capable of building one better?
Surely there will be another Na'man with golden treasures!

THE SECOND MAN. This edifice which you built very high will then look short;
and they will say, for instance, that what Na'man built is smaller in size
than the one Senemar built with the gold of the King of Persia!

NA'MAN. Open your eyes, Na'man, to what you refuse to see!
Why should he not be able to build a better edifice, he who builds this?
I believed that the best in the world was here!
Did I not ask for the best? Where is Senemar?
If you are truly working,
Be like his servants around him.
Learn from him whatever you can!
Yes, pay close attention to his work,
from the walls he builds
to the figures he engraves on the wall!

I will threaten his associates
so they disavow and leave him;
and you—if you are truly builders,
serve him, look over his shoulders,
and become his associates!
Thus, when we divorce the castle from his name,
no task is left undone!
Yes, learn from him as much as you can!
So that when the world is deprived of his name,
and the King of Persia is awed by the wonders of the castle
and asks for the architect,
you do not stick in the mud!

Three men depart. Senemar's hand, holding a letter, drops.

SENEMAR. One day, a traveler came with a letter
from my gray-haired mother
who was asking about my return:
"Your father is ill and asks, 'Where is our lost one?'
I put him to sleep by promising that you will come home soon!
He moans in Persian
And I sigh in Latin.
Come and be the common language of us both, today or tomorrow!"
My mother asks why had I not done this for the Romans,
If I knew how to build such a castle?
"Why did you not take this art to where they wanted it?"
I thought, "Instead of writing back, I will tell her in person"

THE FIRST MAN. Are you really going?

SENEMAR. I asked, "Who am I? Where do I belong?
Am I from Persia, or Rome, or from this desert—since I fell in love here?"

THE SECOND MAN. Was this what you wrote and sent?

SENEMAR. I wrote it on the sand, and the wind wiped it away.

THE THIRD MAN. So, you did not reply?

SENEMAR. What should I write, Mother, how should I respond?
Blazing under the sun, burning on hot sand and in the fire of patience;
at times, I think I would give Rome and Persia for a glimpse of her—
and again, I fear she does not wish it!

Three men cover themselves with clay and dust from the wheelbarrow. Disguised as beggars with sticks in hand, they approach Senemar.

THE FIRST MAN. But of course, you will not recognize us, foreigner;
we are from the remotest areas of the desert!

THE SECOND MAN. We heard news that you employed many people;
the poor people truly adore you
and many pray for you.

THE FIRST MAN. But are you building this for the poor?
No! It is for the rich!
Not even for Na'man, but the great King of Persia!

THE SECOND MAN. We do not even benefit from its shade!

SENEMAR. The King of Persia shall reside here for no longer than a winter,
while the castle shall stand a thousand winters!
No, what I build is not for the King of Persia;
he is but an excuse, and Na'man only the means!

THE THIRD MAN (*scolding the two other beggars*). Stop talking nonsense!
No palace was built for a beggar!
And what palace has been built with no investment?
If you put up money, you will have a castle too;
and if you have none, why not work at the castle to earn something?

THE FIRST MAN. I would rather beg the tribes than work at this castle!

THE SECOND MAN. We are of the ashes and that is our manner of life!

SENEMAR. Working on this castle might teach you to aim high;
otherwise, you will only amount to ashes!

THE FIRST MAN. From the moment you open your eyes to the time you close it forever,
you are always in need!
The colorful garment of independence is worn out
and does not fit the wanting body!
And it is more honorable to beg.

SENEMAR. Who has ever witnessed such an attempt
at sluggishness?
Every excuse I hear
is to avoid working!
Are you looking for the land of lotus eaters?
Truly, you are wrong!
If you roll your sleeves up, we will have a word to say,
otherwise good riddance!

THE SECOND MAN. You are the unconditional supporter of the rich!

SENEMAR. I work and that defines me!
I must work so that I do not feel useless!
Give me something to do if you have it,
otherwise, stop insulting me!

THE FIRST MAN. I wonder at such blather! All this idle talk!

THE SECOND MAN. I laugh at all this nonsense! These trifles!

THE THIRD MAN. We are happy in our carefreeness!

SENEMAR. No—you disdain labor, you are idle!
You are proud of your open mouths and stretched hands for begging!
I am the one whom the kings beg for,
because of the skills I possess!

THE FIRST MAN. Did you hear that? His pride is no less than ours!
We were right that sultans were begging for our carefree lives,
and despite everything we lack, we are free men!

THE SECOND MAN. I have neither territory that an enemy could rob
nor treasure or a harem for which they would kill me in my sleep!

THE THIRD MAN (*to the other two*). That is what I meant; let us go—
of what use is the castle to you
when you only delight in its shade?
What difference does it make to you where you sleep?
The shade of a palm tree which catches the wind
is sweeter than the shade of a castle which blocks it!

They are gone. Na'man crosses in haste with a lamp in hand; he is looking for Senemar.

NA'MAN. Where are you, Senemar?
They report that you are ill. Has a scorpion stung you?
What are these unique figures on the wall?
How handsome and distinctive! When did you create them?
Where did you get them?
This should be Rudabeh on the tower—if I am not mistaken—
hauling Zal up with her long tress![12]
How identical is she to my daughter!
Each one of these is a treasure;
does this mean that you can build grander than this
for better compensation?

SENEMAR. I dreamed that she dreamed about me;
I rubbed my eyes and wondered if it was she, or just her image?

---

12 Two mythological figures from the *Shahnameh*. This story about Zal and Rudabeh is the source for the seventeenth-century German fairy tale *Rapunzel*.

The girl appears gradually.

THE GIRL. I dreamed that she dreamed about me;
she veiled her face when I asked to see her,
yet I had no burqa in my hand!
Others turned into shadows and the tents were taken down,
and I remembered the word I had forgotten.

SENEMAR. We spoke in each other's dreams;
she spoke but only in dream,
and her voice was a song she had never sung!

THE GIRL. I wish I were not famous for my beauty!
I wish they did not see my beauty
the way they do in their dreams!
They sing of me in their songs—
those who know me not.
I am entrapped in my tent and in the desert!
I wish I could take my song
deep into the endless desert and over the raging river!
I wish my pained soul had an image,
so that you could see how it is sickened.
(*Worries for a moment*)
Why am I speaking this,
when I am captive to this desert, because of an antiquated tradition?
(*Slower*) Everyone I see in the desert is below me;
I am a foreigner among my own people.
(*Touches her heart*) What did we add to the world? Nothing.
The days and nights passed by while we were still dwelling in this desert.
But then a foreigner came and shook this sand,
a foreigner greater than his scales!

We have changed,
we are no longer desert dwellers!
We have a castle!
This is what we see from our tents;
the castle has blocked the view of the horizon!
When you climb atop,
you have a broader view
of the endless desert and the raging river,
upon which the sailors sing of you.

THE FIRST MAN. So, you said you had a dream! So much of a dream!
But you did not say what you saw in your dream!

THE SECOND MAN. Interesting! When were you even sleeping so you could dream?

THE THIRD MAN (*secretive*). Do not tell anyone that you see Na'man's daughter in your dreams!

The three men laughingly go to sleep; the girl disappears.

SENEMAR. What should I write, Mother?
Every bone in my body cries out my love for her!
I swear to the gods of this region—to whom I am only an alien—
that the love missing from Rome and Persia
is hidden here in her eyes!
How could a trapped captive come to visit you?
Look at the veiled moon, her furtive looks
guarded by a thousand stars!
And in her proximity, I am still far from her!
Under this low sky, full of dark clouds!
Is she awake and looking at herself in the sky?
Look, the stars in the Big Dipper
are reveling with the Great Bear!
Cancer is drinking water from Aquarius!

FIGURE 12. *The Sacrifice of Senemar*. Directed by Shima Javadpour at the Entezami Theatre at the Iranian Artists Forum, Tehran, 2018. *Photograph by Shahriar Akbarieh.*

Venus is seated among the seven stars of the Big Dipper,
Sagittarius at her service!
That is Gemini, the one torn into two bodies!
Lucky and unlucky stars are at war with each other and the cosmos,
restless in its orbit;
and I am yet Senemar!

NA'MAN. I shall untie you and let you go, if you wish it!
How long should I shield you from the arrows they shoot at you?
Everyone points at you. "Him!"

SENEMAR. Do not untie me, Na'man, unless you let me go to her tent!
Let my gray-haired mother in Rome read my reply in my silence;
or with your blessing, a camel should stop by her door
with two riders!

NA'MAN. Are you insane?
I am surrounded by my own vassals!
Did you not see how they encircled me?
No, you did not hear when the Arab sheikhs
invited me to their tents, to the council of sheikhs, in secret,
and advised me against building this castle—
sometimes with soft words and sometimes with threats!

Three men cover themselves with white flour from the wheelbarrow and play the roles of the sheiks.

THE FIRST MAN. You fancy the paradise of Shaddad,[13] Na'man,

---

13 Shaddad, a descendant of the people of ʿAad, was a king of their nation. Having heard about the afterlife paradise described by prophets of his time, he decided to build a paradise on earth. He built a splendid city from gold and precious gems, aiming to rival the divine. But as he entered the city, a horrific scream from the heavens killed him and his cohort as punishment for his arrogance. The fabled city became a source of inspiration for many legendary stories and adventures.

and the Hanging Gardens of Babylon.
Did they not turn to ashes?

NA'MAN. I was not at a loss for words, no;
and I faced the consequences by all means!
I said—yes I did! "You, my fathers—the sheikhs!
We are created to think and act.
The castle is our endeavor realized in shape!
Is it not preferable to be recognized by study than by sluggishness?"

THE SECOND MAN. Try not to think of the world!
That old world with two gates,
from one of which we enter and the other exit—
and the chance to live is just this short distance!

NA'MAN. Why should we think of demise in advance?
Shall we not live because death is at hand?
And build not because desolation is inevitable?

THE THIRD MAN. Visit the graveyard three times a day
to see the end of man!
Do it three times or more
to forget laughing and begin mourning forever!

NA'MAN. Better to face danger once than to live in fear of it forever!
Why do you mourn over your death when you are still alive?
I have other vocations than mourning!

THE FIRST MAN. You are proud of your power, and what is the castle but a symbol of arrogance?
There are many who have wild wishes but fear vanity!

NA'MAN. And you take pride in your humility
which interests no one!

THE SECOND MAN. You spoke of people's interest?
There are many who have ideas but are in want of means!

And there are many more who are empty-handed
yet have heads full of thoughts.

NA'MAN. Where?
Show me someone with a plan, the measurements, and the skills.
Do you expect me to support any pretender
that has no intention but to loot me?
And make the world mock me for idiocy?
Just because there are a few people
who are worthy of support
—and I am not even sure that there are—
shall I do nothing, because they are still wanting?

THE FIRST MAN. The castle is a thorn in the side of the desert!

THE SECOND MAN. We lacked a mountain and thanks to you we now have it!

THE FIRST MAN. Our gods are displeased!

THE SECOND MAN. Fear the wrath of the supreme gods!

NA'MAN. I said, "What I do is for you Arabs!
Is it not preferable for Arabs to be known for their development rather than destruction?"

THE FIRST MAN. There will be a huge gap between your castle and our huts!

NA'MAN. Not more than the gap between our endeavors!
Come and observe an edifice which is like a mirror held up to the sun
and every hour it turns into one of the colors of the rainbow!

THE SECOND MAN. Learn to show your true, unwavering color, Na'man!

NA'MAN. I swear to the sun and to the moon when they have not eclipsed
that the tribes are greater only with greater gods!
A great man sees wider horizons and the vile man but his own shadow!
Do not fear development!

It is with the castle that we become visible to the world,
not with the wind-stricken tents!
You thought Na'man would be a great man? Yes,
and by gods, it will be you who will achieve greatness if he becomes great!
By the supreme gods, as long as we engage with trifles,
we remain insignificant,
and as long as we bow down,
we suffer from shortsightedness!

THE FIRST MAN. But is he not a stranger you nourish and endear?

THE SECOND MAN. Yes, what of this rumor
about him and that beauty
who, despite her young age, is reputed to tower over the brides of Arabs?

THE FIRST MAN. Woe if he looks at your daughter and boasts about her to Arabs!

THE SECOND MAN (*angry*). He has two foreign bloods in him, Persian and Roman together!

NA'MAN. This is the song I have heard before!
No! He is not here because he is a Roman or a Persian.
He is here because he is Senemar!

THE THIRD MAN. From what I understand, Na'man is endeared to Arabs
and has brought a foreigner to serve them!

NA'MAN. Yes—that is it!
Do all Romans build castles as Senemar does?
Do all Persians toil and strive like him?
No, they lay back and suck the juice from life,
if not sucking its blood.
And did you ever hear me say that Senemar is flawless?

He has numerous defects. Yes,
he wrongs himself and this is his flaw!
He does not sleep at nights and he sketches on sand,
and during the day, he is lost in thoughts!
He is concerned with the swift passage of time!
I have seen no Roman or Persian as restless as he is!
He looks as if he is lost
or has lost something!

SENEMAR. Yes, I knew it—although I did not hear it.
I dreamed about it, even though I did not see it for real!
The desert was in commotion;
people were asking why, why, why.
There was no objection, no claim, no murmur before the castle;
and now everyone was expressing their right to it!
Now that something was happening,
there were many hopes to demolish the castle!

The three men lift up their garments and fix them in their waistband. They rub dust and mud on themselves. They are spongers now, gleeful and happy.

THE THIRD MAN. Hey, you! Do some mud work!
How much longer are you going to fuss with the pot and the stove?

THE FIRST MAN. Why should we complete the castle in time? No!
The longer it takes, the longer I am paid!

THE THIRD MAN. Swindle if you like, but do something too!

THE FIRST MAN. Of course I do—I laugh at you!
I eat twice as much as a gluttonous man
and work half of the lazybones—
This is what it means to profit!

Why should I count the stars
when Na'man's coins are shining before my eyes?

THE SECOND MAN (*drops the spade*). I liked it! Work for a longer time and get paid more!
I do not move a muscle except for stretching out my hand for my wage!

THE FIRST MAN. I try my best not to try! Let others toil to death!

SENEMAR. Hey, you who have crawled to the corners,
you whisper into each other's ear and taunt me.
I fear the bread you win will get stuck in your throat!
You pretend to work
yet you do nothing,
and if I pay you the same as those who work,
I have wronged those who labor honestly!
Have you laid any brick,
or climbed a ladder?
Are you asking for payoff instead of payment?
You roughnecks with your big bellies!
You are fired since you are taking space from real workers!

THE FIRST MAN. Oh! He meant me, and you too!

THE SECOND MAN. Never has a foreigner been so rude to an Arab!

THE FIRST MAN. Why don't we pull his tongue out of his throat, huh? Shall we tear his belly wide open?

THE SECOND MAN. Why did Na'man entitle a foreigner to have authority over us?

THE FIRST MAN. Fired! Ha! That is insolent!
I cannot call myself an Arab if I do not defame him!

THE SECOND MAN. Let us go. I swear to the boiling blood in my body and my honor which pulses on the plate of my temple;

I see no good ending for him!
And it is not unlikely that someday, someone more wrathful than I would smear his hands in his blood!

THE FIRST MAN. Hmm, and if no one does so, how would desert dwellers know
that the same red blood runs in the vessels of the degenerates!

They depart. Na'man approaches from the crowd. He is restless.

NA'MAN. Do not beat around the bush. You did not reply to me!

SENEMAR. I did!

NA'MAN. You did not!—Everyone questions me and I respond,
but no one replies to my question.
Give me a proper answer!

SENEMAR. Then ask a proper question!

NA'MAN (*cries*). Is this the best there is?

SENEMAR. This is the best for now and the best given the resources we had—
from knowledge to ideas, skills, workforce, labor, and art.
We did not have huge tower cranes suitable for tall edifices,
nor did we have protectors and stones!
Given the available resources, we made something unprecedented.
The King of Persia will not blame you!
And the images on this wall
—somewhere next to the battle of Rostam and the Div—[14]
will show him the construction of the castle
and the people who came to visit it!
And among them, he will see someone—
and her eyes!

---

14 One of the Seven Labors of Rostam, in which he kills a white demon during his journey to rescue his king.

NA'MAN. You put my mind at rest!

SENEMAR. There should have been something to assure me too, Na'man;
you did not know me and you never will!
You were lost in your thoughts,
thinking of yourself and caring less about me,
who was neither in his hometown nor had a deserved position!
Any of your archers
could have targeted me with their arrows
while there was no one from my people to avenge my blood!

NA'MAN. Oh, Senemar—you are speaking new words!

THE FIRST MAN. It was too late to speak those words!

THE SECOND MAN. Late too, for Na'man, to hear them!

THE THIRD MAN. Did he want it at all?

THE SECOND MAN. Did he not know anyways?

NA'MAN. What is it that I don't know? Speak, Senemar!

SENEMAR. You never knew what threats I encountered thanks to your people,
who, upon hearing about this establishment,
came from the furthest parts of the desert!

Three men sprinkle ocher dust over themselves. They take off their clothes and wear them inside out. Carrying sacks on their backs, they now become heads of the tribes that have just finished a journey.

THE FIRST MAN. You wrong us, Senemar!
You promote Na'man
and humble us more than ever!
We do not mount anything higher than our camels,
and he who rode a camel like one of us
now mounts to the roof of the castle,

so that from amid the clouds—and out of arrogance—he could look down on us
and humiliate us more!

THE SECOND MAN. No, Senemar, this is not your flaw!
You have fed many with the bricks they laid;
but when the castle is complete, then what?
Now that they know how it feels not to be hungry,
are you going to abandon them in the desert?
What about their tomorrows?
It was easier for them to suffer hunger,
before they knew how it felt to be satiated.

THE THIRD MAN. No, there is no evil in you, but in the castle.
It is upon everyone to make himself worthy of it;
we deserve the desert, the nothingness!
How could we rise and be worthy of the castle?
We are two different worlds,
two worlds next to one another yet dissimilar.

NA'MAN. Oh, this agitates me gravely;
I will not tolerate that they do this to my guest!
They said this, and yet you did not speak of it to me?

SENEMAR. No, Na'man—it was you who did not ask how my days were passed!

THE FIRST MAN. Oh, Senemar—you are building a castle greater than our temples!
Do you not fear earthquakes or floods?
Or the wrath of gods
for the edifice you build higher than their dens?
Our gods—of any tribe and name—
dwell in the darkness of a den, a pit, a crack.

They live on a pile of ashes
while you rise the castle to heavens!

THE SECOND MAN. This is not your vice. It is that you create something everlasting!
We are passengers—
we arrive one day and depart the next—but the castle remains!
Why should it stand and witness our demise?
Why should the castle be when we shall not?

THE THIRD MAN. This is not your vice, Senemar;
it is that you showed us what we could have built but we chose not to.
You held a mirror to our indolence—
a mirror that reflects us as braggarts
who have not moved a muscle in a thousand years!

SENEMAR. This is the end of he who built a castle on the flowing sand!
Who erected a building in mud and mire
and mistook the mirage for the sea!

NA'MAN. We were making something at a time that was not ready for it.

SENEMAR. Neither were you, Na'man;
you were not ready for what you had wished!

NA'MAN. I wanted the best!

SENEMAR. You are mean, Na'man, and you are insular!
You learned the wrath of kings, not their mercy!
You asked for the best, without making yourself worthy of it!
You threw me down—I who promoted you—
and broke the bones of he who strengthened you.

NA'MAN. Speak not—and do not remember—yet;
yes, I did this all, and with my own hands!
And I laugh at your blame!

FIGURE 13. *The Sacrifice of Senemar*. Directed by Shima Javadpour at the Entezami Theatre at the Iranian Artists Forum, Tehran, 2018. *Photograph by Shahriar Akbarieh.*

Why should I go mad?
Why should I get lost in the desert of winds?
If Senemar was alive, he would tyrannize me,
and build a grander castle for others who give better rewards!

THE FIRST MAN. Oh, we should regret twice as much then!
The world suffers for it will never see his next, finer castle!

THE SECOND MAN. There is no art in destroying, Na'man.
True art lives in building and creating!

THE THIRD MAN. Anyone can push anyone off a ledge,
but who is it that can build a castle?

NA'MAN. You speak, and speak too much—but now listen.
A lot was saved;
my best horse and my best camel,
and the seventy best goats of my herds;
and my daughter, who is a jewel among Arabs!

SENEMAR. Why did you not let me go, even if I was heartbroken and empty-handed?
Was I not your guest, whom you summoned and was at your mercy?
Even if I had not built the castle,
or you had not promised me your daughter,
it was not the Arab way to kill an innocent guest.

NA'MAN. The castle was complete, and we were at the roof, with the desert under our feet!

THE FIRST MAN. Oh, Castle! You are visible from everywhere in the desert,
why can one not take his eye off you?
I was riding my camel!

THE SECOND MAN. The castle—this ship grounded in land—was watching me
as I was about to hoist the sails!

THE THIRD MAN. I saw them on the roof;
there was no need for an interpreter;
both were speaking the language of the King of Persia!

NA'MAN. I asked him, "Could you build another castle like this? As good as this one?"
I told him, "This is beyond anyone's imagination.
Tell me, could you ever build anything better than this?"

SENEMAR. I replied, "Yes, I could have, had I known earlier that you would reward me with her
—reputed for her beauty among Arabs—
I would have built a *kushk*,[15] which this castle could never compare to!
We built this castle with craftsmanship, but that castle I would build with love!
A *kushk*, as new as each passing day!
A *kushk*, multicolored like the peacock's tail.
A *kushk* with seven domes and seven floors like the heavens!

NA'MAN. So, there is one better than this in your imagination?
You can build a better one?

SENEMAR. I told him, "Yes, there are hundreds of these in my head
which I dream of like that beautiful girl.
Yes, if there is gold, tools, and support!"

NA'MAN. I asked, "Even better than this one?"

SENEMAR. I replied, "There is no end to imagination.
And perfection is my aspiration.
Yes, Na'man—I am capable of building better than this,
if only life would spare me time!
I am restless and my heart is beating fast;
is it not the time to deliver what you promised?"

---

15 Iranian garden pavilion.

NA'MAN. And I rewarded him!

Everyone shouts at once; they all cover their ears with their hands.

SENEMAR. It was a long way down, and an opportunity
to understand that I will die a painful death.
You who did not like me,
how did you like the sound of my bones breaking?

THE FIRST MAN (*cries*). Why shouldn't he feel regret, he who does good?

THE SECOND MAN (*cries*). Why shouldn't he feel regret, he who thinks?

THE THIRD MAN (*cries*). Why shouldn't he feel regret, he who builds?

SENEMAR. I thought if I lived another life
and knew that I would be pushed down to death
from the top of what I built
—a death equal to dying forty times—
and would hear my breaking bones in every brick of the building,
I would still build the highest castle possible!
soaring as high as man's soul!

NA'MAN. No, Senemar, we are not your problem!
I swear your problem is your honesty!
Why did you not deceive me?
Why did you not say that this was the best possible castle?
Why did you not say you would retire?
Why did you not say that you would only build for me, the sultan of Arabs,
and no one else?

SENEMAR. Remember, Na'man?
Once a storyteller came from Persia
and brought a new story. *One Thousand Tales* was its name,
and the castle workers would listen to it each night to recover from their daily toil.

It was the story of a king who used to wed a damsel every night
and decapitate her the next morning.
Women were all horrified,
and the daughter of the vizir, herself terrified, was after a solution!
And when it was her turn, and the ceremony was performed,
she persuaded the king to demand a story from her—as this was the manner!
Thus, with the magic of stories that she created herself
and left unfinished at the dawn,
she made the executioner wait for her blood till the next night;
and for one thousand nights, with one thousand tales,
she saved one thousand lives!
You Na'man—the son of Amr al-Qeis—would listen and say,
Persians exaggerate!
How would a sultan
respond to kindness with atrocity
and kill an overnight guest the next morning?
You shed my blood and broke my bones—
I, who was your guest for years and months!
You inflicted on me the pain of a death equal to dying forty times
for the service I offered you!
And by heavens, you would not kill me if the castle were not completed;
like the tales of Shahrzad whom the king would keep alive
to hear the end of the story.

NA'MAN. Do not reprimand me, desert dwellers!
Do you have nothing other than blame for me?
Did you not encourage me to push him off?
Do not blame me, you the images on the wall!

I wish I were but an image
to be erased and rewritten anew!

SENEMAR. I said, "I wish the same to you!
I wish your toils go unrecognized!"
I said, "I wish that you receive ingratitude as compensation for your art!"
I said this and yet said nothing as I was upside-down between the two worlds;
the sky was closing its eyes
and the earth was opening its arms!

NA'MAN. Do not take this news to my daughter, for she will cut her hair
and tear at her face!
Do not take this message to her,
she will moan most grievously!
She believed for long she was his betrothed!

SENEMAR. I said, "Look among the images on the walls;
where I engraved my dreams,
there lies a man under the feet of an elephant!
I dreamed a king bearing your name, the offspring of your offspring,
will atone for your sin!
The castle is still upright when that elephant rider,
the King of Persia, will kill him under the feet of his elephant, as a reward for his service!
I wish this does not come true;
I wish it were only a dream, not a curse!
Bury me under the feet of that which did not step on my head!
Bury me in the castle!

The stagehands, clad in black, pick up the body and slowly take it to the castle.

FIGURE 14. *The Sacrifice of Senemar*. Directed by Shima Javadpour at the Entezami Theatre at the Iranian Artists Forum, Tehran, 2018. *Photograph by Shahriar Akbarieh.*

THE THIRD MAN. Rome will not be moved by his death!
And Persia will not rise up to take his revenge!
THE SECOND MAN. His mother will receive nothing other than an anonymous letter!
THE FIRST MAN. His father will moan in Persian!

Sound of drums.

NA'MAN. Apply mud on your head, my daughter, and wear azure!
If this dream comes true,
we should weep blood for a descendent of my descendent,
who bears my name and blood—
he who will atone for my sin!
Why am I trembling?
Why am I shaking, despite this hot sun?
Where is my son, Monzer?
And what was this dream I had last night—a dream I woke up from, terrified?
Where are you, Monzer?
You will never name your son after me.
And you will advise that under no circumstances shall your offspring name their sons Na'man!
And by the supreme gods,
I will curse you if you do not follow!
For I saw that in the farthest part of India, an elephant was impregnated with a calf,
the offspring of which will sire the father of an elephant
that will be ridden by the King of Persia, who will come to al-Hirah
to kill a son of my sons who bears my name and sin!
What is this noise?

The sound of drums and trumpets and horns. Three men return hurriedly, wearing the garments of warriors, carrying flags.

THE THIRD MAN. Oh Na'man, the winter has come, and the King of Persia is arriving.
Put on new clothes!

THE FIRST MAN. And perform new decorum and ceremonies!

THE SECOND MAN. Look, the river is flowing fast!
And their flags are shining in one hundred colors!

THE FIRST MAN. Do you hear their musical instruments, the cries of the bells and drums?

NA'MAN. It is too late to make myself scarce in the desert!
Come ho—the castle is complete!
Do not mention Senemar. Forget his story.
Do not remember this body buried in the heart of the castle!
What is this? I hear the footsteps of the elephants already!
Rest in peace, Senemar;
why should I now begin to bemoan the loss of a son of my sons?
Let us go to greet the King!
No doubt the King of Persia will reward me dearly
for the castle you built!

Darkness. The sounds of the musical instruments climax and then quickly cut out.

OBLIVION

Hamid Amjad

Translated by
Nahid Ahmadian

Original title: *Farāmooshi*

Staged reading in 2011 at Shams Hall, Tehran

Published in Persian by Nila Books, 2013

CAST OF LIVE CHARACTERS

Jiang Rong, Huang, Fusai

CAST OF SHADOWS

Jiang Rong, Huang, Fusai, Father, Mother, Orderlies, the Khagan, Shun Yeo, Messengers, Soldiers, Commanders, Combatants, Attendants, Courtiers, Counselors, Army, Horses, etc.

SETTING

Place: The territory of Qin within the Great Wall, and the desert to the Northwest
Time: Between 221 and 181 BCE

SCENERY

Ivied gateway and part of a mansion in an aging garden; a Chinese scrim for shadow play in the middle of the scene.

PRODUCTION NOTE

The three live characters could stay onstage during the play but in darkness when not speaking. They may also voice other shadow characters.

EDITORS' INTRODUCTION

Hamid Amjad (b. 1968) is an Iranian playwright, novelist, director, and scholar of theater and cinema. Born and raised in Tehran, he is one of the most distinguished playwrights to have emerged after the Revolution. In his plays, Amjad revives indigenous forms of Iranian theater to address Iran's post-revolutionary public and social life. He obtained his bachelor's degree in cinema studies, and master's and PhD in liberal arts studies from the University of Tehran. For over two decades, he has taught theater, cinema, and creative writing at universities and private institutes in the Iranian capital. In the 1990s, he contributed in journals like *Naqd-e Sinamā* and *Donyā-ye Tasvir* as a film critic, and served as the chief editor of the theater quarterly *Faslnāmeh-ye Sahneh* for several years. Amjad is the author of more than twenty plays, most of which he has directed himself. Some of his plays, like *Shab-e Sizdahom* [The Thirteenth Night] (2001) and *Pastoo-khāneh* [The Rear Den] (1999), were prominent among the sensational performances of the Reform Era (1997–2005). In 1997, he and his wife, Jila Esma'ilian, co-founded Nila Books, a Tehran-based publishing house focused on theater, literature, and art. Amjad is also the author of the influential research study, *Te'ātr Qarn-e Sizdahom* [Iranian Theater in the Twentieth Century] (1999), and a winner of several awards for his plays and scripts.

Oblivion uses stylistic elements of Persian classical literature, poetry, and indigenous performance to tell a story far removed from an Iranian context. Like *The Sacrifice of Senemar*, this play is inspired by historical events, tracing the fate of a respected family through the early years of Imperial China around 200 BCE. Both plays begin at the end of the story, then unravel the events that led to that point. *Oblivion* employs several indigenous Persian performance traditions to convey its narrative rooted in both past and present. Central to Amjad's play is the incorporation of *sāyeh-bāzi*, or shadow puppetry, which is performed on a scrim center stage. While the majority of the play's characters are only represented by shadow figures, its three central characters are performed by both shadow puppets and live actors who narrate the story and refer back to what is being staged on the shadow scrim. This complex interplay allows Amjad to deftly jump back and forth between events of the past or dreams (shadows) and those of the present (live actors). This approach to narrative performance directly references *naqqāli* and *pardeh-khāni*, which are used to bridge the gap between past and present.

Much like *The Sacrifice of Senemar*, *Oblivion* incorporates *ta'ziyeh*-inspired techniques, using its symbolic brevity to efficiently represent the play's many characters, settings, and events. For instance, much of the action is narrated by the characters (both live and shadow), instead of being performed in real time for audiences. Meanwhile, the shadow scrim conveys a cinematic aesthetic through its use of slow-motion action, close-ups of characters, and the like, which intensify the epic qualities of the storytelling. Overall, *Oblivion* blends indigenous Persian traditions with modern Western drama and cinematic visuals to create a rich, hybrid aesthetic. This fusion of old and new, global and local invites the audience to rethink how stories are told, history is shaped and power is portrayed.

FIGURE 15. Hamid Amjad reading *Oblivion* aloud to an audience, 2011 at Shams Hall, Tehran. *Photograph courtesy of ISNA.*

OBLIVION

Hamid Amjad

On the shadow scrim, one rider approaches on his horse; there is the terrifying sound of the horse's hoofs, as if it is running on a drum. The rider is Fusai, who paves his way through the moonlit road, mountain and plain; birds and beasts flee from his path.[1]

SHADOW OF FUSAI. Here I come

At last, returning after so many years,
From beyond the hidden scenes,
From beyond the towering battlements and imposing gates,
From beyond the Great Wall,
And all alone, without any company
With no line of devotees,
With no flag or attendant,
With no drummer or army,
No torchbearer or water carrier.

I set off at last,
In my hand only the bridle of the swift Āzarakhsh
—Remember the name of my steed?—
With the fiery beating hoofs of the horse,
I cross the gateway of the setting sun.
Thousands of sparks spraying with each pace,
I cross the rock-ridden dark.
And I pass through the yellow dust, rising from the moonlit trail,
Like a silver flood, intertwined with gold!

---

1 In what follows, Fusai speaks in Jiang's dream. His monologue accompanies the events on the shadow scrim.

—Doesn't it look familiar to your eyes, the stormy mane of my horse?—
I travel to the rhythm of his thundering gallop,
Through the anguished earth
Like the arrow released from a bow;
I pass every strait and plain
Like a tiger through the rings of fire;
And I drown myself
In the depths of short moments and long shadows,
Like an arrow heading for its target!
Riding the scarlet dragon,
I am but a hurricane in the desert.
I pass
Like a bloody sword through yellow silk.

Riding the horse, restless,
I make the blood pump through the thousand vessels of my steed.
And I do so with every roaring whip on his body!
—Do his roars appear familiar to your ears?—
The gem I took from you
Has ignited thousands of memories;
And now I am
The fire itself!

Like lightning in the corridor of night,
I pass through memories and years,
Through fears and hopes,
Through war and peace.
I travel through the memories of cloaks and armor,
Through the dim memories and the bright ones,

Away from pride and past challenges,
Through greetings and farewells,
Schools and taverns,
Temples and graveyards,
Through ivied gateways,
And the gardens of my childhood,
To rage into your heart!
—Where shall I fasten this horse?
Where is the stablehand?
Wasn't the gateway here?
Where, then, are the stairs?—
I turn and come close to you[2]
And I embrace you
Like horrifying news!
I look into your eyes and
Around at my whereabouts,
Searching for glory, which is no longer there,
—The servants who are gone,
The stove which is cold, cupless and potless.
I murmur a name
And many more I remember.
You stare at me, silently,
And look around,
Searching for someone;
A name slips through your lips
And only one name is in your mind.

---

2 "You" here refers to Jiang.

I break through silence and wonder
And overcome the trembling of my hands and heart.
Smiling, I come hither
With news,
The news of I,
Myself!
Oh!
You ask why so sudden, so confused, and in such a haste?
After years—
After yesterday's messenger,
After the gem I took from you,
And through the long journey of night?
Why so unexpected, so anguished, so impatient?
Oh—here I've come—because you finally wished it!
I came as you demanded of me.
Was it not you who wanted me to come
—This past midnight—
In my dream?

With Jiang's cry as he awakens, the scrim darkens and the evening view of the garden with the ivied gateway and the moonlit mansion appears on the stage.

JIANG. No![3]
I have no demands!
Not from you anymore, Fusai!
After asking three times and hearing no response for years.
Oh, what was this dream?
In my own dream,

---

3 This is the physical Jiang on the stage who is now awake.

You spoke of a dream where I asked you something?
No, you saw not a dream but a deception.
And what I saw was a dream shared with yours!
All these years, oh, all these years!
Half of them, I said, I should avoid dreams
For the fear of conspiring,
And in the other half,
As soon as I closed my eyes,
You would appear,
Each time with an excuse,
Each time with a deceit!

Until tonight
—When sleep escaped from my eyes
Like ants from a flood!—
I have not yet worn my nightgown or gone to bed;
I have not even cast an eye on the house or garden
To avoid this colossal void
And the absence of those
Who used to come to learn or serve,
Or the absence of bliss and joy,
Or of father,
Or the raised mound at the corner of the garden, which is
My mother's resting place.

This time I closed my eyes
On the absence of the last gem you took from me.
The long-suffering lady of this house, my sister, Huang.
—The very one
Who awaited your return for years,
Silent to what was biting her like a termite!—

The one who day after day
Would imagine hearing the galloping hoofs of a horse she knew,
And at midday
Would strive to hear the voice of an imagined messenger who never came,
Who was supposed to bring your message,
And night after night
Stared at the road
That extended from the Great Wall to this ivied gateway,
And like a candle,
Stood in the face of the yellow winds of the desert.
And I watched her
Gradually shrinking,
Moment by moment, all these years.
Till today—
When in the evening, a whirling trail of dust from the Great Wall disturbed the landscape.
And the illusion of a hurricane faded soon
Into the image of a chariot!

On the shadow scrim, a swift chariot appears from afar; there are armed riders with dragon flags on it. Behind the chariot is the view of the Great Wall in the twilight before sunset. Huang appears on the threshold of the ivied gateway, looking out.[4]

HUANG (*excited*). I see it!
A chariot with two—no, four—no, six horses!
With a flag in the air.

---

4 This is a memory from Jiang's past, and the actors onstage perform it live alongside the shadow play.

JIANG (*moves forward*). Where is it?

HUANG. Coming from the Great Wall!

JIANG. They are courtiers, traveling with a command.

HUANG. At sunset?

JIANG. Either they carry an urgent command
Or their destination is nearby.

HUANG. They did not turn the other way!

JIANG. They are lost.

HUANG. Isn't that the dragon emblem on the flag?

JIANG. I cannot see clearly.

HUANG. Listen carefully. They are coming this way!

JIANG (*looks at her*). You saw them?
Did they open the great gate?

HUANG. A six-horse chariot with the Khagan's sign crossing the desert?
No, it is probably the Great Wall opening its mouth like a dragon!
Look, they come straight to us!

JIANG. What are they trying to conquer?
Is there any upstanding territory or unburnt farmland left to take?

HUANG. A new message, perhaps!
Or at last, some glad tidings—
A robe for you!
Oh, is it not your birthday?

JIANG. I had all but forgotten it!

HUANG. The fifth day of the fifth month—the day of the tiger!

JIANG. Forty-nine years old!
Look at me. Do you see anything of a mature man in me?

HUANG. I have not heard of anyone more experienced than my tribesmen,
And from them one survives: my brother!

JIANG. Hmm, what luck for a man born on the darkest day of the year!
Would the people on the other side of the Great Wall ever remember that tomorrow, a man on this side, born on the tiger's day in the year of the dragon, will come of age?

HUANG (*her smile vanishes; with new thoughts, she turns to the gate*). Is that him?
Or a message from him?

JIANG. On such a day, a tiger does not offer ransom,
He receives it!

HUANG. The royal chariot is not the messenger of punishment!

JIANG. They don't deliver tidings and robes by cavalry!

HUANG (*worried, stands at the threshold of the gate*). Over my dead body!

JIANG. No! No argument, please! I am ready for anything they seek.

HUANG (*worried*). Anything?

JIANG. Here they are.

HUANG. Is he one of them, shielded by helmet and armor?

The chariot disappears from the scrim, and Huang leaves the stage through the gateway.

JIANG. I was not mistaken; it was not Fusai.
My sister was not mistaken; it was a message—or perhaps a command—from him.
I was not mistaken—his messengers have brought no robe
Or scepter
And no ring with jasper gemstone.
His messengers were here to take.
My sister was wrong. She heard the message gaily, full of hope.
I was wrong. They did not ask for me,

My sister was summoned—and to the court!
Huang, my little sister, asked, "Am I to be summoned alone?"
The messengers replied, "Alone and at once, in this very chariot!"
My sister looked into my eyes—
Her own resembling the god of wonder.
Her hand unconsciously hid the silver lock,
And I turned away.
I was wrong. I was not prepared for the message.
And this was before the sunset.

Oh, where is my little sister? I imagined for a moment that she was here beside me!
I have a sinking feeling.
She has been summoned to the capital.
Is it deceit?
Danger?
A wound intended for me?
Or a true sign of love?
Ay, me! What are you amidst all this, my little sister?
A hostage or a beloved?
All these years,
Your gaze was fixed on this very message.
Shall I now be happy or distressed?
This or that?—When the price is my loneliness!

All the evening
The clawed dragon of the famine stayed on the horizon.
And when it was sunset,

The time for writing the names of ancestors on bones near the fire,[5]
I saw my hands trembling.
I could tell the night was pregnant with fear
By the blood-red eyes of heaven.
Seated next to the hedge,
My hands on the bones of horses and hyenas and wolves,
Restlessly waiting for a response from my forefathers
I could escape sleep but not untether myself from dreaming!
Is there a secret or deceit
In this unwanted dream,
In the vision of this request you said you have brought to me?
Will you come this time?

I am still leaning against this gate in wait.
Next to the ivy and hedges—or what remains of them.
Come and tell me,
What is the game this time?
What shall I call you this time, tell me?—
In what disguise, in what cloak?
Tell me what in this dream,
In that gallop and that cry,
In that unfamiliar look,
Could not be known anymore?
Oh, (*wipes his tears*) but I recognized the horse.

---

5 This practice, known as *jiaguwen*, involved writing names on oracle bones—usually shoulder blades of oxen or turtle shells—and is believed to have been a precursor to the Chinese script. After carving symbols and names on bones, fortune tellers would expose them to fire, causing the bones to crack. They would then interpret the patterns of the cracks to predict future events. *Jiaguwen* dates back to the Shang Dynasty (1766–1122 BCE).

He had truly aged!
(*Fade*)

Huang appears onstage, opposite the shadow scrim; shadows of flags and armed riders on a moving chariot come to life on the scrim.

HUANG. Surrounded by the spearmen cloaked in pewter,
When the scarlet sunset gives way to the silver moon
Where am I going after all these years?
I travel under the vaulted night sky
—With the mixed feelings of anger, sorrow, disgust, and longing—
Through a desert,
Which, when I was young,
Was the landscape before my hopeless eyes,
When I looked through the cracks in the walls and ivied gate.
From my father's country house
To the gate and rampart
Is not a long way;
And yet, I have not trod this path but in dream and desire.

From the very moment my heart beat for you,
All around me
Was but walls.
The Great Wall around my lover,
The small one circling the country house,
And the cold one enclosing my bed.
I am not a stranger to the soothing of the stars,
For spending the lonely night under the vaulted roof is intolerable.
But now I am traveling at night—
Mixed with wonder, disgust, anguish, and desolation.
Come with me, you stars!

Be witness to me,
And what was wasted of me in sorrow and amour.

Oh, there in the sky, three—no, four stars twinkle in the east;
And that is the moon,
Thievishly passing by from atop the Great Wall without permit.
My permits are but these armors emblazoned with dragon,
These daggers from jasper stone,
Hung from hard leather harnesses
With two silver tigers entangled in one another.
These are the talismans on their arms,
And these are pewter helmets
That disguise and make my guardians faceless.
My permit this time
Is this chariot with pheasant feather and scarlet lace,
This is the dragon flag,
And that, the commanding scroll, summoning me.

Countless nights I dreamed of boarding the bridal chariot
On this very road.
But brides are brought
During the day—in the wake of the world!
Countless days, from behind the hedges, I envied the farm girls' laughter,
Farming on the land with their men.
Countless evenings, I withdrew my eyes from the playful maidens near the river,
By the side of their lovers.
But
In the echoing footsteps of night,

There were only memories, waiting and anguished,
And a crack in the wall to the garden,
Which would age with me.
Each harsh winter,
There were only the pine and cedar trees and my heart,
Which was warm with memories,
Saying to a forsaken bird,
"Never make promises with people or the spring!"

Oh, there, above the Great Wall
Four—no, five stars are on the east.
Is my brother now watching me in the mirror of stars?
We didn't exchange questions or replies.
I did not even give him a willow branch as a token of farewell.
When will I see him again?
His loneliness
Was a mirror to my silence all these years.
Now is he lonelier than ever in my absence?
Which one would bear greater burden on his shoulders?
My staying or leaving?
Alas, at this very moment, and on this same moonlit road,
With this bird of fate likely singing my name,
No more doubting or asking this or that!
I have always been bitter! Let me for once be sweet!
On a chariot carried by not one but six horses,
He—the close company of the Khagan—
Has sent for you.
Joy and wonder, love, and longing!
I shall let go of blame,

After all these years spent blaming and battling with the mirror!
I should hide my silver lock in my hair,
And embrace the coming moment.

Rong Jiang—my brother—
Every time I saw him,
The pen was forming a figure of grief in his hand;
When it was time for the new moon,
He would take a deep breath and watch the debris of destiny,
And when he was speaking to the pumpkins,
In his bitter laughter there was a longing for peace.
After Mother's death,
He did not stop talking to her;
After Father's,
He did not stop visiting his resting place.
From now on, he will imagine me
Next to a waterwheel, gazing at the rippling waves on water,
Or by the hedge, under the blooming peach tree,
With eyes full of tears for the gaiety of crickets,
Or when contemplating the grown ivy's blossoms on each rung of the ladder.
I, too, will never forget my brother,
Whether they use me like a stone in the Great Wall
Or seat me like a lady in the place of honor.

Maybe my wheel of fate
Turns and I could reach his star.

Oh, they opened the main gate,
And from atop,

Five—no, six stars are in the east.

(*Fade*)

Jiang appears at the ivied gateway.

JIANG. The moon hides her face behind the clouds;

I fade and the scrim of memories come to light.

(*On the shadow scrim, three teenagers, riding on horseback, pass wheat and millet farms.*)[6]

This was us,
Blissful and blind to the turn of fate,
We have been through a bitter childhood
But have not yet seen battles.
Those two in front are my sister, Huang, and I
On those two taut horses with flying tails and erect necks.

(*Gesturing to the figures on the shadow scrim.*)

These were my stallion and her mare
Noble colts from the legendary aqua horse, that water spirit,
The gem of father's years of youth.
And the other rider
That accompanies on the galloping horse
Was you, Fusai, then with your childhood name,
Riding a short-legged swift Tatar horse,
Which was a memento of your father from the yellow deserts.

Do you remember, Fusai?
Your father and mine were of the same tribe,

6 The physical Jiang on stage describes their childhood by showing the ongoing events on the shadow scrim. Using *pardekh-khāni* techniques, he brings the memories to life in real time alongside the visual storytelling.

Cousins of Rong—
The name that should not be spoken of these days.

As the following lines are spoken, on the shadow scrim, young Fusai and Jiang gallop side by side on horseback along the side of a mountain to its peak, shooting arrows at prey on the ground and in the air. The arrows hit their target and the animal falls. A river appears—the two pace along its bank, bathe in its water, and pull a large fish out of it using a fishing net. Next, they are seated across each other on a gondola, a board game between them. They are overwhelmed with joy, excitement, and laughter. The scene shifts to a fire on which their hunted meat roasts. They amiably drink and play rubab[7] *under willow branches that sway in the breeze. The sound of music and the night raven is heard.*

JIANG. All pass before my eyes,
The same as the shadow plays that we used to sit and watch together in childhood.
Those happy days
Were like the paradise of immortals, with sweet water and a tree that bears jewels, or like the island of happiness!
Those were the times of our blooming; you and I,
Friends in need, friends indeed,
Roommate and kin, company and comrade,
During the night, we would go for a ride
And in the evenings, we would go for a drink
And would treat ourselves to each other's goblet,
Riding our steeds, traveling at the speed of the wind,
Passing by sorrows,

---

7 A stringed musical instrument that originated in Afghan classical music, commonly also found in Pakistan and Kashmir. Today, it is the national musical instrument of Afghanistan.

Walking down the shore,
Wandering through fields of grain,
Lips full of song.
We would board the boats
And bathe in the water
And shoot and hunt.
We would throw dice and play,
Entertain each other with magic and games
And listen to the oracle, the seer of mysteries.
We would play the pipe,
Pluck the stringed instruments,
And time was but an everlasting spring.
The only concern in these nights of joy was
To ask of bliss
Not to let the leaf fall or let the nightingale go silent
So that night and wine may never end.

On the shadow scrim, the yellow river and surrounding millet farms appear. The sun rises above the river and moves west, traveling above the millet farms and eventually giving over to the moon. Then appears the image of the garden at noon, with the aged berry tree. Father is teaching, his pupils are listening, and young Huang is watching from behind a tree.

JIANG. Happiness was a never-ending chant
At dawn and dusk
—Whether it was time for the yellow river to wake up
Or the millet farm to go to sleep—
But between the two
Was the time to attend
Father's classes under the shade of the trees

FIGURE 16. Chinese-style shadow puppet created by puppet artisan Jean-Luc Penso. *Photograph by Hamed Esmailee from the collection of Hamid Amjad.*

Where the local gentry
Was learning
Shoulder to shoulder with the peasantry,
For the big examination, and for success.

Studying Eastern philosophy and arithmetic,
Calligraphy and genealogy,
Learning rituals and manners,
Ethics and poetry,
Under the instruction of the former minister and the debarred secretary—
My father.
Under the shadow of the aged berry tree,
Father was reading to us from the bamboo leaves.
The genealogy of deities from the *Classic Mountains and Seas*
The History of Shu Jing
Or Confucius's *Spring and Autumn Annals*.

In between all these Eastern philosophies,
My eyes, with a playful smile,
Would turn from the bright and carefree students to you, Fusai.
And a little farther,
They would meet my sister's gaze like an arrow,
Who was upset because girls were not allowed to take philosophy classes,
But was enthusiastically looking at you
From behind a tree.
(*On the scrim, the shadow of young Huang gradually emerges.*)
I was thinking that this exile they are speaking of is not a bad thing.
Mirth is permanent and friendship lasting.

Father will no longer depart for battle or travel.
Family, aromatic trees, poultry, caring friends, and agile horses
All have gathered together,
And my sister in new spring
Like peach blossoms,
Was turning rosy in her cheeks.
(*Fade*)

On the other side of the scene, Fusai appears.

FUSAI. Far from the garden,
As if from beyond the world,
I think of this name, Fusai—my childhood name—
Which, like a talisman, defies distance
And transports me to where you are.
Was it truly paradise? Or is that merely your interpretation?
It is an illusion you deceive yourself with
So that you could wish for a return back to childhood.
No, I was not wrong;
I hate doubting this or that!
Paradise disappeared when childhood came to an end.
And in this transition
It left its trace on one face only!
(*Fade*)

On the scrim appears Huang's face and then her body; with two bells in each hand, and following the rhythms of the horse's steps, she crosses from one side of the stage to the other.

HUANG. Roads, roads, roads,
All my life I've been on the road,
If this is the road that takes me to him.

Winds marvel at my haste,
And one more time,
The world is like my dreams.
Advancing but never arriving!
I never wished for a long life—be the nine heavens witness to that!—
Not a long life like cranes
But a short and happy one like ducks.
Which one ends sooner—my life or the road?
Having passed the main gate now,
I am at the gate of the wonderland. Stunned at the sight of the glimmering torches of the big city where I am heading;
The capital!
The place I have never seen before.

She is gone. With the ringing of the camel bells, Fusai is seen in front of the scrim. On the shadow scrim behind him is a group of counselors, seated in a circle.

FUSAI. Now,
I, Kung Fon Su,
To whom the world gave many names, at dear prices,
The wise minister of the Khagan,
Am thinking of a man
Who still remembers me by the name Fusai,
My old companion, Rung Jiang.
—Pity him and his manhood!
He who spent all of his life with one name only.
In the past, we were but shadows to each other.
—Why can we not be so now?—
I know him like the lines on my palms.

I know what memories
This shadow of me
Is remembering.

Here, awaiting the arrival of the guest,
Seated atop the circle of counselors in lapis hall,
I set off on a silent journey to the past
And recall the day the teacher,
Under the shadow of the berry tree,
From the philosophy of *The One Hundred Schools*,
Was teaching us the classic order,
And of the harmony of the earth and heavens, the constancy of the four seasons, and the authority of the King.
And all were resting on the original virtue,
Which, as Confucius had put it,
Was loyalty—
Loyalty of a child to his house and his tribe,
Of a commissioner to his King,
Of the King to the son of the heavens.
The sage Mo-tzu,
Free from relations familiar and foreign,
Had named this virtue
The unconditional love of all human beings.
The pious Laozi
Had found redemption in simplicity
And in the harmony of manners
With the silent river of nature which flows to eternity.
And Yang Zhu, the venerable aged sage,
Had found virtue in loyalty to oneself and in pure pleasure.

The master then, refrained from study and said,
"Now a little discussion!
Tell me, which loyalty is it that leads to the betterment of the world?
The one which concerns itself with the house, the tribe, and the homeland,
Or the one which prefers the interest of the state
To that of others, nature, and self?
This or that? Speak!"

But I was not listening to the lesson and the lecture.
The scented breeze of the east was blowing
And my eyes were, for the first time, resting on the Judas tree in the garden.
Huang,
The master's daughter and my friend's sister.
In the morning I had seen her in grey clothes.
Now, she had changed,
Dressed in purple, like a flower sprouting from the early-morning soil,
She was passing before me
From one side of the garden
Like a blossoming tree which, proving the charms of spring,
Was walking gracefully.
Once with a bucket,
Another time with berry leaves, and silkworms,
And again with a fan
Emitting the aromatic breeze of the orient.
And I thought to myself.

When did this blooming happen,
And where did it come from, all at once!?

The laughter of my classmates
Brought me back to master
Who had called me by my name and asked,
"Tell us, Fusai, is it *this or that*?"
And I could recall nothing
Except the purple blossoms dancing in the breeze.
The master asked his question again,
"Should one have loyalty to oneself,
Or to the tribe, homeland, and King
As it is registered in the history of the ancient states?"
I could barely swallow my saliva
As I answered him, embarrassed.
"Hundreds of years of domestic wars are themselves evidence to
this—
The wise Confucius's life was spent presenting
The doctrines of loyalty
From one state to another
To the princes of Lu, Tesau, Wi,
Tsai, Cha, Ja, Sung and Chu—[8]
Nonetheless,
If there were any benefit to loyalty,
None of the states and princes
Would disappear from the world
One after another!"
(*Fade*)

---

8 Lu, Tesau, Wi, Tsai, Cha, Ja, Sung, and Chu are the names of ancient states in China.

Huang appears on the stage holding bells, the sound of which imitate the rhythm of the chariot's horses as they speed up, slow down, halt and move again. Huang crosses from one side of the stage to the other. She is astonished at the view surrounding her.

HUANG. The capital
Is a city of barriers, soldiers, and battlements.
The view of the long road
Is like the countless flickering torches of the shimmering river of the galaxy
In the seventh evening of the seventh month of the year—
When the Cowherd and the Weaver Girl of heaven meet.[9]
In between the groups of armored guards,
One could count the horse's paces on both hands.
Oh, those pewter mirrors reflecting the flames
—Which look like armored torchbearers—
Have heard nothing of restlessness and longing.
They see nothing in the shade of a far chariot
But the threat of unauthorized passage.
A row of torches blocks the road,
And archers on both sides
Reach for their quivers.
I wish I were a phoenix, with wings spread,
Or a tiger ready to leap over the fire;
But I am merely a girl
Who was forgotten for years and now has been summoned.

---

9 Characters in Chinese mythology whose romance is part of Chinese folklore. Not being allowed to unite, the lovers were exiled to the opposite sides of the Heavenly River. It is believed that they come together once a year on the seventh day of the seventh month with the help of magpies.

As soon as the royal chariot is seen
—With the dragon flag and ceremonial bells—
The night guards, heads lowered in awe, will part to make way.
All that results is the slowing of my heart
When it beats faster than the horses' hoofs.

She is gone. On the stage, Jiang at the threshold of the ivied gateway, turns from the Great Wall.

JIANG. The Great Wall is but a scrim;[10]
Upon it is my sister's shadow
As she travels, escorted by spearmen.
—All my life,
What was my world but shadows on a scrim!—
Would it be better if that shadow never went on that journey?
Would it be better if we had torn up the scroll and disobeyed the command?
But what was the alternative?
Should I have accompanied her?
Or should she have stayed with me?
This or that? Which one was better? Whose heart's desire should we have followed?
What should I have done
When all I learned of military teaching
Was the art of losing!?

For most of his life, my father murmured only of wearying doubt;
My mother whispered in my ears, cursing war.
Oh, wars on top of wars.

---

10 Jiang refers to how the Great Wall is reflected on the shadow scrim. He is also relating the Great Wall to the history of his family.

I remember my childhood.
My oldest memories from this house
And that time of childhood and ignorance.
Despite all this, since the day we stepped into this country house,
News was with us like shadows.
They called it a temporary stay;
—We will stay for a few days in father's hometown
Till the commotion of the war passes—
And no one told me what battle was being fought or why.

(*On the scrim, a child twirls and becomes two—now there are two children next to each other. Near them, the shadows of a mansion, garden, and the ivied gateway gradually emerge.*)

My childhood memories are split in two in this house.
One part concerned myself
And the other a child, the same age as me, the son of a cousin from father's house
—Fusai, the temporary housemate—
Who was entrusted to my mother
The day his father accompanied mine onto the battlefield.

(*On the scrim, next to the shadows of both children, the shadow of Father appears—it is time to embrace and say farewell to the children.*)

My father, an intellectual born a peasant,
Paved his way from secretary of the local nobilities to minister of the nearby kingship.
Now he had no choice but to take to war all his knowledge of combat,
His archery skills,
Whatever he knew of using catapults and siege engines,[11]

---

11 An instrument of battle used in antiquity to break the gates or walls of castles during wars.

Along with his valiance, the remainder of his youthful strength,
To prove his loyalty to his King.
Thus, he was made to leave what he held most dear
—His family, the four of us,
And his multitude of books—
In the garden of his forefathers.
And at the gateway of the garden, he appointed day guards and watchmen
—Some guardsmen in addition to house servants—
And he and his cousin rode their horses to battle.

On the shadow scrim, Mother holds baby Huang in her arms, appearing among the four, while two horses emerge from both sides. Fusai's father sits on his short-legged horse, and Jiang's father gives a willow branch to Mother and bids her farewell before mounting his tall steed. Two riders set off and disappear through the ivied gateway. The shadow of Mother at the threshold of the gateway rocks her daughter and stares out.

SHADOW OF MOTHER. You said our separation would be only for a few days,
And day after day I offered a bowl of millet
With the wine to the dead.
Now,
A day is no longer a day but a week.
The spring blossoms withered with the southern wind.
Your name alone is on your daughter's tongue.
Your favorite meal is no longer in season.
How many times could I read your only letter?
Now,
A day is no longer a day but a month.
In your absence, how could I reach for perfume and rouge?

No millet left, this time I offer the cold wheat
To the living people who starve even more,
And you still do not return with the western wind.
The garden and my heart were both stricken with the blast of cold.
Did the migratory birds not bring my words with you?
I long for you,
For a visit!
Now,
A day is no longer a day but a year.

On stage, Jiang raises his head next to the ivied gateway.

JIANG. We were not left wanting for bread.
There were some peasants in the neighborhood,
Who would, from time to time, take from their reserved store
To bring the master's family a loaf of bread,
To pay back for previous seasons' gifts.
Until autumn, news would come from time to time,
Sometimes with the promise of peace,
But once autumn arrived, hope died with the falling leaves.
The battlefield would shift
From one place to another.
By the end of autumn,
The war was in our neighborhood.
(*On the scrim, the shadow of Mother fades and the shadows of guardians line up beside the ivied gateway.*)
In that harsh winter,
Mother kept us away
From the northern wind,
From the din of the outdoors,

And from seeing her tears.
The entire year
Was an opportunity for her two children
—You and I—
To learn the names
—Of one another, of things and colors and games—
To explore trees and domesticated animals,
The corners of the garden,
Its secrets and hidden paths.

(*On the shadow scrim, two soldiers play with the children. The rest of the guards line up close to the ivied gateway and on a remote road outside the gate, while an enormous shouting army crosses from one side to the other.*)

That day we had asked two of father's orderlies
To hand in their swords and give us piggybacks.
Upon hearing the noise of the army passing outside,
—With hurrahs, fanfares, and battle drums—
Mother hurried with terror to the garden,
Seeing us practicing battle.

Mother, with tears in her eyes,
Whipped our feet with the young boughs from the garden.
Nevertheless,
We knew the color red
Only in the shining leaves of the maple tree
And the juice of the aged blackberry in the garden,
Until the day when once again
We could hear the commotion of soldiers approaching from outside the gates at daybreak,

The clamor of the swift riders and the moaning of the wounded and
fatigued horses
Were shaking the leaves on the spring branches in the garden
And making my mother hot with fever.

(On the shadow scrim, the guards beside the ivied gateway move swiftly, ready to defend. The eastern sun gradually disappears from the scrim as a crimson sunset appears on its western edge.)

It was at twilight
When the neighs and galloping of a horse from outside
Terrified these two little boys—the two of us—in the corner of the
garden.
The orderlies at the gateways reached for their spears,
But they retreated upon seeing the fatigued but swift rider,
Whose cries were robbed by the wind.

(On the scrim, the rider gets off the horse and enters the house; the horse collapses, and the two children approach the beast.)

Worn out, the man rode to the center of the garden,
And upon dismounting,
He slipped, holding onto his chest
And without hesitation,
He raced inside.
You and I rushed forward.
—Do you remember the fall of the horse?
And its beating chest—
The red traces we saw on the ground were fresh.
Drops with warm vapors
The name of which we did not know;
It was red mingled with sweat off the horse's body!

An orderly—who ran to get the saddle and the bridle from the beast—
Cried.
"Blood!"
There was something familiar in that ragged stranger.
Instinctively, we headed for home
When we heard a cry—"Don't!"
The call was coming from the orderly
—The one who gave me a piggyback—
And then he said the same to you.
Frightened, we escaped
Through the hidden paths into the room
And hid behind a curtain.

On the shadow scrim, the interior of the house is displayed, showing the shadow of Mother, the maid, Huang, and the stranger who enters as Jiang narrates.

JIANG. On the scrim was the shadow of my mother who, in fever, had left bed with tears of joy. Standing next to her and in the candle-light was the maid with little Huang in her arms. The shadow of the tired stranger at the door belonged to my father, wiping blood and sweat from his face with his sleeve.

SHADOW OF MOTHER. Is this a fever dream or have you truly returned?

SHADOW OF FATHER. I have come to stay!

JIANG. Mother cried.

The maid took my sister outside so as to not let her see the flood of blood and tears!

On the shadow scrim, the maid exits with Huang.

SHADOW OF MOTHER. The wind brought nothing of your news,

And neither did the migrating bird heed my longing cries.
The only news
Was the scent of death and the sound of plunder
From behind the walls and gates.

SHADOW OF FATHER. The great war
Came to an end,
At the last sunset,
After a battle on the bridge.

SHADOW OF MOTHER. The wound on your chest!

SHADOW OF FATHER. It could have taken me down
If the thought of you
Had not also gushed out of my chest at that very moment!
It was the thought of you that empowered my dagger and my arms, arrows and bident,[12]
The thought of you
Which helped me to survive several times
So that, in the final battle
—That war of destiny on the bridge between hell and victory—
I could drag down the banner of the enemy!

JIANG. Mother had missed him.
She cried, just as she did when she broke the boughs at my feet.

SHADOW OF MOTHER. No more battlefields or battles!
You said you thought of us?
Where was that thought
When the wind was singing a song of terror to this house?
When the children were begging for their father and the wife for her husband?

---

12 A two-pronged weapon in the form of a pitchfork. In Greek mythology, it is associated with Hades.

When with each knock at the door, bad news would tear at our heart like a dagger?
Or when an army with bloodshot eyes passed us from behind the fence
And we were lucky that each time
They postponed their plunder and murder until after victory.

SHADOW OF FATHER. I fought
Out of loyalty to my family—
So that they would take the thought of plunder to their graves!

JIANG. Mother was about to weep.

SHADOW OF MOTHER. Danger was not far from us!
Once I heard myself, and twice the orderlies mentioned
That a rider had approached near this ivied gateway—
On the other side of this very fence!

SHADOW OF FATHER. I was that rider!
When the war was nearby
Three times in darkness,
Once at sunset and twice at midnight,
Alone, disguised and out of sight,
I galloped to this country house
To see if the gate and pillars still stood,
If the defenders were at the door
And the fireplace was burning.

SHADOW OF MOTHER. And what did you see?
Prove it!

SHADOW OF FATHER. What I saw did not torture me so much as what I heard.
I heard your mourning,
Your bitter songs, your lullaby to my daughter,

Your grievances of war and travel,
And my name, spoken in the heart of darkness!

SHADOW OF MOTHER. You heard my woes and went away?

SHADOW OF FATHER. One step further,
One moment of your sight,
And I would have been powerless to return to the battlefield!

SHADOW OF MOTHER. Oh, the wound on your chest!
Was there no physician in the army of the King
That knew of dressing?

SHADOW OF FATHER. I galloped straight from the battlefield to here.
My chest could bear the wound but not the loss—not anymore!

JIANG. Father's callused hands
Wiped tears from Mother's cheek.
As she cried,
Mother removed armor from this statue of exhaustion.

SHADOW OF MOTHER. Speak—tell me of the battlefield!

JIANG. What father said
Remains word for word in my mind;
The very same words that later
He wrote in the *History of Warring States*,
And I memorized in such a way that I never forgot—
And you know why, Fusai!

(*The shadow scrim on which Father and Mother still converse slowly moves away, revealing another scrim behind it, where armies are shown locked in a bloody battle.*)

Father recounted.
After sequential wars with the princes of the four territories
—From mountains and plains to campaigns
With enemies at sea or in castles—

After defeating the tribes of Han, Wei, and Chao,
And after crushing the army of Chu,
It was time to wage war on Yen.
Our army was exhausted,
And Yen's was filled with mighty combatants and exemplary archers.

(*On the shadow scrim, dead bodies are littered across the plain and the exhausted army remains standing.*)

When the time came to oil the drums
For the new battles,
—Using a mixture of holy oil and blood—
Our men, from all the tribes of the King's territory
—Those born in the moors
And those raised in the mountains—
All fatigued with floods of blood and their long journeys,
Groaned,
"We are the eyes of the King, bereft of sight.
It has been a long time that we've been traveling from one battlefield to another,
The shadows of the willows were once aplenty when we trod on the path.
Now, snowflakes are flying in the air.
We are the teeth and claws of the King.
Behold what the chill of cold has done to us!
Leave the catapults!
Who drives our fatigued bodies forward?
We are the claws of the King
And with us no vim and vigor are left."

(*Flags of the opposing army gather and circle the shadow scrim. Gradually, the ranks beneath the enemy flag swell. Little by little, the dead rise, carrying their fallen flags, and join the massive army. Across them, the exhausted and confused army gradually lines up. The two lines start moving; each time one line moves forward the other retreats.)*

The arms of our standard bearer were weakened;
It was a timely moment for the once defeated
—Those survivors of the enemy's tribes—
To pick up their dropped weapons once again
And ally with the refreshed Yen.
A new invasion ushered in all at once and from everywhere.
And as such, of all the territories between the four seas
To the land in the cols,[13]
The battle ended up here,
Where our men had to choose between
Death and a never-ending war!
A moment of hesitation was enough to make it one's last moment!
Every breath was a chance
To wound before an arrow wears you down!
The terror of being torn apart by the five-headed serpent
Washed the need for sleep from our bodies and wiped our heads of fear;
It was because of the greatness of our horror
That our men looked mighty in the eyes of the enemy!

(*On the margin of the scrim, shadows of the capital's bridge and battlements appear; the defending army has gathered in the vicinity. The enemy army approaches from all directions, advancing in step with the steady beat of war drums.*)

---

13 The lowest geographical point between two peaks.

Thus we battled, with the last strength mustered from deep within
our body,
And drove off the enemy that had advanced from all sides.
And thus the last war
Took place today,
On the bridge nearby, next to the battlement.
Early this morning,
When the enemy played their drums—made of Yen crocodile
skin—
Each beat was a warning that a single step would mean death.

On the chariot,
I summoned up my men with a loud voice,
"What you hear now is not my cry
But that of our ancestors, calling in our ears,
Asking for our loyalty—
To our house, our tribe, and our King—
No matter which tribe we come from—
Plain dwellers, mountain folk, city denizens, and peasants, from
shores to cols.
Now, after all of those arduous tests,
We are one house and one tribe.
As souls entwined,
We are at the command of one man, and that is the King of the Qin
territory!
May this bridge be like our promise,
Which will break if the enemy crosses!
The hell of battlefield

Is paradise compared to what will come of our family and tribe
If we are even momentarily idle!
If we do not act quickly,
The curse of our forefathers and the death of our children
Will be like a fire from below and above!
This bridge and battlement
Is our last border—and the King's last territory!
Then let us fight harder than ever
So the promise of loyalty to him is not wasted at the feet of the enemy."
(*On the shadow scrim is seen the great war on the bridge.*)
And so we all transformed into one fist, holding the hilt of a sword
Targeted at the enemy's arteries!

The scrim bearing the large shadow of Mother is replaced by the battle scrim. It is set in front, obscuring the one behind it.

SHADOW OF MOTHER. What you did, then, was a demonstration of loyalty to your King!

On the scrim, the large shadow of Father appears next to the shadow of Mother.

SHADOW OF FATHER. While I'm sure it's due to our separation,
Your sarcasm pains me like another wound in my chest.
Our loyalty was not divided.
My loyalty to this house was part of my loyalty to the King,
And neither were separate from my loyalty to our tribe,
For which our code of warriorship has advocated from the time of our ancestors.
Shoulder to shoulder with the tribes of Qin—the King's own kin—
The men of my tribe fought to their last drops of blood.

And out of the forty-nine men of my bloodline,
Not a single one survived.

SHADOW OF MOTHER. Not even one!
Then your cousin, the father of this little boy!

JIANG. On the other side of the curtain, father went silent.
On this side, you, Fusai, were pale.

Fusai appears on the other side of the stage.

FUSAI. But there was something
Echoing in my head.
My father told me that I was born a peasant but that I would not remain so.
He said he would join the army
So that someday he might see me among the noble.
He said he would come for me,
Or else he would send someone for me with a ring as a token!
I had something
Echoing in my head—
It was a question.
Will I never see my father again?

Jiang and Fusai, positioned at opposite ends of the stage, watch the shadow scrim. On it, the shadow of the bridge and the fallen soldiers pass behind Father and Mother.

SHADOW OF MOTHER. Did you see that?
With your own eyes?

SHADOW OF FATHER. After slaying the last hand to draw a dagger at us,
Beneath the cold light of the cloud-covered sun,
When only the sound of fatigued breaths
Was breaking the wet silence of the scarlet mist,

From over the bridge
I looked into the reed-filled pond.
Within this pond, the ghosts of six generations
Intermingled with the mist,
And moaning,
Clung to the stony columns of the bridge
So that the homeless wind, heading for hell, would not sweep them away with the mist.
My cousin's horse, riderless,
Was neighing, thirsty, beside the pond,
Face to face with the ghosts of the slain.
My cousin was not nearby,
And he was not there,
And he was not there,
Until at last I finally found his body,
Clinging to a slayed Yen commander,
Sewn together by arrows—
And between them was an overturned chariot on fire!

SHADOW OF MOTHER. Oh, each time I saw these two boys
—Busy playing their war games—
Good grief!
I said how could they know that they were practicing death!
I endured and kept silent
So that I wouldn't betray news of their fathers if it may come—oh!
Now, with whom will this child stay?

SHADOW OF FATHER. With us, and he will be like the cherished descendent of a hero.
And—altogether—we will go to the capital!

SHADOW OF MOTHER. No!

Resign from the secretariat!
The day you came to ask me for my hand,
You spoke not of battle or battlefield or serving the King.
I wanted a husband, not a warrior!
You were a secretary and my father was writing history.
He said it would be a blessing if a son-in-law continued his scroll!

SHADOW OF FATHER. Open your eyes—the war is over!
This is not a slumber between everlasting wars!

FUSAI. My father said there was no limit to war,
But men's chances were limited;
One must create opportunities out of war!

JIANG. Father said that since childhood, we have been all too familiar with war—
And throughout history, we have survived massacre.
But now,
The tribes have been defeated in such a way that they
Can no longer mount their horses,
And their survivors, thousands of them, are captive to the King!

SHADOW OF FATHER. Not just the enemy,
But we too conquered countless hostilities;
It was a big battle for great peace!

Sound of fanfare.

JIANG. Then suddenly,
We heard
The call of fanfare from outside.
On the other side of the curtain
Was the hornpipe celebrating the victory father spoke of,
And on this side,

It broke your icy wonder
—Which melted as you burst into tears.
Mother drew the curtain and found us both.
One terrified, the other crying,
Both equally in need of her arms!
Father had turned to the door, through which armored men,
With pheasant-plumed helmets and the jingling sounds of their magnificent belts,
Had entered the room.
One with a trumpet in one hand and a torch in the other,
One with a bow,
And one, a stout man with a bamboo scroll.

(*The shadow of Mother has disappeared from the scrim, and the shadow of Father is seen opposite the three armored men, in torchlight and candlelight.*)

Mother was watching with us.
The torchbearer cried,
"Where is the Prime Minister?"
—He did not know how to speak softly!—
Father asked,
"Who are you?"

SHADOW OF TORCHBEARER (*cries*). We are the special messengers of the Khagan.

JIANG. Confused, Father murmured, "The Khagan?"

(*Fade*)

Huang appears onstage, with two ringing bells in her hands.

HUANG. The court of the Khagan!
I can see that!

Is the man who is sending for me now on the court?
In what position?
Once he told me that I would see him one day in the court of the Khagan!
And that I would see him be wittier than all the men in the legends.
And wittier than the men in lyrics from love songs.
Does he know that
Even the most beautiful flowers will lose their aroma some day?
(The bells stop ringing.)
The court watchmen rush forward and salute—
Not me,
Not my attendants,
But the six-horse chariot, which always hosts a venerable passenger.
From what my attendants—his messengers—say,
In the language from this side of the Wall, the language of the kingdom of the Khagan,
I understand only three words: "the Chancellor's guest!"
Are they speaking of Fusai?—the Chancellor!
A long time ago, he told me that I would finally see him on the grand seat.
Now he is seated where he said he would be,
But I am not where I once was!
(*Fade*)

On the shadow scrim, the shadow of Father appears alongside three armored men. Jiang and Fusai stand on opposite sides of the stage, watching the scrim.

SHADOW OF TORCHBEARER (*cries out*). Where is the Prime Minister?

SHADOW OF FATHER. Who are you?

SHADOW OF TORCHBEARER. The special messenger of the Khagan!

SHADOW OF FATHER. The Khagan?

JIANG. The stout man came closer—

SHADOW OF THE STOUT MAN. Shun Yeo, carrying a command for the Prime Minister!

SHADOW OF FATHER. I am the one you are looking for.

SHADOW OF SHUN YEO. Oh, I know this voice.

JIANG. The stout man bowed—

SHADOW OF SHUN YEO. The Prime Minister should excuse us.
I did not recognize the victorious commander-in-chief in his underclothes!
And it is no wonder that the cherished minister does not recall his subordinate—in armor.

SHADOW OF FATHER. Shun Yeo . . . Your name sounds familiar—
Were you not the paymaster of the King's harem?

JIANG. The stout man bowed once again—

SHADOW OF SHUN YEO. This very year that the able minister and his brave men
Were traveling from one battlefield to another,
The administration of the capital was handed to squat men,
And the cloak of the gentlefolk was adjusted for my humble body.
But now—with honor—I am commanded to come before the Prime Minister
To offer this red bow
As a token of Khagan's trust to his valiant commander
—And a good omen for future wars—

(*On the scrim, the man bows and kneels down to offer the red bow to the shadow of Father.*)

As well as this scroll that contains His Highness' command,
Which invites the cherished minister to a celebration
To be held the day after tomorrow.

On the scrim, Shun Yeo, head down, offers the bamboo scroll.

SHADOW OF FATHER. But wait—
You used the title "Khagan" three times!

SHADOW OF SHUN YEO. And you said "the King."
Excuse this stout man,
But the title of King from henceforth
Suits the sons and commanders of His Highness, who, until yesterday, was called our King.

JIANG. Father was still tasting the flavor of that word-

SHADOW OF FATHER. The Khagan.

SHADOW OF SHUN YEO. The King of kings, the son of heavens
The lord of all territories within the four seas,
Which, in honor of the name of His Highness' tribe
Will be forever called Qin.

JIANG. On this side of the curtain,
Mother's hand clutched my shoulder.
On the other side,
Father reached for the blood on his chest.

SHADOW OF FATHER. The day after tomorrow, I—

SHADOW OF SHUN YEO. The great Khagan
considered your valiance
And forgave you due to your continued loyalty,
And having recalled your wound, he did not take offense
That you hurried home from the battlefield instead of visiting him.
Dress your wound and stay in bed until you are able to move.

No excuse is acceptable for the Khagan,
May this be the last blood of your lineage shed on earth.

SHADOW OF FATHER. Excuse? No!
It is the matter of my family
My spouse, my daughter and now two sons
Who were with me day and night during the war, here in my chest.

SHADOW OF SHUN YEO. I bring good tidings for your highness that the day after tomorrow,
You will hear good news for this country
—Which will be like a cure for your wounds—
And among the news, will be a reward for the Khagan's devoted soldier, your Highness.

JIANG. On the other side of the curtain
Drops of blood flowed from Father's wound.
On this side, Mother's hand sat restlessly on my shoulder.

SHADOW OF FATHER. My family deserves the reward more than I do.
Now that I cannot stay with them,
May my family accompany me to the feast?

SHADOW OF SHUN YEO. Just one—
Of your sons.
As you will soon find, this is a manly feast.
Now, it is time for us to return to the capital.
We have brought along a chariot which will stay
To bring you the day after tomorrow, before noontide to the presence of the Khagan;
Also, this Tatar horse branded with the emblem of the House of Rong will stay here.

FUSAI. My father's horse!

SHADOW OF SHUN YEO. It is best that anything with the Rong emblem
Stays in its land.

Accompanied by the sounds of drums, horns, and bells, colorful lights shine on both sides of the scrim.

JIANG. The coming day was awaiting us behind the eyelid of night
To take us to the capital;
My father and I, alone!
Upon our departure, father did not notice
The saddle and frenum of his favorite horse
On a mounted heap in the garden,
A grave which the orderlies
Had dug and filled in the day he was in bed with fever.
The six-horse chariot
With horses from six colors and breeds
Took us,
And the chariot was the loot for the victory over all ancestries of the land!

(*On the shadow scrim, we watch people hold up bright, colorful flags and a dancing dragon above their heads, accompanied by the sound of musical instruments. The scrim moves slowly as if it transports the dancing dragon across the stage.*)

The capital was shining
With the armors and helmets and shields that glinted in the sun.
I turned from these shining heavy metals to the colorful flags.
In my ears, however,
The hornpipe of victory mingled with the moans of the prisoners of war,
Chained and seated in rows on the sides of the road.

Father was in new garments
—Made of silk and woven by my mother—
That covered his dressed wound.
As the six-horse chariot passed,
The prisoners turned to us,
Some with wanting hands and others with pleading moans.
I wished I had stayed at home
With you, Fusai—
And your new plaything, your Tatar horse.

(The scrim with the dragon's shadow fades in one corner of the stage and in its place on the second scrim, the Khagan's court takes shape. The court has a huge throne at one end of the hall and audiences surrounding it, as Jiang will describe.)

The gates were wide open,
And in the grand hall,
Each group occupied a separate corner.
On one side was the commanders of war; on the other, the allied nobilities;
On one side the administrators in dress clothes for the feast;
On the other the leaders among the prisoners, handcuffed and on their knees—
Surrounded by armored soldiers.
There was also an aged man, as old as the world, next to the throne!
I pulled my father's sleeve. "Is that him?"
Slowly he said, "No, that's his great-uncle."
At noontide, the time of luck,
The dagu drum[14] announced the peak of the sun's arc.

---

14 A Chinese bass drum.

(All at once, the sound of musical instruments dies out. Absolute silence.)

And veils of pure silk
Were lowered, at once, in front of each group.[15]

(On the side scrim, the shadow of young Jiang and Father's torsos appear, both staring at the central scrim.)

Father pressed my hand.
The devotees lined up.
A man appeared silent and serene,
In a robe of golden silk with two dragons on it,
The sun and the moon on his right and left shoulders,
And stars on his chest.
It was the Khagan.

(The shadows of Father and Jiang bow and exit from the side scrim; in their place, the looming, strutting shadow of the Khagan appears. Simultaneously, the central scrim reveals the audience in the hall dropping to their knees and bowing their heads at the Khagan's entrance. On the side scrim, Shun Yeo, standing close to the Khagan, raises his head.)

We all bowed down,
Until someone cried, "Stand up!"
It was the stout man—Shun Yeo—
Next to the throne, his head down, holding a scroll.
We were close to the throne,
And once more, fate was a shadow on the scrim before my eyes.
The Khagan's hand unsealed the scroll.
Shun Yeo read.

---

15 To prevent direct encounter with the Emperor—who was considered heaven's representative on earth—court tradition required that during public gatherings, attendees saw him from behind veiling curtains.

SHADOW OF SHUN YEO. "The son of heavens
Celebrates this great victory."
JIANG. The audience cheered.
The Khagan did not even blink.
SHADOW OF SHUN YEO. "The long war among the territories
Has left confusing and illegible words from the ancient land,
Like letters on bamboo fragments with loosened thread;[16]
The son of heavens intends to rewrite this letter anew.
Thus, His Highness accepts his dominion over all territories with a new name, taken from the great yellow emperor,
Shi Huangdi, the first Khagan,
The founder of a dynasty.
May it last for thousands of generations!"
JIANG. The audience cheered.
The Khagan did not blink.
SHADOW OF SHUN YEO. "Chaos gives way to order,
And autonomous territories to a unified country,
Under the name of the great country of Qin!"
JIANG. They cheered.
The Khagan did not blink.
SHADOW OF SHUN YEO. "Thus, the command is to unify all territories and tribes,
In law and treasury,
Language and script."
JIANG. Cheers!

---

16 Bamboo and wooden slips were the main writing materials in ancient China before the invention of paper. Long, narrow bamboo strips were sewn together with silk, hemp, or leather threads, allowing them to be folded and unfolded like a scroll. These bindings also established the sequence of the strips, in effect creating early books.

The Khagan did not blink.

SHADOW OF SHUN YEO. "To execute the order,
The gates must be closed to strangers
So that we do not have aliens inside.
The nobles from the states and the local princes
Must transfer the authority of the territories
—Including their treasuries and local armies—
To the delegates of the Khagan.
All through the country,
Every weapon must be handed to the commissary of the Khagan and sent to the capital.
Existing roads must be repaired to benefit the Khagan's army.
And new roads must be constructed too,
From the capital to the farthest of the country's borders—
Where civilization ends.
All must speak and write the language of Qin and every other language must be silenced!"

JIANG. When the shock was over, it was too late for cheers.
The Khagan blinked.
Father's hand turned cold.
His face was pale!

SHADOW OF SHUN YEO. And the last order—
"There must be a borderline between us and the foreigners;
A world without walls is impossible.
The Four Mountains at the four corners of the earth are the borders of life,[17]

17 The Four Mountains are a recurring element in the myth of the Great Flood, from the time of Emperor Yao (during whose reign the Great Flood began) to Yu the Great (who finally controlled the flood waters). In ancient Chinese cosmology,

And 'home' is where you circumscribe it with walls.
Thus, there must exist a great wall
To block the invasion of the foreign tribes.
To that end, the command is to construct a giant wall,
Such that the northern fortifications of the country join together.
A wall that reaches east to the sea
And west to the farthest borders where the savage nomads live."

JIANG. Father's hand felt like ice.
The Khagan blinked.
The audience recovered themselves. Cheers!
The Khagan stood up—

SHADOW OF KHAGAN. But now, a celebration!
And happier will the festivity be
Should it begin with an invocation of our war hero.
Where is the valiant minister—
The one who made the bridge of the capital a tomb for the enemies?
(*Fade*)

Huang appears onstage, confused and crossing hastily from one side to the other.

HUANG. Why the backdoor?
What did his messengers and the guards say to each other?
Why do they take me to the court from this back entrance and with two new attendants?
And why with such haste?
My shoe fell off!
What do all these mediators, servants, and retinue want

---

these mountains were thought to mark the four corners of the earth, envisioned as a square.

From the visit of two people, one of whom has invited the other!?
I wish you were not the Chancellor.
I wish you never knew the administration
And never found your way to the capital!
What would have happened if we had lived peasant lives, cousin?
Without the need of attendants and watchmen,
I would keep up with you during harvest time.
We would farm millet and reap mung,
I would age with you,
And fasten your children to my back
And cook over the fire for your unexpected guests,
And avow food for the health of your traveling relatives.
Oh, I was young the last time we said farewell;
You did not age with me,
Could you believe that I aged with you?
Where will these orderlies take me?
Did they open that door for me?
Oh! Why the backdoor?

She is gone. On the central scrim, the shadow of the Khagan approaches the drawn silk veil, behind which are young Jiang and his father. Jiang and Fusai are onstage.

SHADOW OF KHAGAN. I had missed the warrior of all seasons.
Come forth from behind the veil.
You may see the Khagan's face uncovered,
For you have won over my heart.
I confess that the day I entrusted the army to you,
I had doubts.
—What does a man of words want with arrows and sling?—

But the reports from the battlefields
Made you more and more capable in my eyes.
And when I heard your last speech,
With tears of sorrow, I said that he won the last battle with words.

On the central scrim, Father and Jiang have come forth from behind the silk veil. On the side scrim, the shadows of the Khagan, Father, and Jiang are seen.

SHADOW OF FATHER. Great Khagan!

SHADOW OF KHAGAN. Is that your son?
And now a promise to add to your reward!
He will be one of the Khagan's men.
When will he reach the legal age?

SHADOW OF FATHER. He was born on the fifth day of the fifth month—the year of the dragon.

SHADOW OF KHAGAN. Oh, the day of the tiger, the year of the dragon!
The tiger is power and the dragon is the Khagan.
He was born great!
Register this.
Seven years henceforth, on the day of the tiger,
He will be conscripted to serve the administration.
(*On the side scrim, the shadow of Shun Yeo approaches the Khagan.*)
Teach him the language of Qin;
He will someday write the history of the Qin territory!
What is his name?

SHADOW OF FATHER. Rong Jiang

SHADOW OF KHAGAN. Oh—Rong!

SHADOW OF SHUN YEO. May the Great Khagan notice that—

SHADOW OF KHAGAN. Yes, write.

"Some people from outside the country
Will be admitted into the Qin territory,
But only upon scrutiny, test, and proof of ability."

SHADOW OF SHUN YEO. The command says—

SHADOW OF KHAGAN. Do not mount an opposition against my will with my own commandment!
Laws should be modified by other laws.
Write.
"Whosoever from alien lineage is admitted into this territory
Must invert his given and family name
To be recognized by others."
Write his name—Jiang Rong!

SHADOW OF FATHER. Much obliged I am to the Ki—the Khagan.
My son can participate, like others, in the great test if—

SHADOW OF KHAGAN. We will allow it as a reward for the test you passed!

SHADOW OF FATHER. Your humble servant did not mean that.
I have another son—
The truth is, he is the son of a cousin
Who was slain near the battlement of the capital.
He is now living with us in my homestead,
Directly on the other side of the battlement, outside the wall that is to be constructed.
Is he then an alien?
Didn't the men of Rong prove their loyalty in this war?
On the battlefields, we were in one line, regardless of lineage.
Does the Great Khagan
Consider half of his servants as barbarians and foreigners?

JIANG. The Khagan blinked several times.

SHADOW OF KHAGAN. History has been written by you and people like you, not me!
It is scrolled in bamboo volumes
That six hundred years ago, the tribe of Rong
Invaded the capital of Zhou
And overturned the Zhou dynasty.
Who can guarantee that they will not mount their horses for the same craving
If opportunity were to strike one more time?
And remember,
Outside the borders of Qin, this is not the only tribe!
I have heard that throughout the yellow and dust-stricken wilderness,
There are folks who have forked tongues,
Savages who sew buttons on the left sides of their clothes,
Tribes that drink cow's milk!
Will a civilization grow if it mingles with savages?
The law demands drawing borders with the lawless wilderness.
Therefore, our home must be surrounded by fences
So that everyone within yields to the law—

JIANG. The Khagan raised his voice—

SHADOW OF KHAGAN. Anyone from any tribe!
Did everyone hear that?

JIANG. Absolute silence;
Everyone lowered their heads, and the Khagan his voice.

SHADOW OF KHAGAN. Nonetheless,
The Khagan differentiates between a traitor and a servant,
And the path to the Qin domain passes through his heart.
Of your other son, we will again speak,
But for now,

Your reward is our trust,
For which we delegate the construction of the Great Wall to you!

JIANG. Father closed his eyes.

SHADOW OF KHAGAN. This is a greater battle for you to lead for years!

JIANG. Father opened his mouth to speak
But the Khagan had turned away—

SHADOW OF KHAGAN. We missed the celebration of victory,
(*calls*) Shun Yeo!

JIANG. Shun Yeo bowed his head
And opened the scroll.

SHADOW OF SHUN YEO (*reads*). The victorious Khagan,
Shi Huang Di, orders
That before this very sunset,
All the prisoners—from all tribes—
Must be decapitated,
So that the god of victory
Be witness to it,
And be satisfied with this sacrifice. And too, the black-haired folks learn
The consequences of hostility to the newly established state!
Also, the leaders of the prisoners—the broken nobles and the dethroned princes—
Who are here handcuffed and, on their knees,
Must be passed ropes from their nostrils[18]
And in a long queue, this very sunset,
They must set off for exile on foot

---

18 The Khagan commands that the prisoners have their noses pierced and be strung together by threads running through the holes.

To heap up stones for the Great Wall
At the farthest borders in the north.

The side scrim darkens. The following takes place on the central scrim.

JIANG. Father's closed eyelids were trembling.

SHADOW OF KHAGAN. Is it not the time for wine?
Where now is the goblet?

JIANG. Suddenly, a prisoner raised his head!

SHADOW OF PRISONER (*cries*). I have a demand!

JIANG. The Khagan paused.

SHADOW OF KHAGAN. Who was that?

On the central scrim, the handcuffed prisoner is brought forth by two armored soldiers. On the side scrim, the big shadow of the prisoner appears with his companions behind him.

SHADOW OF PRISONER. It is I, the commander-in-chief of Han!

SHADOW OF KHAGAN. A demand for the Khagan?
To give thanks for our victory, we will hear it!

SHADOW OF PRISONER. I doubt that one single soul will return from this exile.
Now that I must go,
I would like to ask the King of Qin,
To pull out my eyes and hang them on the gates of this city.
I would like my eyes to see the day
When the men of Han invade this capital!

JIANG. the Khagan took the goblet,
And stared at the bubbles in the wine.

SHADOW OF KHAGAN. Granted!
And to let everyone know that the Khagan is generous today,
He will endow this blessing on everyone.

He will pull out the eyes of every single soul before they leave this hall.
This will be a chance for all tribes
To wait the turn of their fortune
On the gate of the capital.
And an added benefit.
The last image they take to hell
Will be the glory of the victorious Khagan of Qin.
Serve wine!
(*On the side scrim, prisoners disappear, and the large shadow of Father appears.*)
My wise minister spoke about loyalty—
It will be a sweet entertainment for such a feast,
To pull out an eye from the enemy's socket.
First of all,
I entrust Han's commander-in-chief to my own great commander—

JIANG. He turned to my father—

SHADOW OF KHAGAN. Come before my eyes, holding his!

JIANG. And moved towards the throne.
Father took a step towards the Khagan
But froze.
I saw his hands grab his chest and clench!
He turned.
A dagger was placed before him on a tray
And the commander of the Han was swiftly seated upon a leather hide.[19]

---

19 Piece of leather traditionally used in past executions to avoid the spread of blood.

It was at this very moment that a scarlet flower bloomed on his clothes
And blood ran into the warp and weft of the silk.[20]
He spoke—

SHADOW OF FATHER. May the Khagan excuse his servant.
The wound on my chest has opened up!

A red light shines across the scrims, then fade into darkness.

FUSAI. The wound your father scratched on his chest that day
Determined our fate forever!
Because he did not pull out the eyes on that day,
Our fates were darkened
by the dagger of that untimely softness!

JIANG. What he did was not out of kindness.

FUSAI. You still argue with me, even in this phantasm!
Look at the horror of the night you have fallen into;
Is this not blindness?
Speak—what, then, was it that he did?

JIANG. Did you not ask him?

FUSAI. When?
(*On the central scrim, the shadow of Father is in bed and the shadow of Mother is attending to him.*)
When you returned from the court,
He was speechless and covered in blood!
He was burning with fever for nine days,
As if he had wished the infection on his wound!

JIANG. It was the infection of time heaped on his chest!

---

20 The two main thread positions in weaving. The lengthwise warps are crossed with the vertical weft to keep the threads stationary.

FUSAI. It was complete silence!
Even when your father would open his eyes, they would merely stare at the opening in the roof!
Even though your mother
Was dying to have a word with him—
As she was making eucalyptus tea with one hand
And washing his feet with the other.
And when he got up from bed, he spoke nothing,
Even to me who had gradually come to know
What it means to give up hope for a father's return!

JIANG. Now I understand
That silence was his own punishment for his eloquence on the battlefield;
That fever came from the fire of his words!
Could he not foresee that the fateful battle on the bridge
Led him and the others nowhere but into the burning inferno?!
The infection on his chest was the wound of humiliation
—The wound of alienation—
Of calling him a savage and reversing his family name!

FUSAI. My father fought beside him!
What was his crime other than having hope for me?

JIANG. Father and his tribesmen battled through their loyalty to a king
Who was now drawing a huge wall between himself and them.
Were his feverish nightmares not the eyes of the slain staring back at him?
And the eyes of the survivors turning away from him?

FUSAI. And once he recovered from the nightmares and fevers, he did something strange!

(*On the central scrim, Father gets up from bed and sits down to write a scroll on bamboo. On the side scrim is the ivied gateway, a chariot, and a messenger from the Khagan at the threshold.*)

On the tenth day, a messenger came from the Khagan
To greet and summon him up to the capital.
And Father sat down to write a letter.

SHADOW OF FATHER (*reading what he has written*). May the great Khagan excuse his humble servant,
For whatever youthful power he had
Was spent at war with the enemies.
And now the ministership of as vast a territory as Qin
Is too heavy a burden on these feeble shoulders,
And the supervision over the construction of a wall as tall as that
Demands an abler man than I.
Thus, if His Highness' mercy
Lifts the burden of ministership from the shoulders of this aged and injured man,
The administration of the state will be carried out properly,
And this penman will return to his work in his birthplace—
Teaching, serving as secretariat, and writing history—
So that future generations will know
What has come of this land.

SHADOW OF MOTHER. I am glad you spoke at last, with the best of words,
But look to yourself and your children.
Do you know what you are doing?

SHADOW OF FATHER. Between our home and the throne, there is now a wall.
It is time to ask this or that?
I'll stay on the other side of the Wall so that they don't invert my name!

Father exits the central scrim with a letter while Mother watches him go. On the side scrim, The shadow of Father goes to the gateway and hands the letter to the messenger. The messenger bows, boards the chariot, and rides away. Father returns to the garden. On the central scrim, the shadow of Mother covers her face and weeps.

JIANG. When he handed over the letter,
He turned to the garden.

SHADOW OF FATHER. Oh, fowls!
It is me, the wise minister.
My oxen!
The great minister stays with you.

FUSAI. He had already delivered the letter;
It was too late to ask him anything!
And now it is much too late,
Now that I hold a position
That took much effort to obtain
Although I could have gained it more easily.

JIANG. Then he went to the garden
To water the dust of his beloved horse
With his tears.

SHADOW OF FATHER. What did I do to you,
My loyal company?
And with my other companions—
Plain dwellers, mountain folk, city denizens, and peasants, from shores to cols.
(*Fade*)

Huang appears, standing with her hands outstretched, ready to be dressed in garments.

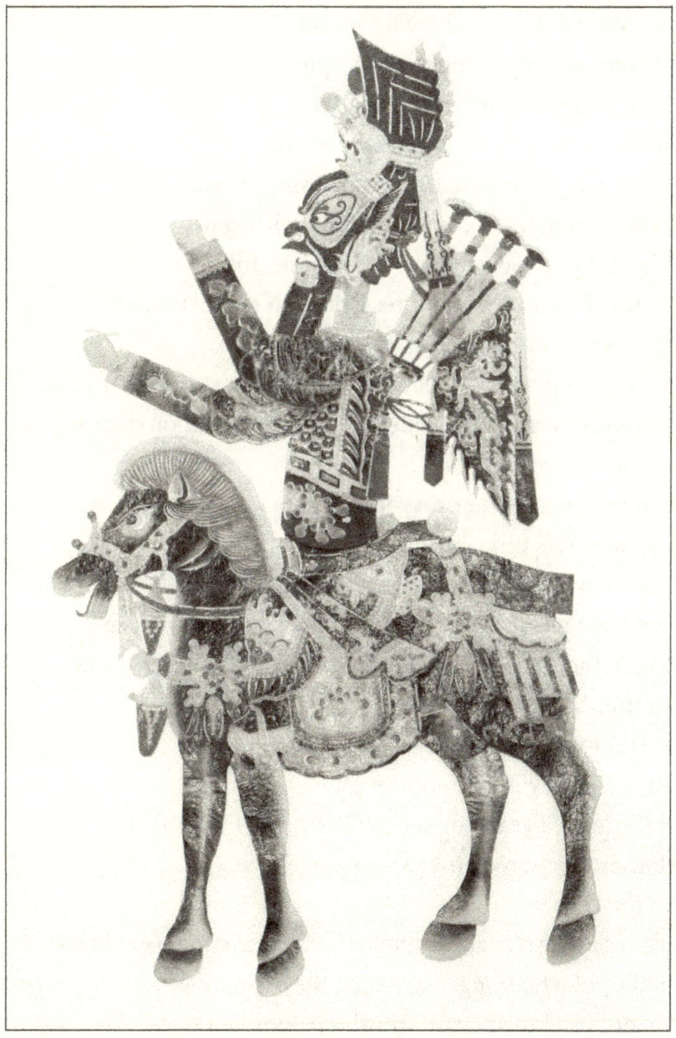

FIGURE 17. Chinese-style shadow puppet created by puppet artisan Jean-Luc Penso. *Photograph by Hamed Esmailee from the collection of Hamid Amjad.*

HUANG. Why did you call me for a visit
If I were not appealing to your sight?
If my burlap clothes dishearten you,
You've plenty of colorful silks to share!
Why have you sent me to this dressing room,
To be among these courtesans of the Khagan?
Why did you leave me to your beauticians
To disrobe me and then dress me with royal clothes?
Oh, I was watching those three women,
Who came from the village at daybreak in shabby attire
And were permitted to enter the palace only upon donning colorful borrowed clothes
And making up their rosy faces.
And now it is time for them to go home
—As they put their shabby dresses back on—
And not one wishes to part with the returned pongee,[21]
Which they stroke as if thinking, "farewell till tomorrow."
Do they bring such guests
To you too, Fusai?
Oh, why did you humiliate me!?
In those grey years, under the berries of the garden,
Mother taught me how to weave and dye silk.
All those years,
I never abhorred silk as much as you make me hate it now,
By the colorful pongee in which they wrap me, at your command.
No, no, you beauticians! Finish up your work.
These tears are from the candle smoke burning my eyes.

---

21 Delicate Chinese fabric made of silk.

Oh, why did you do this to me?

(*Fade*)

On the central scrim, the shadow of a house and garden appears, followed by the teenage Jiang and Fusai, and then Father and Mother with the teenage Huang beside them. On the side scrim is the circle of pupils in the garden. Jiang and Fusai leave the central scrim and move to the side scrim among the students; Father comes and teaches. On the central scrim, Mother and Huang are at work in the garden. Then the pupils disappear from the side scrim and Father teaches only Jiang and Fusai. Onstage the embodied Jiang and Fusai appear.

JIANG. On one of those bright days,
I asked what you did not, Fusai.
Do not say that we did not have happy days,
Do not say that this household was not kind to you.
Remember, you were not a guest here.
You were a son to my mother and my father,
A brother, a friend, and a soulmate to me,
Needless of what father told me—
"Befriend him so
That he forgets his woes."
And we all had seven years' time to love and unite.
And he had had the opportunity to write a record of the warring tribes.
For a few hours he would teach
Under the shade of the aged berry tree,
And for another few hours
—Once the rest of the pupils were dismissed—
He would teach you and me Qin
—Which was the language of the bureau—

And archery, calligraphy, music, and poetry—
Which were the languages of life.
The colts of his deceased horse were now,
Like us, at the age of riding.
Remember?
We were truly happy, you and I,
Despite the fact that within our sight,
On the other side of the passing yellow dust,
They were laying the foundation of the Great Wall, stone upon stone.
Still, our sky was wide
And our life was as colorful
As the colors the spring was leaving behind,
As the colors Mother used to paint the fibers of silk and canvas,
As the colors that time was leaving on Huang's cheek.
The Wheel of Fortune was turning at our will,
And Father was cheering us up with his heavy laughter—
Except for those days when the orderlies at the ivied gateway
Would alert us of a messenger from the Khagan.

Mother and Huang have left the center scrim. In their place now stands a messenger with two soldiers on one side, and the shadow of Father on the other.

SHADOW OF MESSENGER. His highness said that he was looking forward to reading the history you are scribing.
What day will the grand secretary be ready to come before the Khagan?

SHADOW OF FATHER. Inform His Highness that the secretary is ready.
The history book, however, is not.

SHADOW OF MESSENGER. His Highness demands that you name a date
And the special chariot will come to greet you.

SHADOW OF FATHER. Autumn comes with the dusty, freezing winds.
The winter here is very harsh for you.
Come the last day of springtime
And I will tell you a time.

On the scrim, one of the two soldiers comes forward.

SHADOW OF SOLDIER. I have battled beside you hereabouts during the winter;
Do you remember me?
I have a wound from the war, and I take pride
That I have fought under your command.

SHADOW OF FATHER. Take my greetings to the cohort
And say registering each one of the wounds will take a long time.

FUSAI. You see?
The Khagan was still giving him the honor of meeting, and he evaded it.

JIANG. He was not evading;
History is not like a scroll of commands, where you can write a hundred of them every day!

Now the earlier soldier who has been promoted to messenger appears on the side scrim with two soldiers alongside him and Father in front of them.[22] *On the central scrim, young Jiang and Fusai watch them.*

SHADOW OF SOLDIER. I had never seen the start to summer in this area;
It is hot but agreeable!
I am the previous soldier but now in the position of a messenger,

---

22 In *ta'ziyeh,* the passage of time is shown rather than described, particularly by changing costumes or moving around the stage. In this case, the promotion of the soldier to the position of messenger indicates the passage of time.

I have brought the message of the Khagan: "My eagerness is beyond measure.
Where is the book that is supposed to outshine the glory of the scrolls of tribes?"

SHADOW OF FATHER. Scrolls of tribes?

SHADOW OF SOLDIER. The heads of the previous states were moved in groups to areas near the capital, and with them are the ancient scrolls of each tribe's history.

SHADOW OF FATHER. Oh—the history of civil wars recounted by all the tribes involved!
This is the best tidings,
So that I could pore over those scrolls
And rewrite what I have recorded in the book of history.

SHADOW OF SOLDIER. May the wise secretary not blame me;
But it is the command of the Khagan to *receive* the book,
Not to *hand in* scrolls or rewrite history from *the enemies' viewpoint*!

SHADOW OF FATHER. Deliver this message to His Highness: How could I complete a book without evidence?
And if you do not give over the documents, neither can I give you the history!

SHADOW OF SOLDIER. Are those your sons—in the corner—watching us?
They grow fast.
I too have children, who will themselves be fatherless if I take this message.

SHADOW OF FATHER. The record of civil wars is the record of how many children went fatherless.

FUSAI. Such bold responses!

SHADOW OF SOLDIER. The previous messenger whom I have replaced
Was delegated dominion over the Chu territory

Because he never brought negative reports to the Khagan.
What is the most pleasant news from the book that one could take to the Khagan's attention?

SHADOW OF FATHER. This area witnesses harsh winters—
That is the season I call off teaching and devote all my days to taking records.
I hope that next spring *The History of Civil Wars* will be complete.

SHADOW OF SOLDIER. Your cohort sent you greetings with a message—
Do write about the wounds remaining of the bygone days,
But not such that you affect our present and future days.

FUSAI. He could have gone to meet the Khagan
And offered excuses himself!

JIANG. He was still heavy hearted
And was worried that the meeting might cause new bitterness—
A fresh lance on the wound of his humiliated pride.
It was not that the new offense would slow the process of writing further,
But that *The History of Civil Wars* was the fruit of his life
And he did not want it unfinished.

Now the earlier soldier in the position of the special messenger appears on the central scrim, with many in attendance, and Father is in front of them. On the side scrim, the teenage Jiang and Fusai are watching. Young Huang is further away.

SHADOW OF SOLDIER. The spring in this region is altogether different,
Even for the stone-carrying slaves of the Great Wall.

SHADOW OF FATHER. The spring days are not long enough,
And shorter still are one's chances to rest in the blossoming garden.

SHADOW OF SOLDIER. I have less time than even that!
I am now the special messenger—and am in much more haste!

I have been commanded to return with a gift.
The Khagan is impatient to read your masterpiece, *The History of Civil Wars.*

SHADOW OF FATHER. Right this instant?
But this book is unfinished!

SHADOW OF SOLDIER. His Highness said that his patience was exhausted, and yet the book is still incomplete?
The reward for its authorship has rusted in the treasury.

SHADOW OF FATHER. How did His Majesty call it a masterpiece and reward it while still unread?

SHADOW OF SOLDIER. He has heard much about your history lessons from your pupils' recounting.

SHADOW OF FATHER. My pupils? The Khagan said this?

SHADOW OF SOLDIER. The Chancellor Shun Yeo said so, quoting the Khagan.

SHADOW OF FATHER. Oh, I see.

SHADOW OF SOLDIER. Between us, he does not deserve the position that was truly yours.
But—thanks to the Khagan's support—he has measured up to it very well.
And the latest news.
Over one hundred and twenty thousand nobles from various states
Were moved to the suburbs of the capital.

SHADOW OF FATHER. Like the aftermath of war,
That is a report worth mentioning in this record.
Yet there is a lot to register before I write the history of the contemporary period.
This is not a daily letter
But the history of a millennium, cited in the ancient scrolls,

Taken word by word from documents, and summed up line by line from countless records,
Like wine from grapes handpicked from the best vineyards.
Take this message from me: patience still is required.
Unfermented wine causes headache.

SHADOW OF SOLDIERS. Bravo to your sons,
Each time more robust than before!
And that newly bloomed flower must be your daughter.
Have you ever treated them with fatherly anger?
The Khagan likewise stated that
This time, you would bring either the history or the historian,
And we would finish whichever is not ready.

FUSAI. Since Father was not grateful for kindness, they now showed him hostility!

On the central scrim, Father puts several scrolls on a tray, brings them to the ivied gateway, and hands them in. On the side scrim, Mother joins the children and watches.

SHADOW OF FATHER (*displeased*). This draft is untidy;
It is incomplete, full of errors and strikeouts.
And the newly discovered documents are not yet included.

FUSAI. This obsessiveness would not save us!

JIANG. He was always concerned if he was accurate enough.
He was always dissatisfied with himself,
And yet pleased that the fruit of his bygone years was being read.

SHADOW OF SOLDIER. Let me kiss your hand, sir.
You carried out a great task.
Now, I return with my hands full,
And my reward is the kingdom of Han!

FUSAI. Every subordinate used Father as a means for promotion,
And yet he would ruin our own opportunities one by one!
When, then, did you ask him?

JIANG. I did not ask that day out of shame.
My question was left to one summer day
When father was busy teaching,
And you and I were among the pupils,
With Huang watching you, from inside the garden.
All of a sudden, there was a commotion—
Some soldiers were at the gate!

On the central scrim, the ivied gateway is opened, and a line of soldiers enters the garden with a commander riding ahead. On the side scrim are the family and pupils.

SHADOW OF COMMANDER. Class dismissed!
Pupils out!
No one is allowed to enter the garden!

Father approaches the commander.

SHADOW OF FATHER. By what order?

SHADOW OF COMMANDER (*draws sword and swings it in the air*). The order engraved on this blade.
Whoever wants to see must come hither!

SHADOW OF FATHER. Ha! Which kingdom have you been promised,
With such fealty I see in you?
Is it not written on your blade?
What is the problem with this class?

SHADOW OF COMMANDER. Fraudulent history!
You yourself know the crime!

SHADOW OF FATHER. I swear by the Khagan's sword that I do not!

SHADOW OF COMMANDER. The book you scribed,
They analyzed and underlined.
Did you not call the past of Qin barbarous and bloodthirsty?
SHADOW OF FATHER. The ancient documents said so!
SHADOW OF COMMANDER. "The territory of the Qin kingdom,
Has devoured nearby lands year by year,
Like the silkworm devours berry leaves!"
SHADOW OF FATHER. I merely quoted that!
SHADOW OF COMMANDER. His Highness took offense at this line and many similar ones.
And had it not been for the pleading of the nobles,
Your tribe would have disappeared with the yellow wind of the wilderness!
SHADOW OF FATHER. So they interceded!
I need to see the Khagan.
SHADOW OF COMMANDER. Behold—that is the Great Wall rising up,
And there is its gate;
Only your slain body will pass that gate.
SHADOW OF FATHER. I have not yet written the record of this period!
Now where is the book?
How could I edit it if you do not return it?
SHADOW OF SOLDIER. The editing was left to the fire.
If there was any hope for changing you,
You would now be in the fire too.
His Highness stated that savages like you
Would be better left alone,
Now that you are on the other side of the Wall!
FUSAI. Did your father expect better feedback?

The side scrim darkens. On the central scrim, the members of the household cross one after the other.

SHADOW OF HUANG. Was that yelling directed at my father?

She crosses.

SHADOW OF MOTHER. Do not tremble, my daughter,
It's good that they are gone.
And father is alive!

She crosses.

SHADOW OF FATHER. The fruit of many years!

He crosses.

SHADOW OF JIANG. We will write it again—
Together!

He crosses.

SHADOW OF FUSAI. Of course! He had plenty of time under house arrest!

He crosses.

SHADOW OF ORDERLY. Sorry sir,
We have been commanded
To watch the gate from now on, from outside the gateway!

He crosses.

JIANG. That's the very orderly who gave me a piggyback ride!

Father is alone on the central scrim.

SHADOW OF FATHER. So, they finally drew a wall before us too.

FUSAI. Watch him on the scrim of memory;
He was a statue of wonder,
Mulling over what he had done!
And once again, you did not ask him.

JIANG. I did.

When everyone was gone—both pupils and swordsmen—
Father returned to the garden
And breathed deeply.

SHADOW OF FATHER. Oh, pumpkins!

Now the wise secretary has enough time to attend to you.
You autumn sparrows,
From now on we will share morsels of bread with each other.

JIANG. I followed him to the garden.

He was silent like the trees
And restless like birds on the boughs.

(*On the shadow scrim, young Jiang joins Father.*)

I asked him—

SHADOW OF JIANG. Was it worth the price?

SHADOW OF FATHER. I wrote history

The way history revealed itself to me.

SHADOW OF JIANG. I am asking about the beginning.

You could have remained chancellor.

SHADOW OF FATHER. They commissioned me to raise a wall between myself and the world,

And I thought,
Blind loyalty or freedom of choice—this or that?
Woe to the wise man
Who spends his life on history and learns nothing from it.
History is the inventory of choices,
And he who does not choose in life
Might as well have never lived it.

(*Fade*)

Onstage Huang trails a long, loosely flowing gown, as if she is in a royal robe.

HUANG. Now, these borrowed garments are my permit to enter the main gate!
The odor on the stairs greets me
Like a charming smile
On an ugly face!
You are not the one I spoke of to the flowers, birds, and river,
Nor to the fish—those roses of water.
This is not the meeting I expected—
Like an ex-lover asking his sweetheart,
"How is your new beloved?!"
This is not how we should meet—
With my face disguised
And in a garment which still smells of the woman who wore it yesterday!
I wish I could
Destroy the palace with my gaze
Like a rebellious god
Who stared at the waters of the world
And turned them to tempest and stormed the earth!
Or like the moon that is all but water,
I wish I could rise and wash the world from the humiliation you've inflicted upon me!
But I am much like the woman who did not know
She had fallen for a beast,
And upon seeing its face unveiled,
Could only turn to stone.

Now I am a stone,
Stepping on the stone stairs of your palace.
You are not the one that my heart longed for all these years,
Without a word spoken to my brother, mother, or father—
And they, for years, avoided mentioning your name in my presence!
Alas, it was all in vain, for your name was in our eyes
And on our silent tongues.
Oh, why should I come to you through these winding hallways
Full of flowers under candlelight?
It is the first time I've seen a flower and not spoken my secret to it.
Revealing secrets in the presence of strangers?
No, you will not hear it from me, now that you are a stranger to my heart's secrets!
But these attendants do not let me return;
So now that I must see you—No, now that I must see "the Chancellor"—
Let him know that he will be hearing my cries and complaints!
(*Fade*)

On the central scrim, the house and garden are bathed in a dim, cold light as snow begins to fall, gradually covering them in white. Then, the shining sun appears and the snow slowly melts away. On the stage are Jiang and Fusai.

FUSAI. What your father said
Was not an answer for our future.
Time was a steed galloping towards tomorrow,
And your father had fallen from his storming horse,
Still mourning for yesterday!

JIANG. In such a tempest, what face would be free of dust?

Luckily, we were growing anew,
Like the grass after the storm.
We did our best to go our way, like the yellow wind of the desert,
And were happy that we did not yield to grief.

FUSAI. These were your words:
"Be kind to father so that
He forgets his grievances."

JIANG. We wanted him to forget,
And he wanted the same for us.
And mother would give us the elixir to forget our sorrows
With the smell of her cooking over the fireplace.
She dyed silk with the color of her hopes,
And she taught
The language of gardens, skylarks, and silkworms to Huang,
With music tuned from the strings of her heart.
I was glad
That with the colts of father's noble steed
—Given to Huang and I—
We could pass by the yellow wind of the desert
With you on your Tatar horse.
And you were happy,
For when we were back from hunting
Huang would run forth to get the pouch—heavy with prey.
Huang was delighted
That now she had permission
To sit in on father's lessons
With you and me.

On the central scrim, Father is seen teaching Fusai, Huang, and Jiang in the garden. Meanwhile, on the side scrim, the scene shifts inside the house, where young Jiang works beside Father over an open scroll, illuminated by candlelight.

FUSAI. Had the lessons become more difficult or your father more bitter?

JIANG. Your mind was wandering somewhere
Between the master's lessons and his daughter's looks!

FUSAI. And was that the reason you chose private lessons?
By working through the nights with father on what he was writing?

JIANG. I had promised to be his assistant
In rewriting the book of history.

FUSAI. No, you were eager to continue the book,
The book which had disquieted our lives.

JIANG. I was helping him to rewrite it,
For he was worried that he would not live long enough to conclude it,
And I was worried to lose it once again, unread!
I'd rather not sleep at night and lose the pleasure of your company during the day.
But you were right: time was a steed
And it did not ride smoothly.

FUSAI. And then chance knocked on our door!

JIANG. But for whom was it knocking?

FUSAI. Your name was on the letter!

The side scrim darkens. On the central scrim, Father accepts a scroll from a messenger at the ivied gateway and returns.

SHADOW OF FATHER. Inverted!
This is your name, my son,
But the way they prefer it written on the other side of the Wall: Jiang Rong.

Shadow of young Jiang joins Father.

SHADOW OF JIANG. A letter—with my name on it?

SHADOW OF FATHER. An invitation to attend the big contest in the capital
At the command of the Khagan!
Has seven years passed?

Shadow of Mother joins them.

SHADOW OF MOTHER. The test for serving in the administration?
How is it that a son from a banished tribe would be summoned up?

SHADOW OF FATHER. Is it a tribute to the previous command—or perhaps it is a new trick?

Shadow of Fusai approaches.

SHADOW OF FUSAI. A new opportunity maybe!

Shadow of young Huang joins them.

SHADOW OF HUANG. A message of reconciliation, perhaps!

SHADOW OF JIANG. Does the Khagan regret the wrong he did unto his servant?

SHADOW OF FUSAI. Or perhaps it is a test.

SHADOW OF FATHER. A probation

SHADOW OF FUSAI. To see how you respond to the Khagan's command.

SHADOW OF JIANG. I will not go!

SHADOW OF FUSAI. And that is the worst response!

SHADOW OF FATHER. Why should we trust him
After his swordsmen called us savages?

SHADOW OF FUSAI. Why shouldn't we trust him
When they may draw their swords once again—
And this time not just on Father?

SHADOW OF MOTHER. On the family?
For what?

SHADOW OF FUSAI. For ignoring the Khagan's command.

JIANG. I did not feel good about the contest.
Mother was worried about the family and Father was still wounded.
You said they would have no excuse to harm the family if I went,
Only if I did not.
Father said—

SHADOW OF FATHER. You are more than qualified for what they are testing;
And yet, I suspect a new humiliation.
Despite all your wisdom, they may still not admit you.

FUSAI. I said, "Here on the verge of the blustery wilderness,
We are far away.
There is no need to conspire against us or write to us,
Or to issue permission to cross the Wall for the sake of a new humiliation."

SHADOW OF HUANG. In case you are admitted,
Is there any hope to visit the Khagan
And erase the bitterness and call for reconciliation?

SHADOW OF FUSAI. This is a chance to part with years of feuding,
For the Khagan has experienced those same years too,
And perhaps his wrath has been cooled.

JIANG. It was the first time my name was ever on a letter.
A farewell to a life free from the pain of choosing—this or that!

FUSAI. But you decided!

The central scrim darkens. On the side scrim, young Jiang is seen in the darkness of night next to a fire in the garden. A moment later, Father joins him.

JIANG. The night I had to decide,
I escaped everyone to go to the garden,
And I was staring at the fire
When Father interrupted the silence and quelled my doubts.

SHADOW OF FATHER. There is still a way
That we can leave here and escape;
Then you will neither have to go
Nor will they reach the family.

JIANG. What crossed my mind: escaping?
Where to?—Where is it that no hand of the Khagan's could reach?
And how?—When we don't have enough wealth to ask the nomad tribes to assist us?
How far could one go?—With all those books and scrolls which several carts once drew in!
And how could one conclude the book of history while homeless?

SHADOW OF JIANG. I will go to the capital for the test.

The side scrim darkens. The Great Wall with its main gate fills the entire central scrim. Jiang appears on a horse.

JIANG. Then in front of me was the Great Wall, reaching into the sky.
The battlement of the capital was tucked in between.
The closer I went,
The more it appeared like a whirling dragon rising before my humble figure,
Watching the wilderness through the watchtower with sleepy eyes.
The day guard glanced at the scroll and the permit but not at me,
Then the Wall opened its mouth and devoured me.

On the central scrim, Jiang passes through the gate; the image of the Wall and the closed gate remains on the scrim. On the side scrim, a pair of legs appears, wrapped tightly with greaves,[23] *followed by many more draped in long robes.*

JIANG. On the other side of the Wall, I was invisible—
Or perhaps the people—in their long cloaks—pretended that they did not see me,
A man in a short robe, wearing greaves and smelling like a stranger.
All the coins my father had given me on the day of the journey
Were worthless here. Ten coins to one Ban Liang.
And no one would give a bed
To a stranger who had permission to take the exam but not to stay.
I had passed through the main gate,
And yet everywhere I was surrounded by walls.
A teahouse owner, a foreigner with his name inverted,
Gave me a place to stay during the day and offered me a cup of tea,
But he was not allowed to give a stranger a corner to sleep in.
The season was favorable;
All night, the sky—my blanket—spared me the reminder that I am a stranger here.

FUSAI. You did not speak of these!

JIANG. On the day of the exam, the teahouse owner gifted me an old, long robe
So that I would not go to the contest dressed as a nomad.
I asked, "How do you ride your horse with such long robes?"
He replied, "With Qin robes, we fall more than nomads,
But that pain is outweighed by the consequences of being a savage!"

FUSAI. After you returned from the capital,
You never spoke of any of this!

---

23 Piece of fabric or iron worn to protect the shin and the knee.

JIANG. What was the point?

(*On the side scrim, greaves-clad legs of a man seated on a stool peek out from under a robe.*)

During the exam,
I was expecting questions from the hundred schools of philosophy,
And questions from *The Annals of History*, *The Book of Manners*, and *The Book of Poetry*,
But they were never asked.
I was busy answering the questions on music, arithmetic, and medicine,
All in the Qin language,
When I noticed that the examiners were staring at my greaves-clad legs,
Which had slipped out from beneath my robe.
After that, it was time to write a paper.
A one-month period to elaborate and explain
What the most brilliant achievement of the Khagan's reign was!

(*The side scrim darkens.*)

It was difficult to write a treatise on this period
Without referring to the Wall and what had become of the tribes,
Or of history or the classical languages.
The teahouse owner said that they had constructed new roads—nice and flat—
To each corner of the country with such forbidden goods that were previously unreachable.
With the cup of tea in hand,
I wrote of roads—the main roads to the capital—from each direction,
Those that the development of land depends upon.

FUSAI. But you did not stay in the capital for a month!

JIANG. It was not possible!
Neither could one reason and praise the Khagan's roads for a full month,
Nor could one survive on merely cups of tea.
Within fifteen days, I wrote and submitted the paper.
And when they asked which part of the administration I would like to serve in,
I did not hesitate: the Khagan's library—where one would not be admitted easily.

FUSAI. We were not yet expecting you when you returned.

JIANG. That was not my city.
I intended to participate in the exam
And fail without arousing suspicion!

FUSAI. But you passed!

JIANG. It was not my fault that the others tried even less than I did!

FUSAI. All your answers were correct—the highest score!

JIANG. I could not give in,
When their eyes were fixed on the greaves of this nomad!

FUSAI. Speak the truth.
Were you not at all hoping to serve the administration?

JIANG. I told the truth the other day when I said no—
And once I was admitted, I detested it even more!
The long robes
Were too loose on me
And my greaves would be revealed eventually!

FUSAI. We did not read such disgust in your face the day you returned!

JIANG. They had not yet informed me that I would be admitted to serve them.
And I was happy that I could finally eat my mother's cooking!

The central scrim darkens. On the side scrim, Jiang enters with his horse through the ivied gateway. The family gathers around.

SHADOW OF MOTHER. You have lost weight, son!
Has he not, Huang?

SHADOW OF HUANG. Lost weight? Oh, yes.

SHADOW OF FUSAI. Was the exam that difficult?

SHADOW OF FATHER. You should have taken it easy, why did you stay awake?

SHADOW OF MOTHER. My son has suffered hunger!

SHADOW OF JIANG. Me? No! You should have tasted those colorful dishes!
The cooks of the capital have learned a lot in these seven years!

SHADOW OF FUSAI. You should have brought some with you,
So we could also imagine serving at the bureau!
Am I not right, Huang?

SHADOW OF HUANG (*lost in her thoughts*). What? Right—no! Serving at the bureau? Never!

JIANG. I watched her turn rosy in her cheeks.
Between her haste, her absentmindedness,
And her distress at parting from you—
Which would bring a smile to father's face—
My sister had truly fallen in love!
(*Fade*)

On the central scrim appears the Chancellor's seat in Lapis Hall with the circle of counselors around it. Onstage, Fusai is in front of the scrim and Huang appears before him.

FUSAI. Oh, Huang!

HUANG. Do not say Huang's name!
That was the name of a girl in love with Fusai,

—A young boy from the Rong tribe—
Who set a date with her in the springtime!
The simple-hearted girl wishfully endured
The summer and fall too.
In winter she was still waiting
Until she turned to ice and froze to death while keeping her promise!
Poor Huang, how could she know that Fusai would not come?
For he was slaughtered by the Chancellor!
I have come on his behalf
And have no task
But to defame you—as retribution for murdering two lovers!
I have heard your new name: Kung Sun Fu,
—A name particular to the nobles of Qin!
Now that you summoned me overnight to belittle me,
Do you not fear that I might speak your secret
Here in this palace, in a forbidden language?
This makeup and Qin pongee you dressed me in are of no use!
I know not the Qin language,
And let your attendants in the Khagan's court know
That despite your new forged name,
You have come from an alien tribe—
From a land where people fall in love, by any language but Qin!

FUSAI. Welcome to Lapis Hall!
Feel at home, do not fear or frighten!
My attendants—
In grand garments sewn from the best textiles of Qin—
All have disguised their foreign affiliations!
These men, like me, are all from other ancestries;
They have changed their names and disguised themselves anew.

Qin is not any of our language,

It is a language of power—which we have all adopted.

It is not a complicated game.

To enter, one must know the rules.

Do you think there is anyone in this mansion who does not know this?

(*Fade*)

On the side scrim, family members are in the garden while Father reads a scroll. Jiang stands on the stage.

SHADOW OF FATHER. They have admitted you to serve, but not in the library of the Khagan.

Your thesis was on the construction of roads,

So they have summoned you to serve on road construction for the states!

SHADOW OF JIANG. Huh—a weird joke coming from those sullen faces.

SHADOW OF FUSAI. You were admitted!—Do you call the opportunity a joke!

SHADOW OF JIANG. Would you go if it were you?

SHADOW OF HUANG. Have you nothing to speak of other than going?

SHADOW OF FUSAI. I was right;

This is an opportunity to end the exile!

SHADOW OF JIANG. I will not change this exile for that fortune!

SHADOW OF FUSAI. Think of the danger!

The previous letter was an invitation,

This one is a commission.

SHADOW OF JIANG. Is it an opportunity or a threat, then?

SHADOW OF FATHER. Why did I not realize it before?

Those who recall the command from seven years ago

Remember that the Khagan said that someday *you* will write history.
Now they commission you to work on roads.
What they are after is not your service;
You will be their hostage and within their reach,
Without actually giving you a position!

SHADOW OF MOTHER. My son will not go!

SHADOW OF FUSAI. I am worried for the family.
(*Fade*)

Fusai and Huang stand onstage.

FUSAI. No, Huang,
There is no time for your wonder!
I was expecting you to come tonight
For it will be too late to speak tomorrow.
I wanted you to come to this hall
For I had promised that you would see me on the grand seat
And in majestic garments.
It is the law of the court, not mine.
Now enter the sapphire bedchamber,
My private resort,
So that I will hear from you and you from me.
No, do not break into tears! Why are you crying?

HUANG. The tempest of tears breaks against the wall of my will—
Out of my control—
I remember the day I asked you to stay with me!
Why is it that the day of reuniting is the same day for departing?

FUSAI. How could I stay?
Your father said that they had summoned your brother like a hostage—

Do you not remember?
Your brother did not want to go,
And I said, "Convince him that I should go instead!"

HUANG. I realized very late
That you were looking for an opportunity for yourself!

FUSAI. It could have been going to the altar,
Who knew then?

HUANG. I did!
Your departure was death to me!
And yet you insisted, and I asked Father to permit you
Because you said your father's spirit had summoned you!

FUSAI. There was no need to even engrave his name on bones and hold them over the fire
To see his response on the bones;
Father's spirit was always my company
And was always saying "go!"

HUANG. It was *your* spirit that was soaring to this side of the Wall!
(*Fade*)

On the central scrim, young Jiang, Huang, and Fusai drink next to a fire. Jiang is standing onstage.

JIANG. Do you remember the farewell supper?
I did not want you to jeopardize your life for me.

SHADOW OF FUSAI. There is no risk.

SHADOW OF HUANG. When will you return?

SHADOW OF FUSAI (*pouring some drink on the ground as an offering*).
To the ashes for the needs of the deceased.[24]

---

24 A tribute to remember the deceased by honoring them with food and drink. By pouring his drink on the ground, Fusai observes the tradition that is believed to connect the living with their dead ancestors.

SHADOW OF JIANG. If they find out that I am not the one there . . .

SHADOW OF FUSAI. How will they?

SHADOW OF HUANG. When will you return?

SHADOW OF JIANG. If they realize it is you using my name—

SHADOW OF FUSAI. They will not.

SHADOW OF JIANG. Do you really know what you are doing?

SHADOW OF FUSAI. I am not missing this opportunity I have found, that is all.

SHADOW OF JIANG. You are giving yourself as hostage for the sake of the family.

SHADOW OF FUSAI. You're only making an assumption.

SHADOW OF JIANG. And if it turns out to be true?

SHADOW OF FUSAI. Return the favor someday!

SHADOW OF JIANG. To the ashes for the needs of the deceased.

SHADOW OF HUANG. If they find out,
The punishment will not be just for you.

SHADOW OF FUSAI. Are you afraid?

SHADOW OF HUANG. When will you return?

SHADOW OF FUSAI. Soon.

SHADOW OF HUANG. Tell me the day!

SHADOW OF FUSAI. As soon as I am admitted there.

SHADOW OF HUANG. There?
When will you return to stay?

SHADOW OF FUSAI. Or take you with me?
This family was not born to live in exile.

SHADOW OF HUANG. You go to observe the roads,
And someone will keep an eye on your way back home!

SHADOW OF JIANG. Do not upset him on the eve of his departure!

SHADOW OF HUANG. To the ashes for the needs of the deceased.

SHADOW OF JIANG. You know that I can give an excuse
For not going
And the danger would be less than this.
So, what is the reason, honestly?

SHADOW OF FUSAI. My father once said that he would summon me with signs;
Is this not a sign?

SHADOW OF HUANG. Why are all the signs so dark?
Oh, the day breaks!

SHADOW OF JIANG. The horse is ready;
The last goblet too.
(*Fade*)

Huang and Fusai are onstage. On the side scrim, we see young Huang and Fusai saying goodbye.

HUANG. Upon departing
You gave me a plum-tree branch,
And I gave you a fan I had made myself.
You were far away on your horse
When I asked for the last time, "When will you return?"
And when I turned from the road,
The garden was covered with aromatic plants;
The fragrant flowers were hanging from the doorway,
Under the windows, salep orchids were blooming,
And despite all these, the world was suddenly gloomy!
My lover was far away, and plucking flowers was useless . . .

Jiang appears onstage. Behind him, on the central scrim, are the house and garden.

JIANG. And the first gem you robbed me of
Was my name.
Why the silence?

FUSAI. Which should I answer?—
Your sister's accusations?
Or the arrows you shoot at me in this shadow world of phantom and fantasy?

Fusai retrieves the side scrim and carries it to its initial position, obscuring the central scrim, and then turns away from it. Jiang and Huang look at each other and then at the scrim. On the scrim, Father, young Jiang, and young Huang appear. Mother joins them later.

SHADOW OF HUANG. The pond beneath the shade of the willow tree.
A willow leaf fluttering in the wind.[25]
From where does the wind bring news?
Let's not care about the lessons today!

SHADOW OF FATHER. Heed the lesson and the day will pass easier.

SHADOW OF JIANG. Leave her alone, Father!
Let her walk among the flowers and we shall go to the book of history.

SHADOW OF HUANG. Autumn is coming.
How do they deal with the chill on the roads?

SHADOW OF FATHER. The supervisors will not be in the cold,
Their task is with the accounting books and maps on stretched skins
Next to the warming fires.

SHADOW OF MOTHER. What do they eat on the other side of the Wall?
You had become as skinny as a twig.

---

25 Huang describes the scene in the manner of *pardeh-khāni*, in which the solo performer narrates a scene by referring to the painted images on the canvas hung in the background.

SHADOW OF FATHER. The bureau does not suffer hunger.

SHADOW OF HUANG. One month of autumn has passed.
Is the bureau never dismissed?

SHADOW OF FATHER. There were no listeners to today's lesson either!

SHADOW OF MOTHER. The road supervisors are always on the roads, are they not?

SHADOW OF HUANG. There is a biting blast this winter;
Beside each fire,
They probably throw their fans away.[26]

SHADOW OF MOTHER. No silk weaver you will become—
You wave more restlessly than the silk.

SHADOW OF FATHER. Where, now, is the girl?

SHADOW OF JIANG. On the riverside,
Escaping to spring!
She feels better than we do.
Let us study philosophy without her.

SHADOW OF FATHER. The lesson philosophy teaches is:
Do not leave a lover alone by a river,
For she will lose herself in it!

JIANG. He then knew
That there was a secret between the lover and the river.

On the scrim, Huang is plucking flowers by the riverside. Jiang is watching her from afar.

SHADOW OF HUANG. I pick a flower with a smile
And another with tears.

---

26 On the day of departure, Huang and Fusai exchanged mementos as reminders of their feelings for each other. Having given him a fan, Huang now worries that Fusai might have thrown it away.

Between the two,
What thoughts from behind my eyes
And what sobs from inside my throat will come?

JIANG. And two years passed,
Until one sunset
When you appeared at the ivied gateway,
Unexpected, distressed, and disturbed!

HUANG. It was the twenty-second day of the seventh month,
The day village women celebrate their rustic songs.

On the scrim, young Fusai enters the garden. The others approach him.

SHADOW OF FUSAI. Your eyes are not wrong! It is I, myself!

SHADOW OF FATHER. Fusai!

SHADOW OF MOTHER. Covered in dust and dirt!

SHADOW OF FUSAI. My horse is out of breath!

SHADOW OF FATHER. Look at his garments!

SHADOW OF JIANG. You lost your way, I suppose!
Did you not think of the people waiting for you?

SHADOW OF FUSAI. Where are the guards?
I can guess: the orderlies are shirking their responsibilities.

SHADOW OF MOTHER. Did the smell from my stewpot guide you back?
You arrived just in time—hot soup!

SHADOW OF JIANG. How long will it take for you to tell us about these two years?
Start as soon as possible—
Do not skip anything!

SHADOW OF FUSAI. Everything worth talking about is right here!
Where is Huang?

SHADOW OF FATHER. She is out with the new colt, going to the villagers' festivities.

Did you hear? My favorite horse has become a grandfather!
Are you looking for anything off our wall?

SHADOW OF FUSAI. No!—I am tired;
Is there yet a bed for me in this house?

JIANG. You knew there would be;
But we did not know why you were here!

On the scrim, everyone returns home from the garden. Huang enters the garden through the ivied gateway with the colt.

HUANG. I had gone to the festivity to pray;
Unaware of your return, I came back home.
When I saw the old Tatar horse
Tied to the fence,
My heart trembled with joy—
Should I believe it?
Were my prayers answered?
In the sunset sky,
Three—no, four stars were in the east.
And once I saw your hat hung from the porch,
My heart beat fast.
His smell is in the air!
In the sunset sky,
Five—no, six stars were in the east.
Once I saw your shoes next to the door,
A flock of birds fluttered in my heart.
He has come to stay!
In the sunset sky,
Seven—no, tens of stars were in the east.

JIANG. But you stayed one night,
One night only!

FUSAI. Because I feared that they might follow me!

JIANG. That was evident, but you said nothing!!

On the scrim, the family has gathered together on the porch.

SHADOW OF HUANG. Songs were heard from the villagers' festivities.
The first tune: "Migration of the Cranes!"

SHADOW OF MOTHER. A song from when I was young!

SHADOW OF FUSAI. Is progress being made on the book of history?

SHADOW OF FATHER. Better than before, thanks to my new assistant!

SHADOW OF JIANG. I am only learning.

SHADOW OF HUANG. The second song: "The Loneliness of the Bittern!"

SHADOW OF MOTHER. I had not heard this one before.

SHADOW OF FUSAI. Rumors of a new revolt come from the other side of the Wall.
The Chancellor has lost some ground;
Everyday a lot of reports, every minute an order
On changing the writing system.
There are murmurs about changing letters
From the ancient script
To make Qin characters simpler and more uniform.

SHADOW OF FATHER. Oh! Soon no one would be able to read the ancient books!

SHADOW OF JIANG. Now that you are here, teach us the characters one by one
So that we will know them when we write the book.

SHADOW OF FUSAI. There is no time.
I will set off tomorrow.

SHADOW OF MOTHER. Tomorrow?

The shadow of Huang rises and goes to the garden. The shadow scrim darkens.

JIANG. For Huang,
This was more bitter than your absence!
HUANG. My portion
Was merely an hour that night that we spent speaking a few words,
And feeling such agony—that the night passes too swiftly.
You told me not to count this as a visit.
I told you,
"For this one-night chance,
Let us age together."
FUSAI. I said, "The family is in danger.
I was ashamed of speaking this to your father!
In the coming rebellion,
They might make some excuse to invade the country house!
Many lost their lives for not heeding the previous orders,
Like not delivering the war weaponry to the bureau!"
HUANG. I said, "We do not have the weapons of war!"
FUSAI. The red bow, the gift of the Khagan!
Now that your father is neither in the army nor does he serve in the administration,
This could be their best excuse!
HUANG. What shall we do then?
FUSAI. Ask Father to hand the red bow over to me.
I will quietly
Remove it from the house till the turmoil subsides!

On the shadow scrim, Father, Jiang, and Fusai ride across a sunny plain.

JIANG. The next morning, Huang was hovering over the stewpot.
She had promised to receive us with her cooking.
And you and I, Fusai, alongside Father,
With the stallion, mare, and colt

Riding in the wilderness;

Father's red bow hung like a baldric[27] on your horse!

On the shadow scrim, the three companions dismount the horses.

SHADOW OF FUSAI. This is a strong colt

With scarlet sweat on its body!

SHADOW OF FATHER. It is Phoenix, the winged dragon.[28]

SHADOW OF FUSAI. My old Tatar horse is not worth exchanging;

Lend this colt to me in confidence.

SHADOW OF FATHER. It is too soon to put this colt to labor like a riding horse.

It is too young

Even to be branded by the emblem of Rong.

SHADOW OF FUSAI. So much the better!

I prefer to be anonymous, myself,

An anonymous horse suits better!

SHADOW OF FATHER. What is it you are escaping from?

SHADOW OF FUSAI. The shadows of the past!

SHADOW OF JIANG. I have been on the other side of the Wall.

I know what humiliation means.

SHADOW OF FATHER. Let him speak plainly!

SHADOW OF FUSAI. Far from the capital, we were busy working on the roads

When my old subordinate

Recognized the Tatar horse with the emblem of Rong.

He said, "You are the son of the one who betrayed us in the war!"

---

27 A leather strap worn diagonally across the body—from one shoulder to the opposite hip—traditionally used to carry a weapon or support a drum.

28 Phoenix is the name of this horse.

SHADOW OF JIANG. Your father?
He was the hero of the battlefield!

SHADOW OF FUSAI. I said the same to the old man while he was being whipped,
And before dying,
He said there is evidence for my father's infamy!

SHADOW OF JIANG. What evidence?

SHADOW OF FATHER. No,
You are not escaping this!

SHADOW OF FUSAI. The evidence of my tribe's scandal is in the hands of the people.
I was but one step away from being recognized for my fake name.
How can I not escape my true identity?

SHADOW OF JIANG. Stay here!

SHADOW OF FUSAI. To let them find me easier?

SHADOW OF FATHER. There is no proof,
Not with anyone!

SHADOW OF FUSAI. There is!
My father had spoken of a sign
With which, he said, he would send someone for me with a message!

SHADOW OF FATHER (*shows it*). This ring?

SHADOW OF FUSAI. Oh!
Is that with you?

SHADOW OF FATHER. No one knows that it exists and that it is with me—
For years it was in this pouch hung from my neck!

SHADOW OF FUSAI. But how?

SHADOW OF FATHER. I grabbed it
From the closed fist of the enemy's commander
Who was with your father—

And both were shot to death with the arrows
From our own archers.

SHADOW OF JIANG. No!

SHADOW OF FUSAI. From bows like this?

SHADOW OF FATHER. In those hard days of war,
The kin were spying on your father
And his secret give-and-take with the enemy.
They told me, but I did not believe it.
He had sent this ring—with the emblem of his tribe—
To the commander of the enemy
As a token of his vow
On the most difficult day of battle.
On the last battlefield
—When victory was an undecided bird wondering where to land—
The tribesmen saw your father face to face in a dispute with the Commander—
Had he intended to escape with him?
Or did he want to take back that ring, the proof of disgrace from the loser of the battlefield?
I never knew—this or that!
When I arrived, your father was shot to death in the chariot of the enemy
By my comrades, who themselves were killed by the end of the day!

SHADOW OF FUSAI. Was my father—a traitor?

SHADOW OF FATHER. It is not for us to decide about a man who turned to ashes
And blew away with the wind—
Especially now that the battlefield itself is buried under the Wall!

SHADOW OF FUSAI. He had dreams for me!

SHADOW OF FATHER. And fears for his life.
How could I judge him
When I myself may have done more harm to my comrades!
So let us keep this secret,
So that the person remembered does not look evil!

SHADOW OF JIANG. The evidence was forged then
What are you escaping from?

SHADOW OF FUSAI. The far-off road
Is not constructed but the allocated money has been spent;
Instead of building a road, they have brought us dishonor.
Before I can prove it is not my fault, I will be finished!

SHADOW OF FATHER. And now you are escaping?

SHADOW OF FUSAI. To the capital!
In the Qin robe and with an unbranded horse,
And with a new name—not the one I had!

JIANG. I wish there were a scrim revealing the future!
I recognized too late that the other gems you robbed from us were Phoenix and the bow.
And much too late, did I realize that you also robbed me of my good reputation!

SHADOW OF FATHER. And again, you are going to the other side of the Wall?

SHADOW OF FUSAI. The bird of victory my father could not see
Has long landed, and it has done so on the other side!
Now Father's message has reached me with a sign: his ring!

SHADOW OF FATHER. Power is like the goddess of Lu River.
It seduces but does not satisfy.
What is the benefit of running after the grand chariot
Other than facing the dust and falling behind?

FIGURE 18. Chinese-style shadow puppet created by puppet artisan Jean-Luc Penso. *Photograph by Hamed Esmailee from the collection of Hamid Amjad.*

SHADOW OF JIANG. Is it easier to live as an alien
When you are disguised?

SHADOW OF FUSAI. Our dust-ridden wilderness was not interesting for them to conquer,
Otherwise, we would now be counted as one of them;
I will go to them in this dusty garment
And in the coming chaos,
I will ride the grand chariot—
If only I am not late!
Farewell!

On the shadow scrim, Fusai mounts the horse and rides away.

SHADOW OF JIANG. Stay longer!
Huang has prepared food for you!

SHADOW OF FATHER. You did not take your ring!

JIANG. And your distant image was fading before the Great Wall when you cried.
"Keep the ring as a tip for the meal. Leave it with Huang
Till our next meeting!"
I said to father.
"This wall,
Brick by brick,
Is the distance between us, mounting to the sky."

Onstage, Fusai turns away from the shadow scrim and Jiang. The scrim darkens, and Jiang disappears from the stage. Fusai stands face to face with Huang.

HUANG. Why did my heart forgive you despite all the wrongs you committed?!

FUSAI. You all expected me to do an injustice to myself,
And leave the Sapphire Palace for that wilderness
Like your brother, the owl who roams the ruins!
HUANG. Oh, my brother,
What is he doing now?
FUSAI. No doubt he is arguing with me
In that garden
HUANG. The plot to destroy that garden
Was schemed in this Sapphire Palace,
And my brother—woe to me!
My brother!
You summoned me here,
So that you can catch him alone!
FUSAI. No!
I called you here to have a word with you,
And you did not let me have my say
With your complaints, cries, and curses!
HUANG. Speak! I will listen.
(*Fade*)

Jiang comes onstage.

JIANG. Within a year, you came back,
And you were right, it was mealtime.
The History of Civil Wars had just been concluded.
If he were left to himself, Father would be writing and rewriting it forever.
But bitter news was on the way.
The intolerant Chancellor Li Si had taken over Shun Yeo's position.
They had forbidden history, philosophy, and poetry
All over the Khagan's territory

Culminating in book burnings.
We hurried.
The neat and edited version was completed.
We were celebrating a small, homely party with my mother hosting
When you arrived—and this time you were not alone.

On the shadow scrim, a stately chariot with wardens, attendants, and soldiers appears outside the ivied gateway. Fusai enters, donning a Chinese robe.

SHADOW OF FUSAI. Do not fear!
This is a friendly visit,
With an official permit from His Majesty, the Chancellor.
I arrived in time for the meal, did I not?
Well then.
The soldiers will wait outside.

JIANG. The fire under the pot was still burning.
Nothing was being cooked, but there was a burning smell.
All of us were silent,
Staring at the spangles on your new robe.
We sat to eat sheltered within the four walls of our home.

On the shadow scrim, the family members gather around the short tables of food and sit on the ground.

SHADOW OF FUSAI. I have always said
That no place has pumpkins like this garden,
But for carrots, there are better patches on the other side of the Wall.
Why don't you eat?
You might have heard,
The Khagan has endorsed the order of the Chancellor.
They have commanded a thirty-day respite

To collect and burn all books
On history and poetry, on rites and manners, on morality and ideology,
And most harmful of all—*The Philosophy of One Hundred Schools*!
The punishment for whoever disobeys and hides a book
Is death—for himself and for his family.
So far, four hundred and sixty scholars
Who tried to hide classical scrolls
Were sentenced to death.
With me is the list of those houses which need to be inspected.
And every single wall which might hide a book should be destroyed.
I do not see meat from the hunt on the table—
Did my brother not feel like hunting?
Or did his arrows miss the prey?

SHADOW OF FATHER. Where is this household on that list?

SHADOW OF FUSAI. The Khagan eats a lot of cumin;
That might be the reason he forgets nothing.
Your name was at the top of the list.
And I, out of tribute to our friendship,
Made them leave this house to me—
With such insistence that they suspected I was a relative of yours!

SHADOW OF FATHER. And they accepted that you are not?

SHADOW OF FUSAI. Oh, I have a new name there—
A celebrated name—
Shung Chi, the son of a slain commander,
The owner of the red bow!
And I know it is thanks to you that I have it.
Now on the thirtieth day,
In the position of the special steward of His Majesty Li Si,

And out of sight of my company,
I demand that you hand over your books to me
Until the burning ends.
This is all I can do for my family.
Why don't you eat?

JIANG. Your eyes spotted the newly scribed book on the recess,
And my eyes turned to the crack in the doorway opened to the soldiers.

SHADOW OF FATHER. How many of these books has the Khagan read and found harmful?

SHADOW OF FUSAI. His Highness Li Si
Read some extracts from the philosophy of Sun Zi to the Khagan—
And too, from his pupil, Gong Sun Long.

SHADOW OF FATHER. He is not Sun Zi's pupil.
Not even his contemporary!

SHADOW OF FUSAI. The wise Sun Zi has stated that
The nature of man is inclined toward evil.
Gong Sun Long added to this:
"Thus, there must be a force to stop him from doing evil."
He concluded then that:
"The country rules with terror, not with virtue and justice!"

SHADOW OF JIANG. Father taught this lesson, too,
But not with such a conclusion!

SHADOW OF FUSAI. Mother cooks millet like the elixir of peace.
Taste this, brother, and do not rage at me.
The record of Gong Sun Long
Stayed next to the Khagan's bed, and his catch-phrase became:
"Teaching history, philosophy, and poetry is a deadly venom;
The old virtues lead to the collapse of authority,

And morality is a superstition from bygone days
Which is of no use to the state."

SHADOW OF JIANG. Where did Li Si come from?
And why did he read this to the Khagan?

SHADOW OF FUSAI. They believe he could have come from one of several states.
Similar to now, how the news of this indefatigable man
Sometimes comes from the palace,
Sometimes from the city
And time and again from far away states;
But he was appointed the Chancellor by suppressing the protests of the intelligentsia—
Those who would bring historical evidence
To scorn today's achievements
And humiliate the Faqfur state.[29]
His majesty Li Si said,
"The glorification of the past is a harm to the present.
Hence the past must be forgotten!"
The Khagan liked his solution
So much so that he started by setting his own bedside books—written by Sun Zi and Gong Sun Long—on fire.
Then, he ordered to collect all ancient scriptures from nearby and faraway lands
And leave them subject to the scrutiny of seventy scholars
To find out which ones advocate the superiority of the Qin and the barbarism of others,

---

29 The Persian term for Chinese kings, made of two parts: *faq*, meaning 'God', and *fur*, meaning 'son'. Together, they describe the Chinese monarchs as the 'sons of God'.

And which ones are useful like books on medicine or agriculture.
The rest, he thought, would be better not to exist!
As for the books on history, philosophy, and poetry,
They were set on fire from the very beginning,
Without even being read!

SHADOW OF JIANG. And nobody objected?

SHADOW OF FUSAI. The previous Chancellor Shun Yeo lost his position
Because he delayed suppressing the protests of the intelligentsia.
When the command to burn was delivered,
The oldest and wisest on the court—the grand-uncle of the Khagan—
Said there was no rationale in the order.

SHADOW OF FATHER. So someone spoke at last!

SHADOW OF FUSAI. The Khagan replied,
"I have heard that the heart of the wise has seven ventricles."
Then he ordered that his grand-uncle's heart be pulled out.
He looked at it and said, "They have spoken nonsense!"

SHADOW OF JIANG. Those seventy scholars, where have they studied?

SHADOW OF FUSAI. They enjoyed the mentorship of masters like your father.
I am one of the seventy!
This delicious soup tastes like Huang's cooking.
Are you not hungry?

JIANG. Mother was restless.
Secretly and to no avail,
She had thrown a piece of cloth on the new book
Wondering where to hide it.

SHADOW OF HUANG. My father will not burn a book!

SHADOW OF FUSAI. I have come to free not to set afire!

SHADOW OF JIANG. So, we should leave them with you
So that you make them firewood for your furnace!
SHADOW OF FUSAI. Do not waste our limited time by arguing with me!
Outside are soldiers
Who will rush to inspect the house if I go out empty-handed!
SHADOW OF MOTHER. The books and scrolls are the heritage of the family.
Many of them are in my father's handwriting!
SHADOW OF FATHER. Why should I set my reputation and these letters on fire?
If I had done so before,
I would now be in the position of the person you serve as steward!
SHADOW OF FUSAI. It is not your title but our family's life at stake.
And this is not the story of a tall wall but a grave deep in the ground!
SHADOW OF FATHER. What is the shadow of that wall on the ground
But the graves of the slaves
Who mounted stones on top of stones!?
Their deathly moans fill my ears day and night.
Count the stones of the Great Wall. Each stone cost a man's life.
This wall is not built to sort the good carrots from the bad ones!
Don't you see? This is the wall of oblivion.
A wall to forget the past,
What we were
And what has happened to us.
(*Fade*)

Onstage, Huang is across from Fusai.

HUANG. Is that all?
FUSAI. That was my request.
HUANG. You spoke and I listened.
My tears dried and I was freed from years of doubt

That there might still be a little love in you.
As for what you said,
I have no response.
And if you demand my brother's response,
You should have broken your oath and gone to visit him yourself.
Now ask them to return my humble clothes!
Shall I return on foot
Like those peasant mistresses of the Khagan?
(*Fade*)

On the shadow scrim, the family is arguing in the room. Onstage is Jiang.

SHADOW OF FUSAI. Do you think I love this robe and fake name?
I merely wanted to be someone—like the others.
Taking my chance, I went to the other side of the Wall—
For on this side, every chance is withheld!
I changed into these clothes so as not to seem an alien.
That is all!
How can't you see that between the law of the Chancellor and my own family,
I have sided with you!
I am not an advocate for him
But in love with this girl, and you are jeopardizing her life!

JIANG. Huang trembled!

SHADOW OF MOTHER. If your heart is with this house,
Then speak to the Chancellor!

SHADOW OF FUSAI. He lacks the ears to hear.
His highness Li Si is a man of many mouths,
To give orders with!

SHADOW OF MOTHER. Remind him that we are on this side of the Wall—out of their territory!

SHADOW OF FUSAI. But your voice carries beyond!

SHADOW OF FATHER. When I wanted it to, it did not!

SHADOW OF FUSAI. Do not consent to the fire he wishes to set!
Kindle a small fire in the garden
With a couple of illegible manuscripts, some worthless books
So that they may not look for the original ones.
Or at least deliver those books to me—
Those that we know seventy supervisors will testify to their benefits.
The Epistle of Medicine, *The Book on Winds*,
The Book of Stars, *The Scroll of the Ancient Cultivator*—
These will be exempt from the fire.
With this accomplished, I will justify that you delivered whatever you had!

SHADOW OF MOTHER. And they will not attack this house?

SHADOW OF FUSAI. I will delay it as much as I can
As much as is needed for you to find a chance to remove them!

JIANG. Huang was weeping in Mother's arms.
Mother, crying herself, turned to Father.

SHADOW OF MOTHER. Choose between burning all or some!
Whatever the option is,
I am ready to burn them!

SHADOW OF HUANG. Trust him, Father!

JIANG. What else could he do but trust!?
I still see him before my eyes,
Distraught and weeping,
Books and scrolls in his arms,
Standing next to the hearth—

On the shadow scrim, Father appears, distraught, with scrolls, next to a hearth in the garden. The rest of the family stands behind him.

SHADOW OF FATHER. No, this—Shujing's *The Book of Documents*—How can I burn it!?
Li Ji's *The Manners of Chivalry*—I have yet another version,
But alas, this beautiful handwriting!
The Philosophy of Sun Zi! Shall I burn it or give it?
Here, take it!
I Ching's *The Book of Developments*—of this there are plenty.
Ju Li's *The Book of Propriety*—I should think!
Tao Te Ching's *The Book of Path and Virtue*—damn fire!
Shennong's *The Secrets of the Immortal Body*—you take it.
The Khagan will not burn this!
Chunqiu's *The Spring and Autumn Annals*—oh master, forgive me!
Oh! Shih-Ching's *The Book of Poetry*—
What shall I do with this?
For Confucius said,
"He who does not read this book
Has built a wall between himself and the world!"

SHADOW OF FUSAI. And *The History of Civil Wars*?

JIANG. We all went silent.
And Father cried—

SHADOW OF FATHER. I will burn it!
Bring tidings that I've burned it!
(*Fade*)

With the sound of the bells in her hands, Huang mirrors the motion of a chariot as she silently makes her way back home. A look and a pause, then—

HUANG. No; I will not remain silent.

She exits.

On the shadow scrim are the chariot, wardens, and Fusai's soldiers. Onstage, in front of the scrim, Jiang is face to face with Fusai.

JIANG. Following behind the bags of books and scrolls that your soldiers took,
You said near the ivied gateway,
"We have survived so far,
Both you and I.
Your father shouted the word 'burn' in such a way that I believed it myself!
Smile so that the wardens will not suspect."

FUSAI. You said you had a request.

JIANG. I said, "If you still have feelings for the family,
Hear my demand
And let go of power.
You can shelter against the wind,
But once it turns into a storm, you will no longer have shelter."

FUSAI. I said, "You have good fortune;
But I was not born in the year of the tiger,
So what else can I be but like a fox?"

JIANG. Is it not frightful to live by the tiger?

FUSAI. Saliva of the fox has been prescribed for frigidness;
Do you know the reason?
The warm tongue of a fox works on any temperament.
Have you not heard about the fox who told a tiger that he was the King of the woods?
The tiger laughed and said, "Prove it!"
The fox said, "Come with me and see!"
And while the tiger was walking beside the fox (*scoffs*), he saw with his own eyes

That the entire forest was trembling, frightful in its reverence!
I need to be with the tiger to be revered!
And thus, the tiger will believe it too!
Smile—they are looking at us.

JIANG. The day the friendship between the tiger and the fox is muddied,
Who will be torn apart—*this* or *that*?
And you know,
Once someone surrenders to the tiger, he will forever be the tiger's slave
And hunt others to be the tiger's prey.

FUSAI. Whoever fears is the most despicable!
He who fears has no share of luck
Because the god of luck has the tail of a tiger;
The god of wealth rides a tiger,
And so does the spirit of fire,
Who gives every person what they deserve.
Farewell.

JIANG. Wait!
Speak the truth to me.
Your shadow, His Highness Li Si—
Is he not you?

FUSAI. You and I are one, and I have lived for a while with your name,
So I will speak this to you alone—
There is no man with such a name.
His Highness Li Si is a name acquired by all seventy of us!

JIANG. I told you, "Think about what I asked!"

Fusai exits. The shadow scrim darkens.

JIANG. And that was my first request from you.
You stole countless gems!

For three years, there was no news of you
And I knew you had stolen enough—
So much as to sit above all those who are wise,
And not to ask about the girl you promised to love.
But from the very first night,
Our nightmares were the dreams that would wake Father,
Who would roam through the house like a sleepwalker,
As if to count those who are still living, one by one.
He was wordless with us but full of thoughts by himself,
Days in the garden or by the riverside,
Arguing with an invisible person.
Every sound would make him jump with the thought that they had come!
I see him in the garden,
Asking me every minute about my sister
And asking her about me.
And Mother—busy pretending to do the silk work—calls,
"No one has come, we are all fine!"

On the shadow scrim, Father is seen in the garden. Young Jiang approaches him.

JIANG. Father engages himself with the pumpkins in the garden,
And I listen to what he reads—

SHADOW OF JIANG. Is that the book of philosophy you're reading to the patch?

SHADOW OF FATHER. I am reviewing it for myself,
And naturally, the patch benefits from it too.

SHADOW OF JIANG. That might be the reason why the pumpkins are tastier.

SHADOW OF FATHER. Really?
I should remember not to read history to them,
Or they will turn bitter.
Where is Huang?

JIANG. We are all fine, Father.
We are all fine.
(*Turns away from the scrim*)
I missed the book of history that we had written together, and other books as well.
Self-reflection begins from desolation.
Then I tried to see which one I knew by heart.
(*On the scrim*) I have forgotten a sentence.
I know not which the correct one is—this or that?
Where are the records, Father?

SHADOW OF FATHER. You will be safer if you don't know.
Tell me which sentence and which book, and I will speak it with you.
(*Fade*)

Huang crosses the stage with bells in her hands.

HUANG. I am old—as old as the heavens and the earth—
But I am relieved.
Your question was in answer to me.
What haven't you done to harm us!
I could not see. Was that because I loved you?
Or did I love you because I could not see?
This darkness is more pleasant
Than the brightness of the false light.
Now I am freed from you,

On the way back home—
But without a word to my brother!
Blessed it will be to forget the wasted life
If it frees me of you.
(*The bells in her hands stop ringing.*)
The chariot stops by the Great Wall.
There is no sound, save for the horses drinking from the stream,
No light, save for the reflection of the moon on the dark water,
No hope—none!
Is this not freedom?
Blessed is the horse whose rider is in no haste,
Otherwise, it will only suffer from thirst.
That shadow there is from the leaves of the pumpkin ivy
It is like a dream,
Growing and reaching towards one another from two sides of the
 Wall.
And this is
The wandering desert wind,
Which has left yellow dust on the trembling image of the moon.
Oh! The sight of the moon and its distress
Has again returned you to my memory!
How can one free oneself?
(*Fade*)

Jiang and Fusai are onstage.

JIANG. Time was passing differently for you, Fusai.
You measured the days and years through the news you received—
The year of war, the day of victory, the week of celebration.
The garden was cast out of time;

Father measured time with
A plant on which bloomed new petals every day
Until its fifteenth day;
And over the next fifteen,
It lost one petal each day.
Despite all this,
The Great Wall was swelling
From a new report which could not fit within the confines of the Wall anymore.
News was on the way,
And the insurrections had begun.
Time and again, news came saying that the Chancellor was murdered in court.
And yet there was another report saying that His Majesty Li Si had fled to one of the states.
No, I had not yet counted to seventy when you arrived,
The day Father was sick and in bed.

On the shadow scrim, Fusai enters the garden, wearing the garments of nomad hunters. He hoists a deer he hunted while riding his horse.

SHADOW OF FUSAI. Does no one welcome
A nomad hunter with his catch of the day?
My name is Pu.
Such a nomad's name that even my tribe would not use it!
Did you not recognize me?
During the previous visit, I figured my brother was not hunting.
I thought I might want to compensate this time!
Are you startled by my appearance?

JIANG. No, we've gotten used to mistaking any stranger for you.

FUSAI. I ignored your sarcasm and the coldness of everyone's looks,
As well as Huang's indifferent attitude, which lasted the whole visit.

JIANG. I told everyone that you had come to visit Father.
And in the evening,
You revealed the new reports
by his bed.

On the shadow scrim, the family is gathered beside Father's bed. Next to him is a table of meals from the hunt. Huang is standing at a distance.

THE SHADOW OF FUSAI. The first Khagan is dead!
They will announce it in the coming days,
Although he has been dead for a while—
He died unexpectedly on a trip, a trip hidden from everyone else.

SHADOW OF JIANG. He was traveling in disguise?

SHADOW OF FUSAI. Even from one room to another;
And no one but the mistress of that night
Would know in which bedchamber he had slept.
On a journey to the east with a few companies,
He died,
And they secretly brought him back to the capital.
They feared that the stench of the corpse may give away the news,
So they sent carts of rotten fish to travel ahead and behind them.
Jao Kao—the eunuch steward—hid the news
So as to not let the Khagan's Crown Prince and Commander in the north know.
They exchanged a sealed letter with another
That ordered for the Crown Prince to take his own life and that of his commander,
And with their deaths, the Khagan's young son ascended to the throne.

SHADOW OF MOTHER. They did it all in secret.
How do you know this?

SHADOW OF FUSAI. The eunuch was an ally of His Majesty Li Si,
Before they clashed.
And as for the order of the suicide,
I forged it—
In the same handwriting of the Khagan!
Don't you taste it, Father?
The meat of the hunt heals weakness.

SHADOW OF FATHER. That depends on whether you are the hunter or the hunted!
In such a quarrel,
Which one do you side with?

SHADOW OF FUSAI. Staying at court was like standing in the way of the tempest;
Only the young boy, the second Khagan,
Listens to the eunuch.
The insurgences have begun—
The greatest ones are from the Han and the Chu.
And—can you believe it?—
The roads we constructed have become useful to them
For invading the capital!
After displacing the nobles, the states have no commanders-in-chief.
The revolt of the Han is a headless dragon heading toward the capital,
And its commander is a brigand from the south, the roguish Liu Bang.
But the rioting of the Chu has a venerable head, Shiayo,
A noble from the east who intends to restore the past.
It is a seven-day ride to his camp.

SHADOW OF JIANG. Will you join the insurgence?
SHADOW OF FUSAI. The future belongs to Shiayo
And to you and whoever has set their heart on classical virtues.
Are you not happy?
SHADOW OF FATHER. The classical virtues
Were useful for reminding the brazen times of shame and decency.
Do you think anyone remembers anything anymore?
SHADOW OF FUSAI. I will join the one who has a reliable mind.
I brought nothing with me from the court but my horse.
—The books and whatever was with me are safe
'Til the day we conquer the palace!—
With my court name, I wrote a permit
For a local hunter—the disguise that I am in now.
But I need another garment
So that the Shiayo camp accepts me as a noble
(Plus a little amount of money for the seven-day journey)!
SHADOW OF MOTHER. You already know that we have lost everything we had.
The silk Huang and I weave
And the prey your brother hunts
All equal some worthless coins used by villagers and desert nomads—
An amount which is worth nothing on the other side of the gate!
SHADOW OF FUSAI. Huang, my love,
Others sat at the table, even though they did not eat,
But you do not even sit near the food from my hunt?
I have not tasted anything more delicious than a fawn's meat.
SHADOW OF HUANG. I am remembering those far-off days
When you called me your deer!
(*Fade*)

Onstage, in front of the scrim, is Huang, still on her way, bells jingling in her hands. When her bells go silent, the shadow of Fusai appears behind her on the scrim in the attire of a nomad hunter.

HUANG. The road, the bells, and the horse disappear when I remember the day you were joining the insurgents.
Again, after three years of waiting for your return,
There was only one day for us to meet!
I was bitter with you up until your departure.
Near the ivied gateway, I told you,
"I wish I were sick in bed,
Perhaps then you would remember me."

SHADOW OF FUSAI. How could I have remembered you with your position always shifting with the blowing wind?
I was hoping for a stable life that was worthy of spending long years with you
And see now that I have lost everything.

HUANG. I said, "So, now you deserve me!
With me is a token of your trust—your ring. Won't you take it?"

SHADOW OF FUSAI. I am at peace as long as it is with you.

HUANG. Oh! That was like a poem to my soul!
I said, "Here, this is all our savings from these years.
It may suffice for your seven-day journey."

SHADOW OF FUSAI. You will see!
The day Shiayo is crowned,
Fortune will remember your father!

Huang disappears from the stage.

Jiang appears onstage, and on the shadow scrim, Fusai mounts his horse.

JIANG. Upon your departure, I told you my second request—
This horse that you ride

Descends from my sister's horse;
Each time you mount it,
Remember that the girl is awaiting your return!
You went away, and behind you
Was the dust of years of fire and fighting;
Once again, three more years of war!
(*On the shadow scrim, armies fight a bloody war.*)
Father—worn out and resting on his cane—
Would hear the news from the peasant neighbors;
The eunuch steward had murdered the second Khagan and crowned
himself instead,
But his ascension lasted for only forty-three days!
The armies of the Han and Chu
Twisted through the capital like two dragons
And pulled down his throne!
It had been a while since the guards of the ivied gateway had fled—
The watchmen of the Great Wall, too.
News flowed in and out.
The great country was now the hunted body,
Fallen and fragmented in the battlefield!
And again, the war of the territories,
And again, the great conquerors Liu Bang and Shiayo
Drawing their swords at one another
Over the share of this prey,
Comrade face to face with comrade!
Father used to say that had they read *The History of the Civil Wars*,
They would have seen this in their mirror ahead of time!
And outside
Were the armies, marching every day with their banner.

On the shadow scrim, a roaring army passes by the road on the other side of the ivied gateway. Onstage, Jiang disappears and Huang appears, still on her way back home.

HUANG. During the days of war, I was waiting
Through the nights, praying
For the victory of Shiayo!
There was a report that his army would pass this road.
In the cold, I made a pot of soup,
Piping hot, and carried it close to the road.
A fleeing peasant said that Liu Bang's army was approaching.
And I returned the pot!
The other day, it was Shiayo's army.
Once again, the heavy pot, the road, and me.
From a distance, I saw the overflowing anger of the bloodthirsty men, and I fled,
And after they passed, I returned,
But not even the pot was left!

Onstage, Huang disappears and Jiang appears. On the shadow scrim, armies clash in a storm of roars and cries, locked in fierce battle.

JIANG. The brigand of the south was busy dividing the spoils of war amongst the companies
When at quite the same time,
The noble of the east was composing poetry on righteousness!
Thus, Shiayo's men
Joined the generous enemies in groups,
And on the last day, Shiayo
Heard the songs of his tribe from the enemy's line.
And that was the end of him!

My sister bemoaned your loss, Fusai,
For we had heard that the last attendants of Shiayo were all killed.
The Faqfur throne surrendered to the new Khagan
And Liu Bang took control of everything!
It was about time that we heard news from you,
And soon a letter arrived!

On the shadow scrim, the chariot is stopped by the ivied gateway. Huang receives a scroll from the messenger and returns to the garden.

SHADOW OF HUANG. It is a letter from Fusai.
What difference does it even make if it is under a new name?
He is alive—and in the court of the new Khagan!

JIANG. Father said that whoever had read history should have known this would happen.
But I did not need to know history by heart,
For I already knew you very well!

SHADOW OF HUANG. He has invited us all
To the capital!

JIANG. We understood from your letter that
Liu Bang—the new Khagan of Han lineage—
Prefers to let the law remain as it is and keep language the same,
And the entire territory too, now with a name people are used to. China!
As for the Wall, he wanted to maintain—and complete it.
Changing all of this would be difficult;
But the color yellow—the symbol of Shi Huang Di—
Was to be erased from the walls of the palace.
The new son of the heavens paints his palace with the shades of the heavens,
From ultramarine to sapphire.

SHADOW OF HUANG. There is still something else.
Now, the ban on history, philosophy, and poetry is lifted!
So ask father to bring the books out from their hideout
And let them occupy the highest position in the Khagan's library!

On the shadow scrim, Mother takes Huang's place.

JIANG. Mother was weeping with joy.

SHADOW OF MOTHER. What difference does it make
Whether or not you head for the capital?
But the day eventually came to bring back the books and scrolls from the hideout.
That was precious heritage, and most of them in my father's handwriting.
And it too was the fruit of the life we spent together!

On the scrim, Father takes Mother's place.

SHADOW OF FATHER. The books and scrolls?

JIANG. Father was panting.

SHADOW OF FATHER. The books and scrolls?

JIANG. His face blushed!

SHADOW OF FATHER. The scriptures—

JIANG. The cane was shaking in his hand!

SHADOW OF FATHER. I feared for your lives.
And so I left the books and scrolls—one by one—to the water or to the fire!

JIANG. Mother looked fixedly;
Silent and unbelieving,
Her tears flowed.
She went to the silk workroom at the corner of the garden
And shut the door.
Father was still moaning—

SHADOW OF FATHER. I feared for your lives!

(*Fade*)

Huang is onstage in front of the shadow scrim. Behind her on the scrim, the image of a garment gradually takes shape.

HUANG. The last painting of Mother
Was on a garment made of white silk.
On the right shoulder were the sun, the bird, and the eternal tree.
On the left were the rabbit, the crescent moon, and an immortal maiden holding the elixir of youth;
The gatekeepers of paradise were in between.
And below,
The peacock seated on the vault of heavens,
The duck and the owl—soaring from earth,
The upper heaven with its guards,
The world of man with dejection and delight,
And the underworld with its beasts,
And a bridge in between all of this.
A lady with a cane, asking for the path to paradise!
Mother spent nine days on the sketch, silently,
With nine scenes on the imprint of the garment.
When it was concluded, she bathed,
Cut her hair and nails short,
And wore the imprinted silk like a shroud.
Oh, yellow river!
Did she not speak with you?
At the last moment?
Nothing of the secret of the lover with the river?
It seemed as if the words in her heart
Were entirely burned onto her lips!

Huang disappears and Jiang appears onstage. On the shadow scrim, the family is by Mother's grave in the garden. Father gets up from beside the tomb.

SHADOW OF FATHER. Write to Fusai
To send a special permit
To cross the Great Wall.

SHADOW OF JIANG. To the capital?

SHADOW OF FATHER. I have put you to the test several times,
And you know all the books by heart.
Nothing will be lost.

SHADOW OF JIANG. I will not go!
Will you, Huang?

SHADOW OF FATHER. At least come with me to the gate.

JIANG. On the day of his departure,
The chariot was waiting for him
With the special permit from the court.
My sister and I were both silent.

On the shadow scrim, Father stands by the chariot. Jiang and Huang stand beside their horses. Then Father faces Jiang.

SHADOW OF FATHER. A life doesn't even last a hundred years,
And yet in it flows the sorrows of millennia.
Once you asked me if it was worth such a price.
I think,
Sometimes what we do, is itself the price
That we pay for a dream—
Is that dream worth it?
I am desolate.

JIANG. Beside the main gate,
He said to the watchmen, "I have a special permit,

And memories from a battlefield that no longer exists,
And memories from the day of destiny.
Allow me then to have a look from the top of the battlement on the battlefield.
Perhaps a shadow from the day of war still roams in there!"[30]

(*On the shadow scrim are the battlement and the Great Wall. Jiang and Huang, mounted on horses beside the Wall, watch as Father ascends the battlement.*)

He said farewell
And then, "Be my witness!"
He dropped his cane, stood steady on his feet,
Walked inside, and the gate closed.
I knew it!

Huang appears before the scrim onstage. She is still on her way, accompanied by the sound of bells in her hands.

HUANG (*wipes her tears*). I see the garden in the distance.
The road to court felt longer because I was hopeful and anxious,
But the hopeless return makes the trip feel shorter.
Still, I have hope that I might
Visit the resting place of the two bodies.
One who quenched the fire in herself with the water from the river,
And the other
Reviving memories of those lost on the battlefield by choosing to die!

---

30 By shadow, Father implies the ghosts of his comrades slain on the last day of the war. This can also literally mean the shadows of the warriors, which previously appeared on the scrim.

The sound from the bells in Huang's hands gradually increases. As the ringing grows louder, on the scrim behind Huang appears Father, who reaches the top of the battlement and jumps off.

Silence.

Fade.

Jiang is onstage.

JIANG. The last visit
Outside the ivied gateway.
When I saw the pomposity of your chariot from afar
—With grandeur greater than ever—
I stood outside waiting.

On the shadow scrim, the chariot and the attendants stop. As Fusai dismounts, Jiang is in front of him.

SHADOW OF FUSAI. No, no—no formalities!
I have come, unprompted, to offer my condolences
But let the next visit be in my chamber.
You know, from the capital up to here,
The wind of the yellow dust blows into one's eyes,
And from here to the capital
It blows from behind!
Why here?
Inside the garden—

SHADOW OF JIANG. Let us not disturb the peace of the dead.
Speak here.

SHADOW OF FUSAI. I was desolate when I heard what happened to your father.

SHADOW OF JIANG. "Happened?"

SHADOW OF FUSAI. What happened would have been more meaningful
If he had jumped inside rather than outside.
Let us distance ourselves from the attendants.
See my new badge.
My new name is Mong Shi, and I am the Prince of Lu.

JIANG. I asked if you had ever been to the Lu region.

SHADOW OF FUSAI. In the commotion aroused during the interval between the two dynasties—in the capital and the states—
Names and titles came cheap!
There were a few lying around
And I bought some for a rainy day!
I will give one to you if you wish!

SHADOW OF JIANG. Fusai, brother from my childhood, my shadow!
For a long time, I've felt like I don't know you anymore,
In this robe and that chariot!
What are you doing in that palace?

SHADOW OF FUSAI. How could the two sides of the Wall understand each other's language without me?

SHADOW OF JIANG. I see,
You tore the world into two with the Wall.
Order and *honor* became the language on the other side of the Wall,
And *submission* and *humiliation* were left as the language on this side.

SHADOW OF FUSAI. I am the translator in between!

SHADOW OF JIANG. Which itself is a third language with greasy words of flattery and hypocrisy,
And it sounds more pleasant a reply than the tingling of coins.

SHADOW OF FUSAI. I have come with condolences
And you insult me!

SHADOW OF JIANG. No, insults are the names
That they call us with their language from the other side of the Wall—
Alien, savage, barbarian.
Mother drowned herself because of that same fire
And Father's body was crushed because of that same downfall.
And now you name all of this "happenings"!
These names are your translations of who I am,
And I do not approve of them!

SHADOW OF FUSAI. You are mourning!
And I have not come to argue—but to invite.
Now your path is open to the other side
And it is your choice not to be an alien.
Bring the books and master the library!

SHADOW OF JIANG. There is no book—but the one in my head!

SHADOW OF FUSAI. I do not believe that.

JIANG. You are right.
Since childhood, there has never been a paradise,
And I was deceiving myself!
I asked, "What did my father spend his life for?
How many times should he have written histories and left it all to the wind?"

SHADOW OF FUSAI. Now that not a single one of the thousands of ancient books still stands,
Every single line you write
Is worth thousands!

SHADOW OF JIANG. With such an ending, I do not have the intention of writing.
What was our share of history but a curse?

Let whatever is in my mind
Rot with my head.

SHADOW OF FUSAI. The times have changed and yet you fear!

JIANG. I said, "Now that the times have changed,
My third request of you.
Leave me alone with my memories,
So that I might sit in this garden,
Without the need for interpreters and free of fearing my attendants,
And for the sake of breadwinning, teach the natives
So that they do not remain 'barbarians'!"

SHADOW OF FUSAI. The other side of the Wall is the future.
Do you not want a share of that?
One hundred, one thousand, and two thousand years henceforth,
History will praise the civilization of China, which lays down its foundation today.

JIANG (*as if to himself*). You want me to only be a shadow
Among that crowd of shadows that populate your scrim of history;
And the one who speaks for all shadows
Will be you alone.
One hundred, one thousand, and two thousand years henceforth,
No one will know
What the silenced ones could have created.

SHADOW OF FUSAI. The world rushes forward and you hold on to the past!
See? Iron!—From the rich mines to the west of the empire.
And this is paper—have you heard about it?
Writing on it is much easier than writing on bamboo!
This is the civilization on the other side—
Pewter is replaced with iron,
Bamboo with paper!

JIANG. It depends on what one can write on paper
Under the shadow of iron!
No, Fusai—nothing has changed.

SHADOW OF FUSAI. I had come to console you for the loss of your father,
And in your obstinacy,
I see him alive!
Where is Huang?

SHADOW OF JIANG. She has resorted to the graves.

SHADOW OF FUSAI. I must see her.

SHADOW OF JIANG. No! Two victims suffice.
Do not disturb the soul of this house anymore!

SHADOW OF FUSAI. Hah. I came here to revere you, brother,
And I see that nothing is left of reverence and brotherhood.
Now then, I take an oath to not return to this house,
Unless you ask me to come!

SHADOW OF JIANG. Do not wait for that!

SHADOW OF FUSAI. I do not.
It is you who should wait!
(*Fade*)

Onstage, Huang is still on her way. On the shadow scrim is the ivied gateway. Jiang leans against it.

SHADOW OF HUANG. How could one be freed
From you,
From bitter memories,
From vain hopes?
Is there no way out but the path father chose—and mother, too?
Life was like a thread of silk,
Once knotted, how can one unknot it without tearing it apart?

The chariot moves—like an unwieldy ship into the dark sea.
Shall one hope for the shore
When there are no tidings from the one who waits there?
My destination is there,
I see it,
That dark shadow, my old companion—
Who never married
And wasted his life on me as I did on someone else!
My last hope
Is this brother bereft of hope, himself!
(*Fade*)

Onstage, Jiang stands by the ivied gateway, watching.

JIANG. That which is coming this way
Is the chariot that took my sister to the capital at sunset.
Wherever you go on earth,
The earth returns to where you stood.
Like water to a puddle.
There she comes!

Jiang stands at the ivied gateway, staring out. Bells ring nearby; the sound dies, starts again, then fades away. Under Jiang's longing, inquiring gaze, Huang enters through the ivied gateway. She is silent, her eyes avoiding his. Jiang understands what he needs to know; he turns away, just as Huang turns toward him. Then she too turns away from Jiang and heads toward the house. Jiang turns back to say something, but hopeless, he changes his mind and again turns away. Now Huang intends to say something, but she too gives up. Finally, both turn back—facing each other.

HUANG. Again, you did not sleep.

JIANG. I had a long dream, recalling the shadows of life . . .

HUANG. Well done.
The dawn is close,
And soon you will be forty-nine!
How far back did you recall?

JIANG. To Father's death,
Those years when I endeavored to revive his school,
And those years of teaching the villagers.

HUANG. The government officers closed your school
Because an unknown person had revealed documents from years ago showing that
A man by the name of Jiang Rong
Had stolen the road-construction budget and fled!

JIANG. The years of bartering with the villagers
For just a loaf of bread!

HUANG. Tormenting you by banning you from doing business with the villagers
And moving them from the village!

JIANG. The years of laboring for the neighbors by portering, woodcutting, pruning their gardens . . .

HUANG. The neighbors' gardens were all set on fire.

JIANG. The years of loneliness,
Years of devastation, devoid of anyone and anything
But me and my sister.

HUANG. You spoke nothing of dreams—
The struggles you dreamed of and the nightmares you lived through!
And the quarrels you had with yourself,
Your stubborn defiance of the man inside who wanted to write history.

JIANG. For years my father wrote of innumerable people,
But who remained by his side in the end?
Where did his voice reach?
There was a tall wall standing between every word of his and the ears listening!
Who helped him pass the wall of oblivion?

Wearing his long Chinese robe, Fusai enters through the ivied gateway, distraught and panting.

FUSAI. It is I, this time,
I myself, neither a dream nor a vision.
After your sister's departure,
Before the fifth dawn of the fifth month,
I said to myself:
Hold on to my pride or break my oath—this or that?
Here I came
At last, returning after so many years.
With me are the familiar horse, the red bow,
And a book of your ancestors' scripture!

On the scrim, the shadow of an old horse appears. Jiang moves to the scrim and strokes the horse. Then, he moves the scrim to one side of the stage.

JIANG. Oh! My old Phoenix!
You were a memento from Father, with the trace of mother's caress on your body.
Half your blood is mine and the other half my sister's!
You have aged more than my bitter dreams
And labored throughout your life—like me!

Your pale skin conveys that you have been in a dark corner for a long while.
No, you, the wounded and old, had no place in their honorary celebrations.
No doubt they have remembered you in their day of need—
Like me!
Your parents are dead too,
Without ever having a field to gallop in.
Do you recognize my scent?—It is me!
And this is the smell of desolation and loneliness.
On your body are left the traces of scourge,
And your mouth is torn by the bridle and the muzzle.
On your long legs is the residue from long roads,
On your stretched hands, the thorns of many plains.
And beneath this yellow dust,
The traces of repeated burns and marks are on your body.
How erect your neck once was, my Phoenix.
And your eyes—
Oh! This familiar look!

HUANG. See his breath—he is thirsty,
The sign of ceaseless galloping!

FUSAI. Why don't you look at me?
In all that ceaseless galloping, this horse and I were together.

JIANG. No!
You went yourself and he was dragged by the bridle.
You were the rider, and he was the ridden.
The scourge was in your hand, the wounds were his share.
Oh! At last, my soulmate;

A mirror that is broken—
Like me!

FUSAI. Do not waste time!
It is I who has come to have a word—

HUANG. No one is waiting for you here!

FUSAI. Take me as an uninvited guest!

HUANG. Remove those clothes then,
That
Is the law of this house!

FUSAI. Let all laws be broken but the law of brotherhood!
I throw my pride at my feet like this robe
Since I am here to make a request!

HUANG. I said nothing.
Speak what you want with my brother.

FUSAI. We are short of time, listen:
The Great Khagan, the founder of the Han—

JIANG. The very one you used to call a roguish brigand?

FUSAI. That roguish brigand, that brute, that capricious man
Detests the color yellow
For it reminds him of people of the past.
He has painted his palace blue
And placed three enormous shades
Over the palace, painted entirely in the color of the sky!
He wants a civilization of his own—
A history that begins with him.
He extended the Great Wall and displaced the tribes of the Ordos Desert[31] even further,

---

31 A steppe region in Northwest China.

But he is upset
With the yellow wind of the desert
That blows from above the Wall
And covers his land with a layer of yellow dust.
When he asked me for a solution,
I first took it as a joke.
Then he said, "Look into the ancient texts and find a way to resolve it!"
I asked, "Who knows the language of the winds?"
He said that I had to find it!
And he assigned the deadline of the fifth day of the fifth month
—The day of the tiger!—
To find a solution
Or they will stuff and mount my skin with the yellow dust!

JIANG. So on this day,
The tiger skins the fox!
Did you summon my sister for the same reason?

FUSAI. I remembered your father
Who once said that the ancestors had knowledge of many things
Which we do not remember today.
I looked into this—*The Book of Winds*—all illegible
For the classical letters have been wiped from the language;
I have nothing in my mind but Chinese characters!
This is my request.
Read this book and ask, "Is there any solution?"

JIANG. I know this book by heart,
And have felt the wild yellow wind several times on my body—
(*to the horse*) Like you who used to feel it
With your long mane!

FUSAI. Speak—is there any escape for the Khagan's civilization from this wind?

JIANG. Let those on the other side
Who have raised the wall of oblivion,
Between the past and the present,
Between the lover and the beloved,
Between the self and the family,
Let them assume that
Only the traditions they practice can be named "civilization"!
Those thousands of people subjected to your arrows and blades
All had civilizations of their own
And were called barbarians
For they did not know the tradition of sitting on grand seats!

FUSAI. When I went as a hostage in your place,
You said that you would compensate me someday.
Today is that day!
Do not argue with me and do not answer me,
For you have no trust in me!
Come with me to him
And answer him.
I will make sure that they give you a worthy cloak!
He is eager to find a historian to start writing history,
And in your fortune, it is written that
The nobleman who will write the history of this land is you.

JIANG. I will compensate by speaking plainly and honestly;
History does not have a beginning!
It is an extended scene before us
And the Khagan, similar to us, is but a shadow on this scrim.
On the other side of the Great Wall,

Everything from iron to paper is your share.
But as for the winds on this side—
Call them the wild, mad winds, whatever you wish—
The winds are mine—
Familiar to me and to this panting horse,
They are relatives to my savage tribe
And like me, they are exiled to the place which has been my home!

HUANG. Oh! Wind!—
The very one which sweeps the illusion of light from dark waters!
The one which kindly strokes the long mane of the broken Phoenix!
So Father did not leave this world forlorn.

JIANG. You said Father?

On the central scrim, the shadows of Father and Mother appear. Huang approaches the scrim, takes hold of it, and moves it to one end of the stage. As she moves it, a third scrim is revealed behind—still blank.

HUANG. And my mother!
Their lives were not fruitless, and neither were their deaths pointless.
Their kin, the wind, abided by them.
It still mourns over their graves,
Lifts their ashes to the sky,
Passes them over the Wall
And lands them in the Khagan's eyes!
Their forbidden names still resonate in the song of the wind.
And in our memories too,
Such that even this aged horse remembers their scent!
You see?
This Wall is defeatable
—The Wall they mounted to ignore us—
And this wind mocks it!

JIANG. Oh! Speak more,
For your breath gives rise to a tempest in me!
HUANG. You asked who passed Father's words across the wall of oblivion?
You!
Remember? He was confident
That nothing would be lost
As long as you knew them by heart?
Write those words,
I will be your assistant—
In those intervals between weavings (I learned from Mother).
That is the only way to free myself
From what was lost!
No, we are not forlorn—
Though this world was no paradise!
(*to Fusai*) And you have no escape
From this wind which,
battling with oblivion,
Writes the unwritten history all over you.
JIANG. You were right!
(*To Fusai*) You grow oblivion
And the yellow wind of wilderness reaps your harvest!
This wind
—The ashes of the burned ancestries—
Will pass over you like time!
Fearless of your colors,
The boundless wind
Will spread a layer of yellow dust all over your bodies
And will speak with the children of your children

About the world on this side of the Wall.
Raise the Wall higher and you will see
The shying horse of the wind yields to no bridle!

On the third scrim, in the middle of the stage, the plain is lit up. In the sky, yellow dust slowly and persistently blows above the Great Wall.

HUANG. The sun rose;
Now you are a complete man,
In the dawn of your birthday!
And a short time for you, Fusai,
To escape one more time
With a new name, in a new guise!

FUSAI. I have aged too—
I left this house young, and I have returned old.
Shall we start from the beginning?
—Now that I am seated on the summit?
This was our promise, you and I—
Visiting each other by the grand throne!

HUANG. You spoke of compensation and debt.
Take it—this is yours—
The ring
With the sign of the tribe that you denied!
You and your Great Wall were not my choice;
And one who never chooses
Might as well have never lived!

FUSAI. Oh, look!
I see in the light
That the Khagan,
Mounted on his horse,

Blades in hand,
Is coming after me!
How could one find time to escape?

HUANG. My brother's birthday is a great day—
The day he will end quarreling with himself
And write the book of history.
Not the history you desired,
But the history that tells what came to this wounded, handsome man
—This inflicted and persecuted man—
And to all of us.
What his father wrote, he will continue!

JIANG. I am that history, myself.
Not because I have rewritten and reviewed it,
Not because I know it by heart,
But because I have lived it—
I was burned by it and born with it!
Eye to eye with this resurrected half,
—This upright broken body,
The mirror held to our past adventures—
I will scatter the silence on the scrim of time.
Fearless of the rise and fall of the price of history on the other side of the Wall,
I will write your history—
But in my own language!

Fade to black.

THE DANCE OF MARES

Mohammad Charmshir

Translated by
Nahid Ahmadian

Original title: *Raqs-e Mādiyān'hā*

Written in 2003

First performed in 2013 at The Private Stage at the Bāgh-e Asāteer, Kerman, directed by Babak Daghighi

Published in Persian by Ney Publication, 2005

EDITORS' INTRODUCTION

Mohammad Charmshir (b. 1960) is the most prolific playwright of post-revolutionary Iran. Known as the poet of the Iranian stage for his rich free-verse dialogue, Charmshir is the author of more than 150 plays, many of which have been staged and are acclaimed in Iran and abroad. Born in Tehran, he earned his bachelor's degree in dramatic arts from the University of Tehran, and subsequently he has taught and run creative writing workshops and courses at universities and colleges in Iran. From 1980 to 2010, he wrote reviews of and columns on Iranian and world theater for numerous journals and newspapers (such as *Donyā-ye Tasvir*, *Faslnāmeh Te'ātr*, and *Abrār*), and collabor-ated on the jury of theater festivals and creative writing competitions. He is one of the first experimental playwrights to emerge after the Revolution who worked closely with theatrical groups as a dramaturg, pioneering post-revolutionary experimental theater. Charmshir is well versed in world literature and cinema, a feature which is manifested in the diversity of styles in his plays. Among some of his best-known plays are *Masih Hargez Nakhāhad Gerist* [The Messiah Will Never Weep] (1985), *Shām-e Ākhar* [The Last Supper] (1986), *Fātemeh Anbar* (1992), *Divbandān* (1995), *Shabi dar Tehrān* [A Night in Tehran] (1997), *Macbeth* (2000), *Parvāneh-o Yoogh* [The Butterfly and the Yoke] (2005), and *Koshtan-e Kaftar Chāhi* [The Killing of Well-Dwelling Pigeons] (2015).

The Dance of Mares is one of Charmshir's many beloved adapta-tions from the Western dramatic canon. The play takes the characters and plot of Federico García Lorca's *Yerma* (1934) and transposes them onto a fragmented, surrealist piece that defies conventional narrative structures. Told through fifty-nine brief scenes that move forwards and backwards in time, Charmshir's play bears similarities to the experimental theater of Georg Büchner's *Woyzeck* (1836) as well as a style of writing one finds in cinematic screenplays. Some of these scenes convey seemingly insignificant slices of characters' lives while others take the audience deep into these characters' minds as they speak their thoughts aloud. Altogether, these moments convey existential pon-derings on the human condition, critique the entrenched patriarchal structures throughout the world, and explore themes around grief and loss. The expansive cast of characters become an orchestra of voices, a chorus that shares its inner fears and dreams with the audience as they step into the spotlight. Charmshir's free verse flows smoothly, and his use of poetic colloquial language resembles the work of Walt Whitman. Charmshir's poeticism is steeped in symbolism, as he draws connections between the animalistic violence of bullfighting and the gendered violence of patriarchal society. Although such violence only occurs offstage in this play, the characters narrate those moments to the audience in the past tense, as was common in ancient Greek drama. In all, with its hybrid approach to form, structure, language, and storytelling, *The Dance of Mares* finds universality in its treatment of misogyny and motherhood, showing how patriarchal harm connects women across the globe and throughout time.

THE DANCE OF MARES

Mohammad Charmshir

For Dr. Ali Rafie

SCENE ONE. **TAVERN**

JUAN. You should have been there. You should have seen the coming of this Don Guido. He came like a man. Like a real man. The crowd was roaring and calling his name . . . Where was he, this Don Guido? Where was he? . . . All at once, someone opened a gate. The door opened and the crowd fell silent. It was Don Guido who was coming. He was riding a short-legged horse with its eyes covered by its mane. He was wearing a silver shirt . . . Where was he looking at, this Don Guido? Where? . . . He was coming, seated steady on that horse. The crowd was watching in silence. He was now in the bullring. He dismounted the horse. This Don Guido dismounted the horse. He went to the dead bull laid in the middle of the bullring. He knelt down. Don Guido knelt down—right next to the dead bull's horn . . . What was he doing? What was he doing? . . . He bent down. He bent down and kissed the horns of the dead bull. The crowd suddenly erupted. It roared all at once. You should have been there. You should have seen the entrance of this Don Guido. He came like a man. Like a real man . . . I always wanted to be a man like Don Guido.

YERMA. Have you ever seen the dance of mares, Juan? You must see them dance with a stallion. The two of them stand next to each other. They stand and stare into the distance. So long that they start to breathe in and out together. Then, the mare raises her head and rests it on the stallion's mane. She rests her head and slowly snores—slowly and persistently. All at once she falls silent, very silent. As if no sound has ever come out of her throat. Then, she starts slowly shaking her legs. The tremors run into her body, like the fluttering of a leaf on a branch. It starts from her tail and reaches her mane, shaking and trembling on and on. Now it's the stallion's turn to shake with these tremors. Both tremble, slowly and persistently. The stallion gradually grows restless. He grows restless and a white foam sits on the corner of his lips. You must see this restlessness, Juan . . . You must see it. Juan, I have always danced like a mare for you.

SCENE THREE. DONNA MARIA CROSSES

DONNA MARIA. Let men think they are real men, even if they know less about manhood than a mule. Greet them at the door when they come home. Let your eyes smile, even if you were crying nonstop before he arrived. Breathe as if there is a current of fresh air in the house, even if you feel queasy from the smell of his sweat. Seat him on the stool near your fireplace. Let him smell the food you have cooked, even if he does not recognize the difference between its smell and the smell of dung. Remove his boots yourself, even if there is nothing but dung on it. Pile twice as much food on his plate as your own, even if he does not eat it all and you have to leave it for the dogs. Hug him tight in bed, even if you are too tired to keep your eyes open. Do not fall into a stale bed like an un-feathered chicken. Tumble like a cat. Be like a slippery fish. Howl like a dog. Do not let him know you need something more of his manhood . . . Go now! There is someone out there who wants to brag about his manhood. Give him a child so that he thinks he is a real man.

SCENE FOUR. **IN THE SPOTLIGHT**

Yerma is applying makeup to Maria. She finishes.

MARIA. Yerma.

YERMA. Go Maria, now . . . Alejandro is waiting for you.

MARIA. Talk to me, Yerma. Let me hear your voice as I go further and further from you.

Maria goes.

YERMA. Now Alejandro is there, Maria. He is waiting for you to go to him. He searches for you from among the crowd. He wants to be the first to have cast his eyes on you—the Maria she loves. And you appear before him all at once. Alejandro sees you. His eyes are wide open with surprise. How beautiful you look, Maria! Then a flash of light passes his eyes. You blush at his look. You burn in your body. Your heart is bursting out of your chest. You lower your head, Maria. Then you look up again. Now Alejandro is laughing. The laughter you like so much. You laugh too. Alejandro finds his way through the crowd. He comes to you. He comes to hug you. He comes to kiss your lips; he is embarrassed. He extends his hands to you. You hold his hands in yours . . . Oh, Maria, dreams are always good things.

Maria is crossing the space. She and Donna Maria meet. Maria kisses Donna Maria's hands and crosses the stage.

DONNA MARIA. Don't be the woman you want to be. Be the woman that your men desire. Men don't want much. They are like kids; they fuss a lot but are pleased with small things. Fondle them a little. Give them some love. And more than anything, give them arms in which to laugh, to cry, and to sleep peacefully.

SCENE SIX. TAVERN

DON MICHELE. So, our Alejandro is marrying. How strange! As if it was only yesterday that he was pissing in José's geraniums beside the wall of his barbershop . . . Has anyone told the groom how to do it?

THE FIRST WOMAN. Everyone was waiting for you, Don Michele.

DON MICHELE. You mean, no one other than me knows how to do it? . . . Someone ask this groom. if we take men as bullfighters, who should be the bulls in the ring? Let's assume women are the bulls. So now, what should our bullfighter do to the bull?

THE SECOND WOMAN. He should play, Don Michele.

DON MICHELE. We play with our thumbs, or with the kid from next door, but not with a bull, no . . . A bullfighter kills his bull . . . Does he not, Juan? . . . Every bullfighter must pin his bull to the ground someday. Tonight, our Alejandro must pin the strongest bull of this land to the ground.

THE THIRD WOMAN. He will pin him down. Alejandro pins all the bulls down to the ground, Don Michele.

DON MICHELE. You are so sure of it that one might think he has pinned you down too . . . I propose a toast to Alejandro's good health . . .

So, Juan, what about you, have you sowed anything in the belly of your cow?

JUAN. Not yet, Don Michele.

DON MICHELE. Sow it. Sow it before it's too late . . . finish that cow, man!

SCENE SEVEN. IN THE SPOTLIGHT

THE FIRST WOMAN. These words make me feel queasy.

YERMA. But Maria should know.

FIGURE 19. *The Dance of Mares.* Directed by Babak Daghighi at the Private Stage at the Bāgh-e Asāteer, Kerman, 2013. *Photograph by Rahim Bani-Asad Azad.*

THE SECOND WOMAN. Don't worry. She knows. She knows better than us.

YERMA. How could a virgin know these things?

THE THIRD WOMAN. Is she blind or something? What else is there for a girl to see other than these sorts of things?

THE FOURTH WOMAN. She has seen her mother. She has seen all the women of the village. Is it not enough to know about it all?

THE FIFTH WOMAN. What else do we do other than giving our men their manhood?

YERMA. Her husband Alejandro is a good man.

THE SIXTH WOMAN. What difference does it make for a man to be good or bad? It is the women who should be good.

YERMA. Maria is a good girl.

THE SEVENTH WOMAN. Not all good girls become good women.

THE EIGHTH WOMAN. You were a good girl too, Yerma.

YERMA. But I have become a bad woman . . . I do all that they ask me to do.

THE NINTH WOMAN. Why then does your husband avoid coming home?

YERMA. Juan loves his farm. He loves his cows. He loves his sheep. He loves me too.

THE TENTH WOMAN. Don't you ever believe that a man can love all these at once.

THE ELEVENTH WOMAN. His farm grows crops for him. His cows breed calves. So do his sheep. What are *you* doing for him?

YERMA. Is this not enough that I am a good wife to him? That I love him? Is it bad that I do things to make him love me?

THE FIRST WOMAN. Show me a woman who cannot do all these for him.

YERMA. But he wants *me* to do it for him.

THE SECOND WOMAN. He has expectations of the cows he loves. He has other expectations of the sheep he loves. He has expectations of you too.

YERMA. What is it that I should have done and didn't do?

SCENE EIGHT. DONNA MARIA CROSSES

DONNA MARIA. Everything turns old and worn-out so fast in here, and women grow old and worn-out even faster. Everything turns rough and coarse and dry so fast, and men turn rough and coarse and dry faster . . . Men become manly eventually, but let them change with your caress, with the warmth of your bodies, with the love that only you can give them.

SCENE NINE (CONTINUATION OF SCENE SEVEN). IN THE SPOTLIGHT

YERMA. I am as dumb as a mule.

THE THIRD WOMAN. Bear a child for Juan before your hair goes gray.

THE FOURTH WOMAN. Let everyone say Juan is as strong and tough as a bull.

THE FIFTH WOMAN. Make him believe he is a man.

YERMA. Do they realize it only by having a kid?

THE SIXTH WOMAN. Men are as dumb as mules.

YERMA. How then do they know that I am a woman?

Maria comes.

MARIA. I am so scared, Yerma.

SCENE TEN. **DON PIETRO CROSSES**

DON PIETRO. A woman is like a horse. When you mount her, caress her, but when she gallops, whip her . . . A woman is like a horse. Play with your horse's mane but hit her in the forehead occasionally to make her realize that you are her only rider . . . A woman is like a horse. Remove sand cracks from her hoof, but nail her horseshoe more forcibly into her hoof . . . A woman is like a horse. Let her go as far as her bridle allows, but push her bridle back in time . . . A woman is like a horse. Let your horse have fresh grass, but not so much that she forgets the taste of hay . . . A woman is like a horse. Love your horse, but not so much that she thinks she can take you anywhere she desires . . . A woman is like a horse. One should be able to mount and ride her anywhere.

SCENE ELEVEN. **IN THE SPOTLIGHT**

VICTOR. Julieta said yesterday that you were sad these days, Yerma. What's wrong? What's bothering you? It is not hard to guess . . . Yerma, if you ask me, when God cast Adam and Eve out of the Garden of Eden, he placed them on *this* land. This is the land of those who went astray, the land of the outcast. That's why there is no mercy or forgiveness here. That's why everything is so hard here. And love is the hardest of all . . . Here, it's easy to die, Yerma, but it's hard to live, to love, and most importantly to forgive . . . I still talk too much, Yerma. And I still talk to you more than anyone else. I cannot help it, Yerma. There are times I think to myself that I should even forget your name. I should draw a wall between us. I say to myself you are living in that house, with a man who is your husband. I say you are the wife of a man. But that does not help. To me, you are always Yerma. I still love you. I still think you are mine . . . I hate this land, Yerma. This cursed, loveless land . . . Yerma, no single day passes that I do not think of you. Not a day passes that something inside me does not quiver for you. You are still Yerma to me.

SCENE TWELVE. **TAVERN**

DON MICHELE. Have you seen a fallen horse, Juan? . . . Hey, are you listening? Have you?

JUAN. No, Don Michele.

DON MICHELE. What did you say, Juan?

JUAN. No, Don Michele.

DON MICHELE. You must see it. You must see the terror and fear in the eyes of a horse . . . Have you seen it?

JUAN. No, Don Michele.

DON MICHELE. That horse might never stand up again, Juan. Do you have any idea what they do to the horse that could not stand?

JUAN. No, Don Michele.

DON MICHELE. What did you say, Juan?

JUAN. No, Don Michele.

DON MICHELE. It doesn't neigh anymore. Not that it doesn't want to, Juan. It doesn't do so because it knows its first whinny will frighten other horses. Did you know that?

JUAN. No, Don Michele.

DON MICHELE. This is the rule. All horses know this from the very start . . . Have you ever fallen, Juan?

JUAN. No, Don Michele.

DON MICHELE. So you can still neigh? . . . Do you know what happens if you don't neigh?

JUAN. No, Don Michele.

DON MICHELE. Then we should finish you, Juan. Because other horses must not be scared . . . Neigh, Juan. Neigh as loud as you can.

SCENE THIRTEEN. IN THE SPOTLIGHT

MARIA. I have three dresses. One of them is brown. It has a fringe lace on its sleeves. There is a fringe lace around the neck too. It is tight at the bust. It presses my breasts. I know Alejandro will not allow me to wear it. Even if I drop my shawl from my shoulders. I have another dress. It's green. Like this grass that Alejandro and I used to sleep on, when he used to squeeze my breasts hard. I know he will not let me wear it anymore. There is this idea in his head that someone might have squeezed my breasts when I wore it. I don't like my third dress. I don't like the color. I hate black. It depresses me. But I know Alejandro wants me to wear it all the time. I wear it, but I am always depressed.

SCENE FOURTEEN. DONNA MARIA CROSSES

DONNA MARIA. Always ask your men for something, even if you know they could never provide it for you. Let them think you could not survive without them, even if they don't know how to keep their pants on.

SCENE FIFTEEN. TAVERN

VICTOR. I've lost everything, Don Michele. Where were these traditions you talk about, the day I lost everything I had?

DON MICHELE. They were right here. Before your eyes.

VICTOR. Why didn't I see them? Why didn't anyone talk to me about them?

DON MICHELE. We were waiting for your moves.

VICTOR. What should I have done, Don Michele?

DON MICHELE. You should have killed him. You should have killed him the same day he went to Yerma's parents.

VICTOR. But he had their consent. Yerma's father wanted it.

DON MICHELE. Yerma's father consented only after Juan arrived at his door alive . . . Don't you understand, Victor? Juan puts on his hat to go to Yerma's parents. He knows that Victor is waiting for him behind a wall with a small dagger; still, he goes. He goes and arrives at Yerma's house, safe and sound. Yerma's father understands that he is a real man. As much as he gathers that Victor is not going to come forth for Yerma anymore . . . Everything has a meaning here, Victor.

VICTOR. If you don't kill, does it mean you close your eyes to what belongs to you?

DON MICHELE. You must have killed him, Victor.

SCENE SIXTEEN. IN THE SPOTLIGHT

YERMA. Are you asleep, Juan? . . . You were restless all night.

THE FIRST WOMAN. You were breathing heavily, very heavily, Julio.

YERMA. I was terrified, Juan.

THE SECOND WOMAN. You were moaning and talking nonstop, Corta.

YERMA. I couldn't understand what you were saying, Juan. Where were you speaking? Why were you crying?

THE THIRD WOMAN. I called you many times, but you did not wake up, Jose.

YERMA. I was terrified, Juan.

THE FOURTH WOMAN. The bed was wet with your sweat, Salvador.

YERMA. Tell me, Juan. What's the matter?

THE FIFTH WOMAN. Why shouldn't I know about what upsets you, Ignacio?

YERMA. Sometimes I think I am surrounded in this house by the things I do not know, Juan.

THE SIXTH WOMAN. Am I imprisoned in this house, Camilo?

YERMA. Tell me, Juan, what's the matter with you? Why are you so restless?

SCENE SEVENTEEN. **TAVERN**

JUAN. The red cloth was in his hands. In the hands of Don Guido. He was dancing on his feet right in front of the bull. You should have seen his dance with the bull . . . He lifts one of his feet slowly. Very slowly. The red cloth sticks to his waist. All the weight of his body is now balanced on the other foot. Now the free leg moves gently in the air and rests behind his other leg. Don Guido turns slowly. He turns on his waist, this Don Guido. He lands on his two feet again . . . You should have seen his dance with the bull. Now the red cloth arcs in the air. And the bull runs through the arc. Right next to this Don Guido. Those horns tear the air and the arc only . . . You should have seen his dance with that bull. He was dancing on his feet in front of that bull, this Don Guido.

SCENE EIGHTEEN. **IN THE SPOTLIGHT**

DON MICHELE. Mariana, cook tasty food for your husband. He was praising the cooking of Fernando's wife. Amparo, get along better with your mother-in-law. She is a sly woman. She creates conflict

FIGURE 20. *The Dance of Mares*. Directed by Babak Daghighi at the Private Stage at the Bāgh-e Asāteer, Kerman, 2013. *Photograph by Rahim Bani-Asad Azad*.

between you and your husband. Lucia, don't laugh too much. You know how much your husband despises airy women. Isabella, be more attentive to your husband. He is gazing too much at girls' hips. Carmonita, you are nagging too much at home. Men are not patient.

SCENE NINETEEN. **IN THE SPOTLIGHT**

VICTOR. Julieta said yesterday you wanted to go to Donna Maria Alvarez's shrine. I always wished that this land belonged to women. The land of you and those saints. It would be a good land if it were yours, Yerma. One woman would take a candle for another so that her dreams would come true. It's so good that you women confide in one another. We live in a masculine world, Yerma. Men do not confide in anyone, even themselves. That's why everything is so hard in here, Yerma. Words are left unsaid, in closed containers that no one desires to disclose. That's why it is hard to look up and say it's a beautiful sky. Because if you say that, no one will look up at the sky anymore . . . If only you would speak, Yerma. If only you would shout your words.

SCENE TWENTY. **IN THE SPOTLIGHT**

MARIA. Seven pots. Five cups. Four plates. Six spoons. Two candlesticks and twenty candles. A small wooden closet. A mattress cover. A small bundle of my clothes. A wooden barrette. A wide-toothed comb. A kohl container. All I brought to Alejandro's house. Alejandro says I brought my tears too. I cry so much these days in Alejandro's house. Nothing here is like what I fancied. I only moved from our house to Alejandro's. Everything looks the same as our house. Last night, when I was doing the dishes, I realized I am doing them like my mother. I wanted to tell Alejandro. He was fast asleep on the chair. Like my father.

SCENE TWENTY-ONE. **TAVERN**

JUAN. One more shot, Victor. Then we will leave for our nests. We will go to our restless pigeons—they are waiting to flap their wings for us . . . Do you hear their coos, Victor?

VICTOR. We should go, Juan.

JUAN. One more shot, Victor. Just one more . . . What is this smell everywhere, Victor?

VICTOR. I don't smell anything.

JUAN. I do. It's in my head, Victor. In my head.

VICTOR. Let's go get some fresh air.

DON MICHELE. This is the cooing of the pigeons you keep in your nests. They say you don't take care of them . . . Do you have a pigeon, Victor?

THE FIRST WOMAN. Juan took his pigeon, Don Michele.

VICTOR. We must go.

DON MICHELE. Sit. I want to tell you about my dreams, Victor.

THE SECOND WOMAN. He has his own dreams, Don Michele.

DON MICHELE. Do you dream about bulls or pigeons?

VICTOR. You are hurting my wrist, Don Michele.

DON MICHELE. Are you in for arm wrestling?

VICTOR. With you?

THE THIRD WOMAN. Do it with Juan.

THE FOURTH WOMAN. Juan doesn't feel up to these things tonight.

DON MICHELE. We will bet on whatever you say, Victor.

VICTOR. You are complicating simple things.

DON MICHELE. You are not scared, are you, Victor?

(*Victor sits and gets ready.*)

One more shot for Juan and Victor.

VICTOR. Let's wrap it up.

DON MICHELE. Juan, I dream of bullrings with no people. It's only me . . . Has this Don Guido fought a bull in an empty bullring? . . . I guess there is a woman in my dream too. I don't know why, but her face is white. As white as a ghost . . . Juan. What would your Don Guido do to her if it was him?

JUAN. He would watch her long enough to make her smile.

VICTOR. You are drinking too much, Juan.

JUAN. You look like shit, Victor, when you talk like Yerma.

DON MICHELE. I die in those dreams with my intestines torn out from my belly. What happens to your Don Guido?

JUAN. She drops her handkerchief in the middle of the bullring, Don Michele. Don Guido picks it up and kisses it.

VICTOR. Do you want us to finish, Juan? . . . You are ruining yourself.

Juan forcefully shoves Victor's hand down.

JUAN. I told you, you look like shit when you talk like Yerma.

DON MICHELE. Everyone at this table is on me.

(*Juan wants to go. Don Michele stops him.*)

Remember, Juan. The cow that gives milk gets drunk faster than other cows.

SCENE TWENTY-TWO. DON PIETRO CROSSES

DON PIETRO. Don't ever let your wives know when you desire them more than usual. Let them ask for love with their tears, let them beg. Let them come to you with their needs. Don't let them know you need them as much as they need you. Remember, women always want to be winners. They want to win everything, especially in their life with you.

SCENE TWENTY-THREE. IN THE SPOTLIGHT

VICTOR. Julieta said yesterday that your eyes were red, Yerma. As if you had cried. Yerma, I know there are good reasons to cry here, but I want to know why you are crying. Are you crying for things you lost or perhaps things you never had? One can cry for both here, for this is the land of tears. The land of lamenting. There is a drop of tear for everything. It seems this tear alleviates pain. But is there relief, Yerma, when our souls are so wounded and hopeless? No, there is no relief. There is no relief from these wounds. And tears come down because there is no relief. There is nothing other than tears, wounds . . . For what wounds are you crying, Yerma?

SCENE TWENTY-FOUR. **DONNA MARIA CROSSES**

Donna Maria comes. Maria wants to go. Donna Maria blocks her way. She puts her hand on Maria's belly. Maria leaves the scene rapidly.

DONNA MARIA. Bear strong boys for your husbands. Bring them up like your husbands. Let your husbands say: This is my kid. Let them touch your bellies. Let them place their ears on your bellies. Let them feel the movements of the baby under their palms. Let them hear the flow of their children's blood in your bellies. Let them give you tight hugs and whisper into your ears: This is my child, my own child.

SCENE TWENTY-FIVE. **IN THE SPOTLIGHT**

MARIA. Well, how should I tell you? . . . Have you ever held a live sparrow in your hands, Yerma?

YERMA. Yes, yes.

MARIA. It is the same . . . only the sparrow is in your belly.

YERMA. A sparrow? As tiny as that? . . . You speak highly of it. My mother used to say it is like a crab. When she was pregnant with the last ones, she would describe them as cats scratching on the wall . . . She used those very words. It scared me.

MARIA. I am scared, Yerma.

YERMA. Of what? A little sparrow? . . . What's the matter with you, Maria?

MARIA. Who is this that is growing in me? . . . What am I supposed to do with it?

YERMA. Hug it. Sing a lullaby to it. Speak to it. Tell it you love it.

MARIA. It grows up, and then what? Will it look like me or Alejandro? What man or woman in this village will it look like? . . . What do I have to give it?

YERMA. You are so good, Maria.

MARIA. Everyone keeps telling me I am so good. Why then can't I live the life I like, with all the goodness in me? Why can't *you* live it?

YERMA. I am neither good nor do I want anything from life.

MARIA. Don't you?

YERMA. No, not if I cannot have it. All I wanted is what you have now.

MARIA. I don't know what to do with it. I know nothing . . . I want to go to my mother, but then I tell myself she is old. She has forgotten them all.

YERMA. We don't need to bother your mother. We will make it, girl!

MARIA. How?

YERMA. Get up and walk . . . Not too fast, slowly. Like you are walking on the clouds. On your toes. Don't take big steps. No long strides. Short ones. Let your weight fall on your toes, not on your heels. That way, your belly becomes a cradle, and it gently rocks the baby . . . Now breathe. Slowly. Very slowly but deeply. Fill your lungs with air. As if you are in a garden with clovers and almond blossoms. Like you want to fill your lungs with their fragrance . . . Now, hold your shoulders back. Straighten up your spine. Like you are holding a flower between your lips. Like you fear its petals may fall . . . Oh, Maria, you walk like a mother.

MARIA. Yerma, is that true that it kicks one's belly with its feet?

YERMA. Like a horse trotting on the damp grass, swiftly and playfully . . . Maria, there will be days his laughter will fill your ears. Someday you will put an olive in his mouth and you will hear the sounds of him tasting it . . . Oh Maria, what beautiful days you will have with this little sparrow.

MARIA. How do you know all this, Yerma?

YERMA. From my dreams, Maria, from my dreams.

SCENE TWENTY-SIX. **DON PIETRO CROSSES**

DON PIETRO. Let your children drink milk from their mother's breasts like a horse, but don't let them smell like their mother. Let their mother groom them like a horse, but don't let them learn galloping from their mother. Let your children nicker beside their mother, but don't let them learn to neigh from her. Let their mother cuddle them, but don't let her bring them up in her own way.

SCENE TWENTY-SEVEN. **IN THE SPOTLIGHT**

THE FIRST WOMAN. What are you sewing, girl?

YERMA. Some stuff for the baby.

THE SECOND WOMAN. This house needs a baby.

YERMA. These are not mine; they are for Maria's baby.

THE THIRD WOMAN. What about you?

YERMA. We have not decided yet. Juan says: When the time comes, Yerma.

THE FOURTH WOMAN. And when is that?

YERMA. He says one of these days, perhaps . . . I have prepared everything; I've sewn clothes for the baby.

THE FIFTH WOMAN. What for, when there is no child to wear them?

THE SIXTH WOMAN. Look at Maria. She is just married, yet she has a bump in her belly.

THE SEVENTH WOMAN. Have you seen her walk? That flushed face? Those relentlessly smiling lips?

YERMA. I want the baby. It is Juan who doesn't.

THE EIGHTH WOMAN. Pet him, girl. Get him out of this mood.

YERMA. I want the same but don't know what to do.

SCENE TWENTY-EIGHT. TAVERN

JUAN. It was a huge bull. The biggest bull one could find in Spain, very strong. There was no black in its eyes. It looked completely white. There were red veins in the white part. As if the eyes were burning with flames. Don Guido had struck five of his spears into its neck. Blood was pouring out of its body. The crowd had gone mad. It was roaring; the bull was still on its feet. It was still attacking Don Guido. Don Guido's clothes were soaked in blood. He stared at the bull. He waved the red cloth slowly. Very slowly. Then he was whirling round with the red cloth. The crowd had gone mad. It was roaring. And the bull was coming to Don Guido. It was a huge bull. The biggest bull one could find in Spain. Very strong. Don Guido was whirling, the bull was approaching. Don Guido stopped all at once. Now the bull was in front of him. The sword was shaking in its neck. And there was blood flowing like a fountain all over the bull and Don Guido.

SCENE TWENTY-NINE. **DONNA MARIA CROSSES**

DONNA MARIA. Scream when your baby is coming. Scare your men as much as you can. Let them think they committed the biggest sin in the world when they asked you to bear kids for them. But you should enjoy the labor. Tell yourself that you would do it again, ten times over, no matter how difficult it is. But don't let your men know that. Make them believe that you would only endure the pain ten times more for them.

SCENE THIRTY. **IN THE SPOTLIGHT**

MARIA. Give me your hands, Alejandro. No power is left in me.

THE FIRST WOMAN. Shut the windows, Julio. I don't want anyone to know I am in pain . . . Go for my mother. Don't panic. Just come back soon.

MARIA. Do you remember our wedding night? You whispered into my ear about the son you wanted. He is coming now.

THE SECOND WOMAN. Wipe off my sweat, Corta. Put that pot on the fire. Put my white sheets within reach . . . I want to cry.

MARIA. Give him any name you want, Alejandro. But to me, he will always be a little sparrow.

THE THIRD WOMAN. I want to scream, Jose. Give me the pillow. I want to bury my face in the pillow and scream.

MARIA. I will never let you raise your hand against him, Alejandro. I won't let you shout at him. You must always be kind to him.

THE FOURTH WOMAN. Don't you ever ask me to bear a son for you, Salvador. I am in hell with this pain.

MARIA. Let's bring him up well, Alejandro.

THE FIFTH WOMAN. Ignacio, this son of yours doesn't seem to be coming out of my belly. It feels like he's gradually busting out of my head, from behind my eyes.

MARIA. Come, Alejandro. Let's tell him we brought him into the world.

THE SIXTH WOMAN. I can already hear his cries, Camillo. I hope he laughs as loudly.

MARIA. Ask me for more sons, Alejandro. Let me have more of this pain.

SCENE THIRTY-ONE. DONNA MARIA CROSSES

DONNA MARIA. Clean your babies. Wrap them up in the whitest of all your sheets. Hold them close to your breasts. Let them voraciously suck at them. Let them drink from your breasts until they're full. Then call your men. Put their babies in their arms. Then lean against the bed proudly. Let them understand that you have done them the biggest favor in the world—even if your men tell you tomorrow that life should be as it always was.

SCENE THIRTY-TWO. TAVERN

JUAN. That's enough, Don Michele. I don't want to drink anymore . . . I love her so much, Don Michele. I love her to the point of frustration. I feel frustrated because I am afraid. It frightens me to someday realize that she doesn't love me . . . That's enough, Don Michele. I don't want anymore. I always talk to her in a way that hides how much I love her. But I know I love her. There are times my head fills with the memory of her scent. As if a thousand bulls were released in my chest. I can't bear it. I rush home panting. I ask myself if a thousand bulls are kicking against her chest, too. I open the door and find her there. She is right there, sitting quietly, attending to something. Why is it that those bulls are so calm and quiet in Yerma's chest, Don Michele? . . . That's enough, Don Michele. I don't want to have any more . . . Sometimes I think I must tell her everything. I must show it to her. But again, I fear, Don Michele. I fear that she looks at me, cuddles me like a kid, and rests my head on her breasts to comfort me. Don Michele, I don't want any of this love to recede in her. I want her to burn with passion like I do.

Victor arrives.

DON MICHELE. Don't let those thousand bulls kick against Yerma's chest for anyone else.

SCENE THIRTY-THREE. DON PIETRO CROSSES

DON PIETRO. Do not let your women go out without headscarves. Be jealous of the hearts that desire their hair. Don't let them remove their shawls from their shoulders. Be jealous of the eyes that look at them with regret. Don't let your women laugh or speak loudly. Be jealous of the hearts that tremble with their laughs and words. Don't let your wives look at other eyes or lips. Be jealous of the sigh they may let out . . . Women are like rain—once they begin to pour, they drench everything in sight.

SCENE THIRTY-FOUR. IN THE SPOTLIGHT

VICTOR. Julieta said yesterday that you had not left home for days. Why have you locked yourself in, Yerma? Why do you hide behind those doors? Is it possible to hide anything here? Don't ever imagine you cannot be seen from behind those doors, Yerma. We are all face-to-face in this land. Come out from behind those doors. Open the door, Yerma. There is no place to hide in this land. We all have wounds, Yerma. Some of them are deep, some are small. But we all suffer from our wounds. This is the land of pain and suffering, Yerma. Why are you hiding your wounds from us?

SCENE THIRTY-FIVE. **IN THE SPOTLIGHT**

JUAN. Now the bull is standing in front of Don Guido. It has lowered its head. It is breathing heavily. Gently, Don Guido brings the red cloth from behind his back. Very gently. He keeps it in front of himself. In front of his waist and legs. He holds his sword in his right hand. Now, the bull raises its head. Does it look at Don Guido or the red cloth? No one knows. The bull paws at the ground with its hoofs. Don Guido knows the bull is coming at him. It is coming vociferously to kill him. It is coming right now. Don Guido must be on his toes. He must let the bull come closer. He must keep the bull at arm's length. And now he must lean forward with all his weight. And now the sword cuts deep into the flesh of the bull's neck. He must thrust. He must push that sword in with all his might. Now the bull lowers its head, folds its hind legs into its belly. Slowly, the bull sinks into the ground. Don Guido looks into its eyes—eyes that emit nothing but the darkness of death.

SCENE THIRTY-SIX. **IN THE SPOTLIGHT**

YERMA. How could you leave him alone? What if he wakes up? What if he gets scared and asks for you?

MARIA. Yerma, he is clean and warm. He drank like a calf. He just needs some good sleep.

YERMA. Did you shut the doors? What about the windows?

MARIA. Yes, I closed them all.

YERMA. Maybe you should have left one window unlatched?

MARIA. I did.

YERMA. The stove . . .

MARIA. Yes, I turned it off . . . Yerma, I am his mother. I know my job.

YERMA. You are right. I keep forgetting that you are a mother.

MARIA. It's not just you who forgets. Everyone does.

YERMA. Why are you taking that tone with me, Maria? Who forgets you? . . . Come, give me your hands. Put your head here.

MARIA. Forgive me, Yerma. Everyone is trying to teach me how to be a mother.

YERMA. I was just concerned, Maria.

MARIA. Have I changed too much? Why is it like this, Yerma? Why does everything become monotonous so fast? Did you and Juan become like what Alejandro and I are now? So cold and remote? . . . Why don't you ever tell me about yourself, Yerma?

YERMA. Maybe because I don't have much to say . . . Juan comes in every day and says: Hello Yerma. I reply: Hello Juan. Then there is nothing. Sometimes we convey our neighbors' greetings. Maybe . . . there is not much to talk about.

MARIA. Why is everything so difficult here, Yerma?

SCENE THIRTY-SEVEN. IN THE SPOTLIGHT

VICTOR. I asked Julieta to tell you that I am leaving, Yerma. It's very difficult to go, but perhaps it's for the best. I am not leaving for myself. I am going for you. I don't want you to have a miserable life.

Yerma, this is the land of bitterness. The land of regrets. Dreams are soon forgotten. Tomorrow is no different from today. There is no yesterday. Yerma, one must submit to so many things here. This is the land of submission. You must either live it or leave it. I am leaving, Yerma. I don't know how to live it. Do you have any idea how we should live here? I wish I could ask you to come with me. Let's go together. I am not saying this for myself or even you. Perhaps it's for the child that you wish to bring into this cursed land against Juan's wishes. That child is hope. Your grand hope. Yerma, I never understood why your father accepted Juan when he knew that I loved you. I never understood why I should have killed Juan in a dark, empty street when everyone knew that I loved you. Or why must I now die by Juan's hands, when I know Yerma is no longer mine, when losing you is a pain I carry, the burden in my loneliness. I am going, Yerma. But no matter where I go, you will still be my girl—the Yerma I wanted with every bone in my body . . . Yerma, I will not write to you. But I want you to live. Live a good life, Yerma.

SCENE THIRTY-EIGHT. **IN THE SPOTLIGHT**

DON MICHELE. If you look at the body, you will know that he was stabbed in the back. Struck right between his shoulder blades. They killed him in the traditional manner, if you see the body. It means that our laws were violated, and someone should have fixed them. You will find that everything is back to normal if you see the body. He has suffered beyond measure. He painfully clawed at the soil. It is evident from looking at the body that he turned after he was struck. He turned his face to the person who struck him. He came to learn why he was dying. His eyes were still open when they found him. If you see the body, you will realize that he understood the traditional manner of his death. He knew he should expect to hear about the laws for which they were killing him. It's good that everyone knows the laws of killing and dying. He pressed his lips as if he did not want to talk or scream out of pain. If you see the body, you will realize that the blows came one after another. They did not strike him on the chest. They struck him in his belly. Of course, it had to be like this. The laws require it. Then he dragged himself on the ground. One can tell from the line of blood on the ground. If you see the body, you will realize that they were speaking to him with each blow. They reminded him of the laws surrounding such deaths. Three strikes; they only struck him three times. Three times only. He was leaving. One could guess it from the bundle dropped next to him. If you see the body, you will realize that someone killed him out of ceremony. A law had to be obeyed, so it was carried through. The street was empty and dark. No one saw what happened. He was a good man, this Victor. But no one saw anything. No one saw how he was killed. Of course, no one dared to witness it.

SCENE THIRTY-NINE. **TAVERN**

JUAN. The bull fell before Don Guido. Blood was flowing from its neck. Don Guido was standing still, watching it. The crowd was roaring. Don Guido moved his hand to his hat and took it off. He put his feet together. His body straightened up. He bowed his head for the dead bull. The crowd was roaring. With his other hand, he pulled the red cloth over the dead bull's face. The crowd was roaring. Don Guido turned to the crowd, his hat waving in his hand. The crowd was roaring.

SCENE FORTY. IN THE SPOTLIGHT

YERMA. Are you asleep, Juan?

THE FIRST WOMAN. He is not.

YERMA. I want to have a word with you.

THE SECOND WOMAN. He does not want to talk to you.

YERMA. It's been a long time since I wanted to talk to you. I always carried these words within me. I always wanted to speak them aloud, but I never did. I always said to myself: Later, tell him all of this later, Yerma.

THE THIRD WOMAN. Tell him this later as well.

YERMA. Juan, the longer I wait, the later it becomes.

THE FOURTH WOMAN. What is becoming late? Nothing is ever too late.

YERMA. It is, Juan. Everything is coming to an end. Our life is so cold and empty . . . I always begged you for everything.

THE FIFTH WOMAN. You must beg for everything.

YERMA. Juan, I want a baby. I've wanted to be a mother for so long . . . Did you hear that?

THE SIXTH WOMAN. You must beg him more, Yerma. You must beg him still—much more.

SCENE FORTY-ONE. DON PIETRO CROSSES

DON PIETRO. Women are born with tears. They live with their tears. They die with their tears. They give away everything with tears. They take everything with tears. Women laugh with their tears. They grieve with tears. They fall for someone with tears. They attract men's attention with their tears . . . Don't let women own your homes, your sons, and yourselves with their tears. Their tears should only wet their handkerchiefs.

SCENE FORTY-TWO. IN THE SPOTLIGHT

DON MICHELE. Don't laugh, Mariana. Don't cry, Amparo. Don't shout, Lucia. Don't grieve, Isabella. Do nothing, Carmenita. Shut your mouths. Be quiet. Shut your eyes. Be quiet. Don't forget, women are born to listen, not talk.

SCENE FORTY-THREE. DONNA MARIA CROSSES

DONNA MARIA. Put your husbands to sleep on your chests. Let them confide in you. Let them speak of their agonies to you. Their

FIGURE 21. *The Dance of Mares*. Directed by Babak Daghighi at the Private Stage at the Bāgh-e Asāteer, Kerman, 2013. *Photograph by Rahim Bani-Asad Azad*.

desolations and—more than anything—their hopes and wishes. Let them believe that you listen to all of them. But never talk to anyone yourself. Don't believe that someone is listening to you. Don't forget that you belong to your husbands, like your houses, your children, your tables, chairs, and walls that all belong to them. Your men demand faith, patience, and a closed mouth. Be jolly at home and confine your grievances to your hearts.

SCENE FORTY-FOUR. IN THE SPOTLIGHT

YERMA. Maria's baby died today, Juan.

THE FIRST WOMAN. Julio, today I realized that the worst thing in this world is not death but loss.

YERMA. Juan, Maria doesn't cry. She doesn't do anything else. She just holds her baby tight to her chest. Her dead baby.

THE SECOND WOMAN. I love my kids more than before, Jose. Now I know how easily one can lose them.

YERMA. Which one is worse, Juan—losing something or never having it to begin with?

THE THIRD WOMAN. Salvador, today I saw a woman who could breathe and walk while dead.

YERMA. One must first have something in order to cry over losing it, Juan. I have nothing to cry or laugh for.

THE FOURTH WOMAN. I cried today, Ignacio. Not for the dead baby, but because I was happy that I still had something.

YERMA. Give me something, Juan. Something I could delight in having and cry over losing.

THE FIFTH WOMAN. I wore my best clothes for you, Camelio, so that you might give me one more son. Maybe this way, we can forget death.

JUAN. Don Guido was standing over the dead bull. The crowd was still roaring. Don Guido's sword was still in its neck. Blood was still running. Don Guido bent down. His hand rested on his sword. He pulled at the sword. He pulled at it to take it out of the bull's neck. The sword did not move. He pulled again. It would not move. The crowd was no longer roaring. They were silent. Don Guido pinned his feet to the ground. He gripped the hilt more tightly. He pulled. Suddenly the sword came free. It was broken. The sword was broken. Don Guido looked at the broken sword. He dropped it. The crowd erupted again. It looked like Don Guido couldn't hear any of it. As if he was deaf to the crowd. His head hung low. The red cloth trailed behind him. It dragged along the dust of the bullring, along the path Don Guido had chosen.

SCENE FORTY-SIX. **IN THE SPOTLIGHT**

YERMA. On the way to the shrine, Maria, you will see many women. Some of them are so old that you think they might not survive the trip. Some of them are so young that you ask why they are coming all this way. All these women have wishes, Maria. Wishes that might even make you laugh. But you must not laugh at them, Maria. They have longings—just like you and me. You cannot imagine what you might see on the way. Women who hold lighted candles in their hands. They all sing the same prayers in a loud voice, on a winding road lit by those flickering candles. The sound of prayers comes from every direction. You must take slow steps when you carry that candle. You should not let it be extinguished. As you are climbing up the trail, Maria, you must make a wish in your heart.

A good wish. It does not matter if it is big or small, it just has to be a good wish.

MARIA. Yerma, is it a good wish to want to die?

YERMA. You look much better, Maria.

MARIA. Are you listening to me, Yerma?

YERMA. When you cry, the kohl rolls down your face, Maria.

MARIA. What do I want all of this for? (*She wipes her makeup*) You don't understand anything, Yerma. You are an ignorant woman.

YERMA. You are right, Maria. I don't understand anything. I am like a piece of stone.

They hug.

MARIA. I was a mother. I lost my baby. Do you understand?

YERMA. No. I never had anything to lose.

MARIA. I want to die.

YERMA. Don't say that, Maria. You must live. You must give birth to other sons.

MARIA. So that they die too? There is no breath left in me to endure other losses, Yerma . . . Nowadays I am telling myself: Good for Yerma, who never had and will never have to lose anything. It hurts so much to lose. It hurts as much as dying, but once you lose, dying is not so difficult.

YERMA. Let's talk about life.

MARIA. Not when death is so close to us. Let's talk about death . . . I will carry a lighted candle on that road. I say the prayers like all women. I walk slowly so that the light doesn't go out. Then I make my biggest wish, Yerma. The biggest wish a woman in my condition can make . . . Let me go with the angel of death everywhere he goes.

Let me paint death on my chest by looking at the face of that little sparrow in my arms.

SCENE FORTY-SEVEN. **DONNA MARIA CROSSES**

DONNA MARIA. Hide your tears in your handkerchiefs. And your laughter in your wrinkles. Men don't like tears. They want the laughs. Let them wake up to your laughter. Let them eat with the sound of your laughter. Let them hear it when they work. Let them go to sleep to the sound of you laughing. Make them believe that grief will never cross your thresholds. But cry as soon as they turn their faces. It is only these tears that can wash away unfulfilled wishes from a woman's heart. One can shed tears for everything in this world.

Maria comes and stops in front of Donna Maria, who kisses her on the forehead. Maria crosses.

SCENE FORTY-EIGHT. **DON PIETRO CROSSES**

DON PIETRO. Women don't suffer. They hurt. They are not fatigued. They tire you out. They do not suffer. They make you suffer. Empty your hearts of them. Empty your heads of them. Only remember them in bed as much as you could forget them again. Dream about horses and lands. Dream about a flock of sheep, but not of women. They rob you of sleep. They steal your hearts. They replace it with wrath, with hatred. Women take life and give death.

SCENE FORTY-NINE. **IN THE SPOTLIGHT**

MARIA. I am not going to wear my brown dress, Alejandro. The green dress—I am not going to wear that one either. I tore all the dresses I had brought to your house. Except for the one you always wanted me to wear. I am happy you never let me wear anything other than that dress. I now love the color black. It reminds me of something I once had that I have no longer. Something I cry about losing every single day. I lost the biggest thing in my life, Alejandro. You only lost your child. I lost my love. I never loved you, Alejandro. Not you, not your home, not even all the dreams I had in my father's house. I understand now that it was all for gaining something that I no longer have. That baby wasn't merely a baby to me. He was everything I had. Everything I had ever wished for. We used to talk about everything. About things that exist but should not. About things that do not exist but should . . . You cannot imagine, the baby and I used to laugh at you when you were trying to be a father and a husband. You were neither. The baby and I laughed at everything. At all the things you men were and we were not. I am now loveless, Alejandro. I am loveless for the rest of my life. Until the end of my days.

SCENE FIFTY. **TAVERN**

JUAN. The bull was on the ground. On the ground that was red, red with its own blood. No one was left in the crowd to roar. Don Guido was still in the bullring, watching the bull. Riders on short-legged horses approached. They brought ropes. Don Guido didn't look at them. They fastened the ropes to the bull's horns and dragged it away. Don Guido didn't watch them. A long line of blood was drawn on the ground. The dead bull was dragged away and Don Guido just stared at that long line of blood.

YERMA. They brought Maria's body today.

THE FIRST WOMAN. From all that youth and life, nothing was left but broken bones and crushed flesh, Julio.

YERMA. I am not crying for Maria, Juan. She rushed to her baby like a mother.

THE SECOND WOMAN. Let me kiss you, Corta. Let me feel I am still alive.

YERMA. I am asking you, Juan. If we don't wish to cry for Maria, for whom and for what else could we cry in this land?

THE THIRD WOMAN. Hug me, Jose. Let the cold out of my heart.

YERMA. For whom should I shed tears, Juan? Or for what?

THE FOURTH WOMAN. Let me look at you, again and again, Salvador. It's so good to be alive.

YERMA. Today I cried for myself, Juan. I now know that I am neither a woman nor a mother.

THE FIFTH WOMAN. Ask the kids today to only laugh. Tell me something, Ignacio. I want to hear voices under this roof.

YERMA. I have hidden all of my unfulfilled wishes in my heart, Juan. I did so to be the lowest thing I could be in this world for you: a woman.

THE SIXTH WOMAN. I want to be alive, Camilo. I want to live.

YERMA. I wish you had a chest that I could rest my head on for all my life, Juan. I wish there were arms I could give all my womanhood to . . . Why is it that the more I think, the more I realize I am nothing, Juan?

SCENE FIFTY-TWO. **DON PIETRO CROSSES**

DON PIETRO. Wake them up when they are asleep. Put them to sleep when they are awake. Stand them up when they are seated. Sit them down when they are standing. Make them laugh when they are crying. Make them cry when they are laughing. Don't let them get used to anything. Don't let them get used to speaking. Don't let them get used to looking. Don't let them get used to their household chores. Don't let them do anything they desire. Hold the world on your own shoulders. The world would be worse off on the shoulders of women.

SCENE FIFTY-THREE. **IN THE SPOTLIGHT**

THE FIRST WOMAN. We have come to say: We have a word with you, Don Michele.

THE SECOND WOMAN. We have come to ask: How long is Maria's body going to remain there, Don Michele?

THE THIRD WOMAN. We have come to say: A woman's body must be buried in the cemetery, Don Michele, not in a remote wilderness.

THE FOURTH WOMAN. We have come to say: Maria was a mother, Don Michele. Mothers should be buried near their children.

THE FIFTH WOMAN. We have come to ask: What difference does it make how a woman dies, Don Michele?

THE SIXTH WOMAN. We have come to say: You must be a woman, Don Michele, to understand why a woman would do this to herself.

THE SEVENTH WOMAN. We have come to say: Burying a woman will not change anything in this world, Don Michele.

THE EIGHTH WOMAN. We have come to ask: Are you listening to us, Don Michele?

DONNA MARIA. Men get used to things quickly. You must not get used to anything. Men always maintain their habits. You must not get used to anything. Men are happy with their habits. You must not get used to anything. Don't fight their bad habits. Change them slowly. Don't let the men know they are changing. Change them slowly. Don't ask your men if they wish to change. Change them slowly. Tell your men that you love their habits. Change them slowly.

SCENE FIFTY-FIVE. DON PIETRO CROSSES

DON PIETRO. Men never realize how much they change every day once they live with a woman.

SCENE FIFTY-SIX. TAVERN

DON MICHELE. Have you ever seen the gelding[1] of a colt?

JUAN. No, Don Michele.

DON MICHELE. I have, Juan. Several times . . . They tie the front and back legs of the colt and pull from all four sides to make the colt fall to the ground. Then they bring a sledgehammer and an anvil. They place the testicle of the colt on the anvil and hit with it the sledgehammer. Just once . . . Do you know why they only hit it once, Juan?

JUAN. No, Don Michele.

DON MICHELE. Because if they don't crush the testicles on the first strike, then the colt is not going to survive the second . . . Did you know there is no sound more terrifying than the neighing of that colt?

---

1 The process of castrating a male horse.

JUAN. No, Don Michele.

DON MICHELE. Do you know why they castrate colts, Juan?

JUAN. No, Don Michele.

DON MICHELE. They want the colt to be strong and big. So that it could run fast in a race, faster than any other horse . . . Have you ever heard the neighing of a gelded colt?

JUAN. No, Don Michele.

DON MICHELE. Its neighing fills the world . . . Unless it does not suffer that pain, no colt could run that fast in a race. This is required to win the race . . . You don't want to be a loser, Juan. Do you?

JUAN. No, Don Michele.

Don Michele puts a dagger on the table.

DON MICHELE. We should let everything stay as is. You don't want to change anything, Juan. Do you?

JUAN. No, Don Michele.

DON MICHELE. Well done, Juan!

Don Michele wants to go.

JUAN. They become good horses, those colts. Don't they, Don Michele?

DON MICHELE. Very good ones. Only they cannot be used for breeding.

SCENE FIFTY-SEVEN. DONNA MARIA CROSSES

DONNA MARIA. Give love to your men, and gather the hate in your hearts. Give love to your homes, and hide your hate behind the words in your eyes—words you never speak. Let your men get intoxicated with your love. Let them fear the hate in your breath. It's only with these breaths that they realize there is always a woman waiting for them at home. A woman who can give them love or hate.

DON MICHELE. Mariana, Amparo, Lucia, Isabella, Carmenita, you were all in my dreams last night. There was dried blood on your hands. The scarlet color of blood was all over your clothes. Your eyes were glowing like the eyes of a cat in the darkness. I was asleep in my bed. My eyes were shut but I could see you all. I saw you, Amparo, placing my feet in a washbowl. The water was cool, the coolest water one could find in this land. You were washing my feet, Mariana. You were washing my feet while the washbowl was filling with the blood on your hands. I wanted to wake up. I wanted to open my eyes. I couldn't, Lucia. You removed my clothes, Lucia. I was naked before your eyes. You laid a white cloth on my face, Isabella. I could still see from beneath the white cloth with closed eyes. I was naked, Isabella. I was never naked like this before, Carmenita. You, Carmenita, you touched my body. You washed me, Mariana. You washed all of my body. You, Amparo, you dressed me in white clothes I never had. You all kissed my forehead—such a warm kiss that you planted on my forehead.

SCENE FIFTY-NINE. IN THE SPOTLIGHT

YERMA. I taste the dust in my mouth. My eyes are filled with dust. There is nothing on my hands but dust, Juan. On my clothes, on my shoes. Everywhere there is only dust. This tough and barren soil. Everywhere I turn I see nothing but dust, Juan. I turn the soil upside down—this tough and barren soil. I want to give my love to the dust even though I never had love in my life. At last, I am doing something with my life. Something I want. Something I love. I was never like my mother, Juan. I might never grow to be like her. But I am a woman. Even if no one acknowledges that. Even if you never realized it. Juan, I buried Maria next to her baby. In this tough, barren earth—even if they exhume her a thousand times and throw her away. I play with this soil, Juan. I breathe in it. I speak to it. I make it love me. Maybe this becomes a land of kindness because of the piece of earth where a mother lies. Maybe this land learns forgiveness from the very hands that dig it. I am giving myself to the earth, Juan. I am giving all the mothers of this land to the earth. I am giving all the women of this land to this earth. Let this soil be our father. Let it be our husband and our son.

JUAN. I want to cry, Yerma. I want to cry all my tears.

YERMA. Come, Juan. Rest your head on my lap and cry.

JUAN. I always wanted to be a man. I always wanted to die like a man.

YERMA. I feel bitter in my throat. There is bitterness in my bones, Juan. I now believe in things one can touch with their hands. I believe in things one can see with their eyes. I now know the truth is somewhere nearby. Dreams are far, however. Farther than you could imagine. I just look around me. Victor was right. This is a land of bitterness. The land of growing old with regrets. Everything grows old too fast here—women even faster than everything else. And I, the fastest. I don't want anything from you, Juan. There is nothing you can give me. I don't want a son from you. I imagine you are my son. For this, you must die like a man, Juan. My son must die like a man.

(*She strikes Juan in the chest with a dagger.*)

Now I have something to lose. You have something to gain. Have you ever seen the dance of mares, Juan? You must see their dance . . . I have always danced like a mare in this world.

JUAN. Don Guido died today. By the horns of a Grenadian bull. His guts were spilling out. You should have been there, Yerma. You should have seen his death. He died like a man. Like a real man. The bull's horn was in his belly. Yet he raised his sword and pushed it into the bull's neck. The bull died instantly. Immediately. The crowd was roaring. Blood flowed from both the bull and Don Guido. He knelt down in that blood. Right next to the horns of the dead bull. Then he slowly collected his intestines from the ground and pushed them back into his belly. The crowd was roaring, but he was deaf to it all. He had knelt down to gather his innards back into his belly. Then he got up, he stood on his feet. Don Guido raised himself and stood up. He pressed one of his hands on his belly to hold his guts in. With the other hand, he waved his white handkerchief in the air, circling the ring. The crowd was roaring, while Don Guido was going round and round . . . Oh, Yerma, I always wanted to die a man's death.

Fade into darkness.

THE CHILD

Naghmeh Samini

Translated by
Ali-Reza Mirsajadi

Original title: *Bacheh*

Written in 2019

First performed in 2020 at Chaharsou Hall, Tehran, directed by Afsaneh Mahian

Published in Persian by Ney Publication, 2021

THE PEOPLE

Man: Immigration Officer; he should be a native of the country in which the play is being performed; around 35 to 40 years old

Mina #1: An Izadi Kurd woman

Mina #2: An Afghan woman

Mina #3: An African woman

Interpreter: An Iranian woman, about 35 years old

EDITORS' INTRODUCTION

Naghmeh Samini (b. 1973) is a distinguished Iranian playwright, theater scholar, and screenwriter. Born and raised in Tehran, she received her PhD in art research from the University of Tarbiyat Modares, and has taught at universities in Iran and the US. Alongside her nearly twenty plays, Samini is the author of monographs on Persian literature, mythology, and drama, such as *The Book of Love and Magic* (2000) and *The Theatre of Myths* (2008). She is also the co-writer of *Shahrzad*, the immensely popular historical drama television series (2015–18). Samini began writing plays in the late 1990s, and some of her most acclaimed works include *Sheklak* [Mimicry] (2006), *Rāz'hā va Dorugh'hā* [Secrets and Lies] (2002), *Khāneh* [Home] (2009), *Khāb dar Fenjān-e Khāli* [Dream in the Empty Cup] (2011) and *Hayoola-khāni* (2017). Samini runs creative writing workshops and delivers lectures on cinema and theater across the world. Her plays, which articulate local and global social issues while experimenting with form and structure, have been staged in Iran, France, India, and the US.

With *The Child*, Samini explores the fraught relationship between power and the female body. Centering on three refugee women who all share the name Mina, the play follows their interrogation at the hands of an unnamed, petulant border officer (referred to as "Man" in the script). With the aid of an interpreter, the officer is tasked with determining which Mina is the mother of a child that was born in the refugee encampment. Throughout their testimonies, the Minas scoff at the officer's misogynistic threats, refusing to play along so that the baby stays in the country, even if its mother is deported. Each woman's story reveals a past in which their bodies were treated as disposable commodities for male pleasure, and pregnancy as an unfortunate, recurring consequence of this exploitation. But with the female solidarity built by their shared act of maternal disavowal, the Minas are able to reclaim power. Paradoxically, by denying their motherhood, the three women collectively share in this deeply maternal labor of protecting the child from deportation. The interpreter—whose voice we hear at the end of the penultimate scene—supports the Minas in her own way, speaking in languages that the officer cannot understand. As a largely silent surrogate for the playwright, she amplifies the Minas' struggles and advocates for a politics rooted in compassion, challenging the masculine nationalism that values borders over human beings.

Samini's use of the three Minas also brings to light the particular form of precarity that plagues immigrants, refugees, and sex workers who attempt to flee their dangerous homelands but are turned away or held in a dehumanizing limbo upon crossing a border. These issues are certainly timely and necessary for Iran (which has struggled to navigate an influx of refugees from Afghanistan, Syria, and other neighboring countries, particularly over the past decade), but Samini aims for the play to speak more universally by never naming the country the Minas are hoping to enter or the border officer's nationality. Although the interpreter is identified as an Iranian woman, Samini pushes further against the notion that this play is meant as solely a critique of Iran by including offhand references to other countries' treatment of refugees. For instance, Mina #3 warns the border officer of the consequences he would face if the titular child is put away in a cage, a statement that alludes to how the US border patrol infamously caged undocumented Mexican children in 2019. In all, with *The Child*, Samini has crafted a vital play that confronts the global treatment of refugees and the ubiquity of violence against women, while exem-plifying the hallmark of Iranian political theater: biting criticism, layers of ambiguity, and emotional depth.

THE CHILD

Naghmeh Samini

For my mother, with love

SCENE ONE. MINA #1: AN IZADI KURD[1]

The interrogation room. It is unimaginative and cold—a room with no spirit. Upstage is a window into another room, which is dark. One would assume that no one is in the room. The officer and Mina #1 are opposite one another. Both are wearing headphones. The Man speaks in his native tongue andf Mina speaks in Kurdish. Naturally they cannot communicate without the help of an interpreter who has not yet arrived. Mina #1 seems to be murmuring something repeatedly. She paces nervously and looks toward the room behind the window.

MINA #1. That child isn't mine. You can ask me a thousand times and I'll say the same thing. That child is not mine. I did not give birth to it. That child isn't mine. Do you understand? I'm not the mother of that child. Is there anyone who can translate what I'm telling you?

The Man listens calmly. He approaches Mina #1. She falls silent.

---

1 Izadi, or Yazidi, are a Kurdish community native to parts of Iran, Iraq, Turkey, and Syria, with the majority now living in Iraq. In 2014, the Izadi people of Shangal suffered a devastating genocide in the hands of Daesh—as the ISIS or ISIL is generally called in the Middle East. Nearly 5,000 men were murdered, while 7,000 Izadi women and girls were abducted, sold at slave markets, and subjected to rape or forced marriages to Daesh commanders.

FIGURE 22. *The Child*. Directed by Afsaneh Mahian at the Chaharsou Hall, Tehran, 2020. *Photograph by Akhtar Tajik.*

MAN. I can't understand what you're saying. Unless the light goes on in that room, unless this headphone connects, unless somebody translates word for word what you're saying, I won't be able to understand you. So, it really doesn't matter what you're saying. It could be meaningless sounds, or poetry, or some kind of confession that might impact your fate. Do you understand?

MINA #1. That child isn't mine.

MAN. I don't understand.

MINA #1. That child isn't mine.

MAN. Do you not get that I can't understand what you're saying? We won't understand each other until that light comes on. I could say anything right now and you wouldn't get it. I could share with you my deepest secrets and you wouldn't understand. I could say that I was in a dark place last night. A dark crypt full of gunpowder, dynamites and TNT. Someone asked me for a cigarette. I gave him one. And then I put one up to my own lips and lit it. Do you understand what I'm saying? No, you don't! I'm trying to say that you're just wasting your words and the energy it takes to say them. You're really going to need that energy soon.

MINA #1. I don't understand what you're saying. But if it's about the child, then that child isn't mine.

MAN. The interview won't happen today. They'll show you the way to the camp outside.

At that very moment, the light goes on in the Interpreter's room. The Man realizes this and returns. The silhouette of the woman is now visible behind the glass window. Her face is obscured; we can only see her shadow. We can't hear her voice. We are aware of her presence through the words of the woman and the officer.

MAN (*to the Interpreter*). You are half an hour late, this is unprecedented! (*Surprised*) You?! . . . What happened to the usual interpreter? . . . They transferred him this week? . . . They didn't tell me anything . . . Did they say I need an experienced interpreter for this case? . . . Are you experienced? . . . How's your Arabic? You know Arabic too? . . . But just knowing the language isn't enough for this. You have to understand *exactly* what they're saying, and you have to communicate the *exact* meaning to me. Sometimes a single word out of place can completely change everyone's fate . . . We had been working together for three years. Why did they have to transfer him to a new camp? . . . You must translate what I say precisely, word for word, "He said, he's saying, now he's trying to say . . . " None of that! Exactly what I say, with the same pronouns, the same grammar, the same verbs and the same adverbs. And vice versa . . . Got it?! (*To Mina #1*) It's necessary for you to know that anything you say here is going to be recorded and afterwards it can affect the decision they make about your case. Do you understand?

MINA #1. I understand. But the things you said earlier weren't translated for me. And what I was saying earlier wasn't translated for you either.

MAN. Things that don't need to be translated won't be.

MINA #1. But I want to know what you were saying. I also want *you* to know what *I* was saying.

MAN. I decide what gets translated or not here.

MINA #1. Did you know that the wind can even blow the spots off a cow's body?

MAN. What are you saying? (*To the Interpreter*) What is she saying?

MINA#1. The wind can blow the spots off a cow's body.

MAN. Why do all the Kurdish refugees waste their time reciting poetry?

MINA #1. Because there's four thousand years' worth of history behind us that can't be put into the words of any language. Because our past is as old as the sun, and the sun itself is a poem. And because our lives from the time we are born is a sad poem. Our children, they're all tired. From the moment they enter this world, they're too tired to even cry. They laugh from all of this exhaustion. This is why that child isn't mine. Because he isn't worn out.

MAN. We get to the child just in time.

MINA #1. Hasn't this whole interrogation been about the child?

MAN. I said we would talk about the child in due course.

MINA #1. It's so nice that gravity exists.

MAN. I don't understand you! What is it that is supporting the immigrants? (*To the Interpreter*) Are you translating it right? Your accent's getting in the way of me understanding exactly what you're saying.

MINA #1. Gravity won't allow you to cast us away from this planet. If you could, all of us would be floating around in the sky by now. With our little bundles and our muddy shoes, with our frostbitten children and our worn-out suitcases, we would float in the sky. Then, all the news reporters would surround us and would take our pictures. Our pictures would be so valuable. And you would shed tears for us, but you would be happy that we were far away from you and we wouldn't cause you any trouble. Did you see the picture of that child? Suffocated and bruised on the beach?

MAN. I'm the one asking questions here.

MINA #1. You like our children more as pictures rather than as living beings.

MAN. Did you know that by wasting our time, it is likely that you will stay seated in that chair years from now, just like this, answering the same old questions.

MINA #1. No! I'm sorry, my mind is jumbled. I haven't been able to sleep well for several nights. I cannot express myself . . . I'm not trying to waste anyone's time. I want these days to pass more quickly, I want to get to the city. I want to walk through the alleyways. I want to sleep somewhere with a window that opens out onto the street. A place where the windows don't have bars. I want a little bit of light. Not lamplight! Lamplight bothers my eyes.

MAN. If you want to get out of here, you must answer me clearly. Be precise, not poetic. A week ago, the Immigration Police arrested you and two other women, as well as a newborn baby, on the beach, and took all of you to a camp for illegal immigrants. All three of you deny that you are the mother of that baby. Meanwhile, none of you three have any travel documents. You claim that you are thirty-five years old.

MINA #1. I'm three hundred and fifty years old. I'm three thousand five hundred years old.

MAN. Please don't interrupt me until I finish asking the question . . . You claim that you are thirty-five years old, your name is Mina, and that you are an Izadi Kurd. You're from Iraq. That's it! No address, no identifiable name or last name.

MINA #1. My name is Mina because the smugglers would give this name to one out of every three women. I don't have a home, so I don't have an address. I don't have any relatives, so I don't have a last name. I don't have a family because all of them are dead. My father was buried under the rubble, my husband was gunned down, my brother was killed in battle, my sister and mother were made wives for Daesh.

MAN. What about children?

MINA #1. I don't have any.

MAN. Do you have any evidence to support the veracity of your claims and to prove that you are not aligned with terrorist organizations?

MINA #1. You're asking a sick, frail patient if she's been colluding with her virus?

MAN. I can't fill out these forms with poetry.

MINA #1. Show me a member of Daesh and I'll show you how I beat them and crush their bones beneath my feet.

MAN. That's what they all say. Even those women who willingly serve them say the same.

MINA #1. Just think how miserable those women must have been that they'd willingly become wives to Daesh.

MAN. I'm going to have to write that down on your form. As a refugee, defending the wives of terrorists can be detrimental for you, of course.

MINA #1. I'm not a refugee, I'm an immigrant.

MAN. This form is for refugees.

MINA #1. "Refugee" is your word, not ours! You invented it because it gives you power. The power to give refuge.

MAN. Whatever this form is, it's going to decide whether or not you should be deported. And I can't convince the court to keep you with an incomplete form.

MINA #1. Do you think I care whether I'm deported?

MAN. You don't?

MINA #1. No.

MAN. Then why did you become a refugee . . . or immigrate here?

MINA #1. Because taking one's own life is a grave sin.

MAN (*to the Interpreter*). Are you translating this correctly? What is she saying? . . . No, please don't try to explain it yourself, ask her to do so.

MINA #1. If I had stayed, I would have definitely died. Life is meaningless and empty, but it is on loan to us from God. The debt must be preserved, until that moment when God is ready to take it back.

MAN. What a heavy burden you've accepted from your God!

MINA #1. The debt of our God was in the warm, scarlet blood that pulsed through our veins and the black oil that lived under our feet. But you reversed them. Everywhere in Iraq is red with blood and our bodies are black from fire and smoke.

MAN. We reversed them? This "you" that you're referring to in your question is confusing—who exactly are you talking about?

MINA #1. "You" is a scary pronoun. It can point to whoever is opposite you. You understand the smell of its body, its stench. It can torture you, assault you, and when you try to escape it, you get snagged by another "you" who might think that you've destroyed their homeland. So you despise her.

It seems as if she can hear the voice of the Interpreter. For a moment she turns to face the direction of the Interpreter, then she looks at the Man while her words are being translated. She tries to play.

MINA #1. No, I don't want to say anything that might hurt my case. Say whatever you like. Say that I took back my statement. Say that by "you" I meant "no one."

MAN (*to the Interpreter*). She took her statement back?! So, what exactly was she saying in the statement she retracted? . . . "No one"?! . . . This kind of translation isn't useful here. Precision in words is important to me. Even pauses and silences. (*To Mina #1*) Let's continue.

MINA #1. Why should you fear a newborn baby? There are no bombs in its onesie.

MAN. For illegal immigrants, the law doesn't provide an age restriction.

MINA #1. Immigrants are neither legal nor illegal. One day your land will also be exhausted, at war, chaotic, and it'll be your children who must go from one place to another. All that matters is for the immigrant to get to a place that is safe.

MAN. So that they can make this new place unsafe?

MINA #1. I don't make any place unsafe. I work. I've worked my entire life. In Şingal,[2] I delivered more than a hundred babies.

MAN. Midwife?

MINA #1. OB/GYN.

MAN. Yes, that's written here!

MINA #1. But misery makes us all look identical.

MAN. You're not telling me the truth.

MINA #1. Everything I said was true.

MAN. As for the great sin . . . what did you say . . . (*Towards the Interpreter's room*) Yes, the mighty sin. (*To Mina #1*) You're not here for the mighty sin.

MINA #1. So why am I here?

MAN. When, precisely, did you leave Iraqi soil?

MINA #1. I don't remember. It seems like a thousand years ago.

MAN. How many days, approximately? How many months?

MINA #1. Maybe seven months . . .

MAN. You took the immigration route?

MINA #1. With three hundred dollars, from the border to Urfa, in Turkey. Then Lesbos, Greece. Fifty-two people in a boat made for fifteen. The boat sank and only the three of us survived, and we ended up here.

MAN. How many days did you wait for the smugglers at the border?

MINA #1. Twenty days . . . with no water or food, with three other women, shivering from the cold in our ragged clothes. We huddled together to find warmth in each other's bodies.

---

2 Also known as Shangal, Sinjar, and Shingal, this is an Izadi-populated district in present-day northern Iraq.

MAN. And how many days were you on the water?

MINA #1. I don't know . . . maybe five days or more.

MAN. Wasn't it difficult with a pregnant stomach?

MINA #1. That child isn't mine. You can't deport it with me.

MAN. No one said anything about deporting you.

MINA #1. But it's a possibility!

MAN. How could a mother ever abandon her child—for any reason? Although you probably don't know either. Because you confessed that you never had a child.

MINA #1. I was such a rotten mother that my children hated me.

MAN. More poetry?

MINA #1. It's reality, not poetry. I delivered one hundred babies. One day, all of those hundred Şingali children would come searching for me and would tear me apart piece by piece for dragging them out of their mother's safe bellies to suffer in this hell.

MAN. The court needs convincing evidence.

MINA #1. That child doesn't look like me. Its skin is soft and white. It's like a mirror. When they turn off the lights at night, we keep him in front of a small opening on the roof. A beam of light slips from the moon onto its body and the entire camp shines brightly. In that light, all of the women in the camp are beautiful. Their skin shines. Their rotten teeth vanish, their crooked bones straighten. He beautifies the eyes of the women in the camp with the light.

MAN. Look, lady! If you don't support your claims with evidence, they will decide your case based on the other Izadi women's cases. And right now, you are the first defendant.

MINA #1. This child, it's not a result of rape. A child of rape looks like the rapist. If I were impregnated by rape, I would have aborted the fetus.

MAN. So you would throw away God's loan?

MINA #1. God never forces a loan upon you.

MAN. Is life not a forced loan?

MINA #1. This is not a child of rape.

MAN. Fine! Calm down! (*To the Interpreter*) Am I making her upset?! . . . Where did you work before this? I mean what's your employment history? . . . That's quite clear! I must remind you that you don't have permission to give any hints to anyone on either side of this. Do you understand? (*To Mina #1*) Right now that child is bereft of any identity and past. Is that what you really want? Do you think someone without a past can still have a future?

MINA #1. I just don't want that child to share my own past, because then they will share my future too.

The Man shows a photograph to Mina #1. Maybe we see it too. The picture is of three women, three Minas in the dark. Their faces are indistinguishable, but one of the three women is pregnant.

MINA #1. What's this?

MAN. The border security cameras reported that one of the three of you was pregnant when you arrived on Greek soil.

MINA #1. You can't make out any faces in this. How could someone be certain this was us?

MAN. These three women are the three of you.

MINA #1. And how would someone be able to tell if I'm the pregnant one?

MAN. Then could you tell me which one of you was pregnant?

MINA #1. Sometimes all three of us. Sometimes just one of us. And sometimes only two. (*To the Interpreter*) Yes, that's precisely what I said. (*To the Man*) Women refugees flee with a pillow under their clothes. When traffickers have to choose between a pregnant woman or a young man, they choose the young man.

A moment of silence.

MAN. Can you put that pillow under your clothes?

MINA #1. This is against the law! You have no right . . .

MAN. You could choose not to do it. It's up to you. But in that case, this will probably take a long time to resolve.

Mina #1 looks at the pillow hesitantly. This is not easy for her.

MAN. I'll wait. I will look away if you're uncomfortable. (*To the Interpreter*) No! You can't tell me on your first day what is illegal . . .

Mina #1 uneasily stuffs the pillow under her clothes. It gives her the appearance of a pregnant woman. She is unhappy. It revives some memories for her. The Man stares at her.

MINA #1. Should I take it out?

MAN. Not yet. Wait a little longer.

MINA #1. Are you reconstructing the scene of a crime? Is an immigrant a criminal?

The Man takes a picture of her. He compares it with the picture of the three women.

MAN. Can you please walk a few steps?

Mina #1 stands up and takes a few steps.

MINA #1. Do you have any children?

MAN. I never wanted to have any kids. Can you please match the pose in this picture?

(*Mina #1 poses with disgust.*)

Could you please sit down, the way a pregnant woman might sit in a crowded boat?

(*Mina #1 sits down with disgust.*)

And could you please lie down? The way a pregnant woman might at a shelter?

(*Mina #1 lies down with disgust.*)

And if I may, act like you're in labor . . . I mean like you're in pain.

MINA #1 (*angrily*). No! I can't.

MAN. According to your file, you were a prisoner of Daesh for some time.

MINA #1. There were always enough young virginal girls around so that each night they could lie with a different one. They didn't need a thing from me.

MAN. The medical forensics report noted wounds, bruises, and sexually transmitted infections that typically result from having multiple partners.

MINA #1. I don't want to listen to this.

MAN. Can't this child be the result of one of those encounters?

MINA #1 (*distressed*). No, it can't be! Because when I'm raped, I know how to get rid of that filthy sperm and not let it grow inside me. Because by God, if anyone knew how to save herself from the sperm of a rapist, it's me. You lose your temper if someone hits you on the street, but it's so easy for you to talk about the most secret and private wounds on my body . . .

MAN. I'm sorry!

MINA #1. What's the difference between you and them? For either of you, women are just there to be impregnated.

MAN. I know it must have been very difficult.

MINA #1. Is that it?! "It must have been"? It was "probably" difficult to be turned into a prostitute overnight? How dare you say it was "probably" tough for you when men with the scent of sweat and war and the blood of your father and brother and husband use your body like a public toilet?

MAN. I said I was sorry.

MINA #1. That's not enough. Not even poetry is enough here anymore. No damn language can do this justice!

Mina #1 angrily removes the pillow from under her clothes. She is speechless. The Man is remorseful. He gives her a glass of water. The Man is silent.

FIGURE 23. *The Child.* Directed by Afsaneh Mahian at the Chaharsou Hall, Tehran, 2020. *Photograph by Akhtar Tajik.*

MAN. I think we should leave it to a DNA test.

MINA #1 (*worried*). A DNA test? I have the right to deny you permission.

MAN. Of course, I would need your permission, although for special circumstances . . .

Mina #1 falls silent. It seems that she is having an internal struggle. She glances at the Interpreter's room. The Man looks suspiciously at the Interpreter's room. It is as if they are exchanging words that the Man cannot hear.

MINA #1. I can tell you who the mother of the child is.

The Man falls silent; he was not expecting to hear this from the woman.

MAN. I'm waiting!

MINA #1. It's the woman in the blue niqab. The Afghan Mina.

MAN. And what's your reasoning?

MINA #1. Every night she sings a lullaby to the child. The child can only sleep in her arms.

MAN. That's not enough. Did you see the birth?

MINA #1. It was nighttime. Absolute darkness. Someone was crying in pain in one of the secret huts. They asked me to visit her. Her whole hijab was drenched with sweat and blood. I didn't see her face. I delivered the baby in the dark—the light was full of danger. But her voice . . . was the voice of that woman.

MAN. You're not worried that the child will be deported alongside the Afghan woman?

MINA #1. I'm not that child's mother.

MAN. Alright then. I think that's enough for today.

MINA #1. So there is no more need for a DNA test?

MAN. . . .

MINA #1. Have you ever crossed the border illegally?

MAN. No! Luckily.

MINA #1. Don't be so casual about "luck" . . . Did you know that I used to walk through the bazaar of Şingal, buy myself a red beaded shawl? I would hang out in small cafes and drink Arabian coffee with pistachio baklava . . . You know that they used to sell the most sensual and alluring clothes in our city?

(*The Man is stunned by Mina #1's question.*)

Clothes meant to reveal, not meant for wearing. Clothes made from Arab silk that could transform the ugliest bodies into the Queen of Sheba. Clothes that could drive any man mad even without being worn by women. We wished to get pregnant. We wanted children. Because we were happy and we were as assured of our happiness as you are now. I used to deliver those babies to bring happiness into the world, but as the wind blows, it takes with it the spots on cows . . . At the very least try to find meaning in this.

Silence. The Man gets up. He walks agitatedly. He approaches the woman.

MAN. Until we find out the identity of this child, your case won't be processed. Sometimes people have to wait around for years.

MINA #1. And their lips are sewn shut.

The Man falls silent. Darkness.

The Afghan Mina is now at the spot where the Kurdish Mina was. She is wearing a blue niqab.[3] *She is very scared and crouched in a fetal position. She can barely stand on her feet. The figure of the Interpreter can be seen on the other side of the glass. The Man takes a look at Mina #2's case file.*

MAN. Name?

MINA #2 (*to the Interpreter, excitedly*). Are you Iranian?! I could tell from your accent. For some time I worked with my husband in Iran.

MAN. Look only at me. (*To the Interpreter*) Emphasize that she may not talk to you . . . I don't care what she said or whether what she said was important. She is not allowed to speak with the Interpreter.

MINA #2 (*to the Interpreter*) I understand, Miss.

MAN. I'll ask again. Name!

MINA #2. Mina!

MAN. What is your real name?

MINA #2. My real name?

MAN. Your real name.

MINA #2. My real name?

Beat.

MAN. Your last name?

MINA #2. I am fine, sir! I'm cold, that's why I am trembling. But I am just fine.

MAN. Your last name?

---

3 Niqāb is a form of hijab that covers the face completely, leaving only a narrow slit for the eyes.

MINA #2. Ask me to go and climb Mount Qaf[4] and find a Simorgh egg and bring it back for you—I'll do it! Could a pregnant woman go and bring you back a Simorgh egg from Qaf?!

MAN. I don't know these stories. (*To the Interpreter*) No, I don't want you to explain them to me.

MINA #2. Can a woman in the last month of her pregnancy tell you a story? She doesn't even have the strength to drink a tarkari. (*To the Interpreter*) It's a kind of soup, a kind of Afghan soup.

MAN (*to the Interpreter*). Please only translate what I am saying. I already warned you that any communication with the immigrant is prohibited . . . I have no idea why they sent you again today . . .

MINA #2 (*ignoring him*). Or even me, being here! Just imagine! Can a woman in the last month of her pregnancy hide in a sheepskin? Can she ever endure all these nails and thorns? Hills and mountains?

MAN. Where is your family?

MINA #2. I don't have one. I don't have any family.

MAN. How can you not have a family?

MINA #2. When an Afghan woman marries, she loses her father and mother and siblings. Her husband's family becomes her own.

MAN. Are you married?

MINA #2. Yes, sir.

MAN. Where is your husband's family?

MINA #2. I don't have one, sir.

MAN. What don't you have?

MINA #2. I don't have any family.

---

4 An imaginary mountain in the Middle Eastern culture that surrounds the world. In Iranian myth and literature, it is one of the dwelling places of the legendary bird Simorgh. In Persian culture, it symbolizes inaccessibility and remoteness.

MAN. Pull your niqab down, I need to see your face.

Mina #2 hesitantly pulls down her niqab. There is great fear in her eyes.

MAN (*to the Interpreter*) I'm confused. I want to know where her husband's family is.

MINA #2. They are in Afghanistan . . .

MAN. And where is your husband?

MINA #2. My husband is a bandit. He stands on the top of hills and measures the beards of Afghan men.[5]

MAN. Is your husband in the Taliban?

MINA #2. No, sir.

MAN (*to the Interpreter*). I don't understand what she means. Are you translating correctly? . . . No, you're not translating it right. You have to translate whatever she says precisely.

MINA #2. My husband died.

MAN. You said your husband was in Afghanistan.

MINA #2. My husband is in Afghanistan.

MAN. What are you saying? (*To the Interpreter*) Translate correctly!

MINA #2. My husband died from a land mine. I loved him. My husband has two barren wives; I didn't want to marry him. It was forced. I was forced to become his wife. My husband tricked my husband to walk on a land mine so that he could take his brother's wife.[6] (*Fearfully*) If you send me back, they'll chop off my nose and tongue. They'll stick a hot skewer through one of my eyes . . . They'll leave

---

5 One of the demands of the Taliban is that men should grow out their beards. The Taliban takes punitive actions against those who do not comply.

6 Mina #2 refers to two husbands here. The first husband she talks about is in fact her second husband, who murdered his brother (Rashid, Mina #2's first husband) to marry Mina.

me with one eye so that I can do their work for them in that awful cold . . . Have you seen what they do to the nose of an adulterous woman? They lay her on the ground like this, they bind their hands and feet like this. They heat the blunt knife over the fire . . .

MAN. That's enough. This isn't relevant to your case file.

MINA #2. A pregnant woman is a captive of Āl.[7] Do I look like I am the prisoner of Āl?! If I'm shivering, it's just because I'm cold. The Afghan chill penetrates one's bones.

MAN. This is just a waste of time. (*To the Interpreter*) I see that she's sick. I understand she is scared. There's no need for you to remind me of that. (*To Mina #2*) How long did you live with your husband? When did you run away?

MINA #2. I lived with him for six months. I was escaping from him for nine months.

MAN. Where were you during these nine months?

MINA #2. I was hiding, first in my aunt's barn, then in the mountains, alone, then I made it to the border, and for three months I was in Iran. I worked as a laborer. In men's clothes. Until I wasn't able to anymore . . . I decided to escape to a safe place.

MAN. Why weren't you able to?

Mina #2 falls silent.

MAN. What happened?

MINA #2 (*to the Interpreter*). You should see that child. How could you be a woman and not want to be its mother? Is that possible?!

MAN. Don't talk to her. Did you give birth to the child in the camp?

---

7 Āl is a folkloric demon in the cultures of the Caucasus region, Iran, Armenia, and Central Asia. It is believed to be an evil entity that disrupts childbirth and frequently visits pregnant women to frighten them.

MINA #2. Which child? Whose child are you even talking about?

MAN. Your husband's.

MINA #2. Would he rape me if he was my husband?

MAN. What, a child can't be born of rape?

MINA #2. The child of rape comes out the color of wall plaster. It's pale and icy. This child has color. Its color is warm. Its body is warm. The child of rape becomes blind, sir.

MAN. Was your child blind?

MINA #2. I got pregnant a couple of times, but I would either abort them or give birth to dead babies. All of them were blind. There were two empty cavities where their eyes should have been. The child who is conceived while others watch has enough evil eyes on him to become blind. That's what the Afghans say. Is this child blind?

MAN (*to the Interpreter*). What is she saying? I don't understand.

MINA #2. His two barren wives were forced to watch us when he was on top of me, teaching them a lesson for their barren bellies. This child isn't blind. Have you seen his eyes? They're like two pieces of diamond. Completely black. The light in his eyes takes a person's breath away. This child is warm. If this child weren't there in that freezing cold water, we would have turned to ice. We held the baby's hands to stay warm. In the freezing cold of the camp, everyone would gather around the child to get some warmth from his body.

(*The Man is quiet. He jots down some notes.*)

Have you ever been obsessed with someone?

MAN. Not more than a week! (*To the Interpreter*) Don't translate that.

MINA #2. That child might have been mine if its father were my husband. When my husband was on top of me, I used to close my eyes and imagine my husband Rashid, who would hug me and keep me warm. One time I said his name under my breath. He pulled his pants up, picked up his cane, and he hit me every place he thought Rashid used to hold me. From head to toe. (*To the Interpreter*) No, miss, don't translate that. It's wrong. I'm ashamed.

MAN (*to the Interpreter*). I'm awaiting your translation . . . What did she say? . . . I mean what did she say that she doesn't want translated?! . . . No, a refugee has no right to say something and then insist it shouldn't be translated . . . It's my right, because I have to fill out these forms . . . Yes, because this is my country! . . . Fine! Let's continue. (*To Mina #2*) It's been reported that only you can put this child to sleep.

MINA #2. No one else in this camp knew any lullabies to sing to it. I sing and it falls asleep. You would go to sleep too if I sang for you. (*Toward the Interpreter's room*) Did you know, miss, when I sing the lullaby, it looks at me with its big eyes, and sucks my fingers. It sucks the cold straight from my bones.

MAN. Look at me, woman! Take that pillow and stuff it under your clothes. Please. (*To the Interpreter*) Translate exactly what I said.

Mina #2 reluctantly picks up the pillow and sniffs it.

MINA #2. It smells like the baby.

MAN. Put it under your clothes.

Mina #2 puts the pillow under her clothes. The Man takes a photo of her.

MINA #2. Don't force that baby on me, sir! It didn't come out of me. Would you have liked to be born of me? It's possible! If it were God's will, you could have been born of me. No matter how big you are. They blind her eyes. She's pretty. She becomes a man's sex toy before she even reaches puberty. They put rouge on her face, tie bells to her feet; it doesn't matter if it's a boy or girl; they make them dance; as they dance, men fondle them . . . Those boys and girls, they hide their pain either under their burqas or under their beards.

MAN. So what do you think happens to the baby here?

MINA #2. It's free here, sir!

MAN. No, it's not. This is the delusion of freedom. I shouldn't be saying this. Speaking it is against the law. But when you're this delusional . . . This child here is captive to its appearance. It is a prisoner to its fate. Best-case scenario, some White parents will adopt the child. But he will never feel like he belongs with them. At school, he will be hurt, he will get beaten. Children are cruel. They are the cruelest creatures on Earth. Every night those kids will see their fathers and brothers being attacked by people who look like this child, and then the next day they'll make him pay for it. They will gather around him and beat him.

MINA #2 (*restless*). No, sir . . . That's not what will happen . . . This child is strong . . .

MAN. He will grow up. He will get hurt in the street. No woman will pay him any attention. As soon as they find out where he's from, they will abandon him. His heart will be broken a thousand times. Your child's heart will be torn to pieces.

MINA #2. Stop it, sir . . . (*To the Interpreter*) Miss, tell him that's enough!

MAN. Look at me! (*To the Interpreter*) Tell her to look at me.

(*Mina #2 does not break her gaze from the Interpreter.*)

Tell her to look at me.

(*Mina #2 does not break her gaze from the Interpreter. The Man goes to stand in her line of sight.*)

All that'll be left of him is a thug who'll go out on Christmas Eve and attack those same women who humiliated him, rip their clothes off, and force himself onto them.

MINA #2. That's enough, sir . . .

MAN. Then the electric chair . . . and execution.

Mina #2 becomes extremely weak and collapses.

MINA #2. Where can we escape to, then?

MAN. I've been asking myself that same question for a long time. (*To the Interpreter*) You don't need to translate that . . . No, it's best that you don't translate it.

MINA #2 (*to the Man*). What are you trying to escape from?

Silence. The Man looks toward the Interpreter's room with doubt and anger. Mina #2 becomes dizzy. She wants to get up. But she can't. Her eyes are on the Interpreter's room. She seems to hear something.

MAN. That's enough for today. The DNA test will clear everything up.

MINA #2. I know whose child that is . . . The tall woman. At camp they call her the Black Mina.

MAN. Is this her?

The Man shows a photograph to Mina #2.

MINA #2. It is, sir.

MAN. And how do you know this?

MINA #2. I saw it.

MAN. What did you see?

MINA #2. I saw her breastfeeding. I saw the baby clinging to her, and then she held him beneath her clothes to feed.

MAN. That's not convincing enough. Did you see her in labor?

MINA #2. I think I did.

MAN. Did you see her, or do you just *think* you did?

MINA #2. I saw her . . .

MAN. Where?

MINA #2. On the boat.

MAN. This child was born on a boat?

MINA #2. Yes, sir.

MAN. I want you to tell me exactly what you remember about the birth.

MINA #2. It was foggy, sir. A thick fog. A lady was screaming, and it sounded like it was in that woman's language. The boat was so full that no one could move. Then came the sound of the baby crying. I'm cold, sir.

MAN. That's not enough. I need more detailed accounts in order to convince the court.

MINA #2. You saw her picture, sir. They call her the Syrian Monarlees. Do you know why they call her Monarlees?

MAN. Please don't derail the subject.

Mina #2 seems to hear something from the receiver.

MINA #2 (*to the Interpreter*). Mona Lisa?! . . . If this child grows to that age and his crying and laughter mixes together, I would be heartbroken, miss. I swear to Muhammad's God, my heart would break. (*To the Man*) I'm so cold, sir.

MAN (*to the Interpreter*). Can you tell me what's going on here? Are you an interpreter or Wikipedia?! Tell her that I need some clear answers to close the child's case file.

Mina #2 seems to have not heard him. She doesn't move.

MAN (*to the Interpreter*). Did you translate that? . . . I can see that she's not doing well, but there is a child left in this country's hands. His fate is unknown, and the law is unable to determine what to do with him. That child has a right to a mother, to an identity, to a past. Tell her what I said . . . The old interpreter never argued this much . . . This is my method. I've done it this way for years. It will take you a long time to realize that lies are the immigrants' tools. The will to survival can bring about anything in a person . . . Translate what I told you to translate.

(*Silence. Mina #2 doesn't react.*)

(*To the Interpreter*) I'm going to demand a new interpreter this minute.

Suddenly, Mina #2 gets up, takes the pillow out from under her clothes, and holds it as if she wants to put it to sleep. She sings a sad Dari Persian song to the pillow.

FIGURE 24. *The Child.* Directed by Afsaneh Mahian at the Chaharsou Hall, Tehran, 2020. *Photograph by Akhtar Tajik.*

Mina #3 is furious, restless, and impatient. She wears a headscarf in the style of Libyan women. The Man is more tired than before. The figure of the Interpreter can be seen on the other side of the glass.

MAN (*to the Interpreter*). I thought I wouldn't be seeing you today after all of the reports I filed against you . . . No, this isn't personal at all. You are working against them. I have to come to a decision. For, if I don't, their case file remains open and gets buried under a hundred other case files, and it's possible that they'll never get out of here . . . Listen! Either you act like you're a translating machine or it's best that you go. And I don't want to hear another word about it.

Mina #3 checks her headphones. She gets up, restlessly.

MINA #3. There's no sound coming out of the headphone. What are you saying? . . . I didn't do anything wrong. I want to leave. (*To the Man and towards the Interpreter's room*) I don't have anything to say. There are only a handful of words in my language: sandstorm, drought, hunger, thirst, death. And one sentence: the Earth is round. The Earth is round, meaning that it has no bottom, meaning that not everyone has to stay forever in the same hell they've always been in. It means that it's possible to rotate, just like the Earth rotates. You can ask me a thousand times, a thousand questions, and my answer will be this: the Earth is round, and I am not going back to Libya. And that's not my child.

MAN (*suddenly*). Sit down!

(*Mina #3 immediately falls silent. Then she hears something on the headphone. She understands the meaning of that sound. She sits down. The Man is quiet. Both are enraged.*)

Pick up that pillow.

MINA #3. Do you want me to smother you with it?

MAN. Pick it up.

(*Mina #3 picks up the pillow.*)

Hold it like it's a baby. Your baby . . . Do what I said!

Mina #3 cuddles the pillow as if a baby, squeezing it to her chest, and then she suddenly rips the pillow open. Feathers fill the space. Mina #3 approaches the Man menacingly.

MINA #3. You can't trap me with these games. This may make your pale White women emotional, not us, though! The hungry woman of the desert is like a wild animal. I want you to know something. Libyan means the Berber people. I've been in the pits of hell; nothing can get worse than that. I've been through thick and thin. I died of thirst, I froze to death, I drowned, I was shot, and if after dying four times I'm still alive, it means that I'm a monster and I'm going to take what you owe me. Now, if you try to deport me, then I'll set this place on fire so that both of us will go to hell, because nothing matters to me anymore. But if you want to make that child share my fate, then I will set the whole world on fire, watch me, I can do it. I breathe fire.

Mina #3 gets up and crosses to the glass wall of the Interpreter's room and punches it.

MINA #3. Tell him that I breathe fire. Even with the little Arabic that you know, you can still tell him that.

MAN (*to Mina #3*). Sit in your chair! And don't get up again from that seat, woman. (*To the Interpreter*) No! You absolutely cannot leave the translation room in the middle of work. You may choose not to come back to work tomorrow, but you can't go now . . . A translator is not allowed to run out of breath in the middle of translating!

These things are normal in this room. Now tell me. What did she say? I want to know word for word . . . Exactly . . . Is that it?

MINA #3. You don't understand that a woman's womb is a borderless land. The child inside her belongs to no land, not even to the homeland of its mother. Don't you understand that you could have been born in any hellscape on this planet, if your mother's belly had risen anywhere but here? Your mother never asked you where you'd like to be popped out, did she? No mother asks that. It only takes a moment—two thrusts back and forth and the baby is conceived! In any place, in any gutter, any hell. Now what if you switched places with me . . . Why do you want to send that child back to rot?

MAN. I don't want to do that. We are not here to discuss whether you'll be deported or not.

MINA #3. Of course, you are here for that! You're lying. You're all lying.

MAN. It is my obligation to gather information and clarify the situation.

MINA #3. If you had been born to one of us three, would you still have tried to clarify the situation?

MAN. I ask the questions here.

MINA #3. You're not asking questions. You're pissing on me. Then you return me to the gutter where I come from. There, where I come from, is the toilet for your neat and pretty country. You've planted toilets here and there all over the world so that you never forget how lucky and happy you are.

MAN (*to the Interpreter*). Tell her to be quiet or I'll send a blank case file to the court, and that won't be in her best interest, or the baby's. (*To Mina #3*) What you just said could be interpreted as a terrorist threat, which would mean they'd have to deport you.

(*Mina #3 sits down. She is nervous and restless. The Man is quiet for some time. He tries to regain his composure.*)

(*To Mina #3*) Which among the three of you breastfeeds that baby?

MINA #3. I don't breastfeed him. I just let him bite at my dry chest.

MAN. Why you, of the three women?

MINA #3. Because he smells me and I smell like his mother.

MAN. Why should you smell like his mother?

MINA #3. Because I smell like his mother.

MAN (*to the Interpreter*). Translate my question correctly! Why should you smell like his mother?

MINA #3. Because I smell like his mother.

MAN. Why should you smell like his mother?

MINA #3. Because I had a miscarriage on the road.

MAN. You never mentioned that in the earlier interviews.

MINA #3. For a starving woman, having a miscarriage is like eating food.

MAN. Hunger makes you have a miscarriage?

MINA #3. Hunger makes you sell your body off!

MAN. Did the miscarriage happen on the boat?

MINA #3. No! It was on a dark night. In a room at camp.

MAN. Did they bring someone to visit you? A woman, I mean, that might have wanted to help you?

MINA #3. I don't remember. Maybe there was.

MAN. Was there also a child born on the boat?

MINA #3. Possibly. Everyone was screaming on the boat. It seemed like all the women were in labor.

MAN. Did you see a child being born on that boat?

MINA #3. There was a baby, covered in its mother's placenta. He was passed among a couple of people and was finally put into my hands.

MAN. How would you convince me that your child was actually miscarried and this isn't your baby?

MINA #3. The children of prostitutes in the Fazan region[8] are either born dead or disfigured, and their bodies are as hot as a furnace. It's like they arrived from hell, and they do nothing but cry. This child's body is cool like a cloud. He is not hot, he has descended from above and he only laughs. Even when he is hungry, he laughs. And when he laughs, the whole camp laughs. They dance to the sound of his laughter. A strange dance. Everyone dances in a different style. At nights in the camp, everyone dances to its laughter. Everyone in their own way.

Mina #3 does a melancholy dance. It is as if this dance reveals her anger.

MAN. I think our only option is to do the test. That's enough for today.

Mina #3 stares at the Interpreter's room.

MINA #3. And what if I lied? If the mother of the child is one of us three? A woman who could ease the child's pain . . .

The Man stares at Mina #3. Silence.

MAN. Imagine this. It might have been a Kurdish woman who gave birth to him in a fog, or at night, and you didn't see that moment. Or maybe the child grew simultaneously in three wombs. One woman gave birth to his hands, you his feet, and an Afghan woman his body. Sure, go ahead and translate this for her.

---

8 A dry region in southwest Libya.

The Man laughs. He is nervous. Mina #3 approaches the Interpreter's room. She punches the glass.

MINA #3. Tell him that that child is not one hand and one foot and one body. Do you understand what I'm saying? Tell him that we three saved him through thick and thin. Get out of there, I want for you to look him in the eyes when you are telling him what I'm saying. I want you to tell him that I will set him on fire if he decides to put that child in a cage, or if he returns him to that hell we came from. I will tear him apart. I breathe fire. I will destroy him. I'll rip apart his body and hands and feet. We will eat him alive. Each of us will become pregnant with a piece of him. (*To the Man*) Do you hear me? We'll become pregnant from pieces of you. One with your hand, one with your foot, me with your body . . . And we'll be deported back to that hell where we came from and each part of you will be delivered on those soils. A piece of you in Iraq, a piece of you in Afghanistan, a piece of you in Libya. Then you'll understand what you should be laughing at.

MAN. Get out! Now! Someone will lead you back to camp.

(*The Man practically shoves Mina #3 toward the door. Now he is left alone.*)

(*To the Interpreter*) It's your fault if this woman or any of them gets deported. This will happen to them because of the stories you made up in that dark room and whispered into their ears. How else would they be able to communicate with one another, when they don't understand each other's languages? This is the danger; this is the threat. You all stick to one another like drops of mercury, you multiply like ants, you cross the border like grasshoppers, until one day we open our eyes and see that you've conquered the whole country that we toiled to build . . . One day you won't see anyone on the street who looks like you . . . No! I won't stop! . . . I'm still talking . . . This is what an interpreter does, ma'am. No one has ever asked an interpreter whether they believe in what they're saying. An interpreter is a machine. Like a typewriter . . . What?!

The Man angrily yanks off the headphones and the sound of a woman comes up on the speaker. Now we can hear her voice, and she speaks in the same accent as the Man.

INTERPRETER'S VOICE. Tell me, if you could choose where you had been born, where would you have chosen?

MAN. There's no reason for me to answer that question.

INTERPRETER'S VOICE. You don't answer because you're afraid! Because this question forces you to face the fact that no one is to blame for where they were born. Because maybe everyone's wish is to be born someplace else.

MAN. Today's session is over!

INTERPRETER'S VOICE. Seriously, why won't you let go of this child when no one else claims him? Do you want to force that child to be tied to his doomed fate? If you were in that child's place, and all of these women would have given their lives to let you have the impossible chance to determine the place of your birth, and there was one person who wanted to take this chance away from you, wouldn't you have wanted him to be torn to pieces? Why can't you understand that these three women are giving their lives so that their child wouldn't be born on a border or in a war zone or be starving or living in destitution? Why don't you understand?

Darkness.

The same room. Three months later. The Man and the Interpreter are seated across from one another. Next to each of them is a cup of coffee.

MAN. I thought you'd never come back.

INTERPRETER. I didn't come back.

MAN. But you're here now.

INTERPRETER. I didn't come here to work. I am not made for this job. I learned that three months ago.

MAN. I was thinking about you all this time. "I was your mouthpiece for one week, and I said things that I never believed."

INTERPRETER. Did I really say that? I don't remember.

MAN. You really said that.

INTERPRETER. Maybe I did.

MAN. I've interviewed them many times since, and they've never been as truthful as they were on those days with you. When you defended them.

INTERPRETER. I did not defend them. I protected them. I was afraid of what they could become. I had the feeling that they could transform into any shape. They could turn into a whale in the ocean and swallow all the water in the world, or become tiny worms and seek refuge in the hottest spot of the Earth's core. A place where no one could reach them.

(*The Man is confused to hear her talk about things that resemble his dreams. He stares at the Interpreter. Silence.*)

It seems that sometimes it's easier to translate than to come up with your own words. I don't know how to talk about it. Or maybe I do, but I'm afraid.

MAN. Does it concern me?

INTERPRETER. Yes . . . but not directly.

MAN. I admit that I am disappointed.

The Interpreter puts her hands on the folder in front of the Man.

INTERPRETER. I think my answer is in here.

MAN. How did you know that today was the day?

INTERPRETER. It wasn't difficult to guess.

MAN. So that's why you're here, then?

INTERPRETER. It can change my entire life. It's hard to explain. I'm really scared. But I've been thinking about it night and day for three months. This is the only thing that . . . did I say it could change my life? Much more, even. It could save me.

MAN. Now I really need someone to translate what you're saying.

(*He wants to open the folder. The Interpreter stops him.*)

No?!

INTERPRETER. No!

MAN. So if you didn't want to know, why did you come here?

INTERPRETER. For a very small possibility . . . For a very distant hope. For the child.

The Man seems to realize what she means.

MAN. Is that why you tried to get them to constantly deny that they are the mother?

INTERPRETER. I didn't do that.

MAN. Yes, you did just that.

INTERPRETER. I didn't do that.

MAN. Denying it doesn't change anything. The case is now closed. And you wouldn't be here, if it weren't for this.

INTERPRETER. I've been here for ten years. I sat in a chair, waiting. What difference does it make, whether it were a chair in a bar on ____ street, or some wobbly chair in a dark restaurant in the ____ neighborhood, or a rented metal chair in a small, rented house in the ____ back alleys.[9] All of these chairs put me in a situation where I'm lonely and waiting. As I get up from each chair, I feel even more alone. Relationships last a year when you are young, then they become shorter and shorter as you get older. My last lover left me after three weeks. Of course, the problem is with me. Iranians are strangers to me. Every year I become less Iranian. Foreigners find me to be a stranger too. Every year we are here less and less. Every year I understand better that I am not like you. I'm lost and alone. That child can free me from these chairs. He can bring meaning to my days. I can find myself in him. I could at least become two persons with him—a land that has a population of two people. My homeland, with my self-defined borders . . . It's hard to explain. But I am ruined if these documents prove that the mother of that child is any of those three women.

MAN. Why does it have to be this child?

INTERPRETER. Because it has to be this child. Because every word that those three women said to deny the child made me want him more. Because on that very day, ______, I conceived that child through those three women and through you.[10]

MAN. Through me?!

---

9 The blank spaces are intended to be filled in with names of streets and neighborhoods reflective of the city in which the play is being performed. [Playwright's note]

10 The blank space should be replaced with the date of the performance. [Playwright's note]

(*A long silence. The Man gets up. He takes out the folder.*)

You know that it's not simple. You'll have to wait for many days, and then you'll have to answer a lot of questions. You may become very disappointed at times . . . Are you not afraid of the effects of genetics and how it might shape the child's character?

INTERPRETER. I don't know.

MAN. We inherit everything from our parents. Many things, actually.

INTERPRETER. But I didn't return to my origins. To what my mother and father were like. Otherwise, I would be a patient in a mental hospital right now, or depressed and isolated in a room filled with books. But I'm sitting here instead, and every bit of me is yearning to care for that child . . . I know that if he cries, I should put my hand on his tiny belly until he calms down, and if I want to give him milk, I have to let him smell me first, and if I want to put him to sleep . . .

(*The Interpreter begins to sing the Afghan lullaby, the same one that the Afghan Mina sang. The Man opens the folder in front of the Interpreter. She turns away.*)

I can't face it . . . I've lived with this dream for three months.

MAN. Look!

The Interpreter turns around. There is no paper in the folder. The folder is empty.

INTERPRETER. Did I make a mistake? Is today not the day?

MAN. It is my job to report the results to the court. And I won't do it. I'd already decided this. The child will go to the orphanage. The report explains that none of those three women is the child's mother. No one can track the test results amidst all these immigrants, all these case files, all these tests. So the child will go to the orphanage.

But you shouldn't let him stay there. The pain that this child would feel at the orphanage is deep, perhaps even deeper than the pain he suffered amidst blood, war, hunger, and fire.

INTERPRETER. I don't understand.

MAN. It's difficult to explain, and I'm not really connected to my past, except in dreams. It's hard to explain, but I saw the child. For the test, I had to be there and I saw him. I saw the child.

INTERPRETER. If hearing about him drives me so crazy, why shouldn't seeing him drive you mad?

MAN. Those three women's cases are so complicated. Maybe they'll be able to stay, or maybe they'll be deported. They will be lucky if they hear an answer soon, with all those hundreds of cases being added every day.

(*A ringing is heard.*)

You have to go. Just yesterday, three illegal immigrants were brought to the camp. Three men who don't have any documents. I have to work all night on this . . . You have to hurry. For the child.

The Interpreter gets up.

INTERPRETER. It's just that . . . Can I know who the real mother is?

MAN. Maybe it's best that you don't. Then you can raise him more easily. You won't spend every moment thinking that he's becoming like one of them. If you don't know, then day by day, the child will grow to be more like you.

INTERPRETER. Thank you!

MAN. Maybe we'll see each other again.

INTERPRETER. Maybe!

MAN. And to answer your question . . . I don't know of any place on Earth where I wish I'd been born.

INTERPRETER. So it's clear that we messed up all of history.

The Man and the Interpreter both laugh. The Interpreter leaves. The Man is alone. He gets up. He paces, anxiously. He goes and sits in the immigrant's chair. He stares at the place where he once stood. It's as if he is talking to the empty chair.

MAN. I had a strange dream last night. I dreamt that my mother was a small marten in a tree. I dreamt that my mother was a fox in a forest, I dreamt that my mother was a whale in the ocean, I dreamt that my mother was a tiny worm burrowing into the ends of the Earth. I go after her. I lose her along the way. I go back and the ground keeps getting darker and darker and darker and I'm alone and scared and lonelier. I call out for my mother, and she's not there. I dig through layer after layer of the soil until I reach the center of the Earth. It's a place that is hot, filled with fire, on the verge of explosion due to its mass. The Earth is heavy. And it is cracking open at its core. My mother is there with the same smile on her face that she carried through her death. My mother talks to me in her own language, asking if I have a cigarette? Her language is strange. I never wanted her to speak in this language. I hated the looks others would give me when I would speak in that language. When I was bullied by the children at school for speaking a different language. Because it revealed that I'm a stranger. One night I went to sleep and the next morning when I woke up, I had completely forgotten my mother's tongue. I couldn't understand her anymore. But this time, in this dream, I remember my mother's language—without a translator—and I have a cigarette. I light her cigarette. It's as if only one spark is needed to set fire to all that is already burning. And then . . . BOOM. I see that the Earth has become thousands of little planets without any borders. My mother and I have a planet to ourselves, and we are alone on it. And I tell my mother in her tongue how much I've missed her. Is there anyone that can translate what I say?

Darkness.

BIRD OF DAWN

Sepideh Khosrowjah

Translated by
Hesam Sharifian

Original title; *Morgh-e Sahar*

Written in 1995

First performed in 1997, Berkeley, CA, directed by Hamid Ehya

First performed in Iran in 2012 at the Entezami Theatre at the Iranian Artists' Forum, Tehran, directed by Ahmad Asoudeh

Published in Persian by Nila Books, 2007

CHARACTERS

Ms. Arjumand, in her 70s

Sima, 35 years old

Camille, in her 20s

Time: The year 1995

EDITORS' INTRODUCTION

Sepideh Khosrowjah (b. 1965) is an Iranian-American playwright, theater director, actress, and the co-founder of Darvag Theater group, an Iranian troupe based in Berkeley, CA. Born and raised in Tehran, she is the author and translator of more than fifteen plays and an accomplished director. Khosrowjah moved to the US in 1978 but never lost her close contact with Iran. Since 1985, she has acted in plays directed by distinguished Iranian directors in Iran and the US, such as *Marg-e Yazdgerd* [The Death of Yazdgerd] (1985), *Mosāhebeh* [Interview] (2013), *Negin* (2015), and *Tarabnāmeh* [The Book of Revelry] (2016). She has also directed her own plays, staged in both countries: *Āyeneh* [Mirror] (1985), *Mard, Chāhār Zanash va Mādarash* [The Man, His Four Wives, and His Mother] (1994), *Morgh-e Sahar* [Bird of Dawn] (1997), and *Dar Soog-e Kāzem Ashtari* [In Memory of Kazem Ashtari] (2003). Holding bachelor's and master's degrees in mathematics, economics, and cinema studies, she is the writer and director of the short film, *Lemon Cake* (2019).

With *Bird of Dawn*, Khosrowjah explores the lives of Iranian women living in the diaspora as they navigate complex relationships with their homeland, the men in their lives, and seek community. Inspired by Marsha Norman's play, *Third and Oak: The Laundromat* (1980), the title of Khosrowjah's play functions on multiple levels. On the one hand, it is a metaphor for the three central women, who bump into one another at a laundromat at three o'clock in the morning. For many Iranians, however, the title *Morgh-e Sahar* would immediately connote the famous song of the same name that has played a significant role in their cultural memory. This song originated as a poem by Mohammad-Taqi Bahar (1886–1951), who was a prominent Iranian writer, journalist, politician, and professor of literature, and it was later set to music by Morteza Neydavoud (1900–90) and first recorded in 1927. Bahar's poem is thought to be a reaction to the tumultuous political situation surrounding the Persian Constitutional Revolution (1905–11), and the song manifests the collective aspiration of Iranians for freedom and justice. Khosrowjah's play begins and ends with the titular song. As each woman tells her own story, we hear their individual "songs" that tie them back to Iran and a feeling of (be)longing. The play is mostly written in Persian, although the women jump back and forth between speaking Persian and English (sometimes juggling both in the same sentence), and their differing masteries of each language speaks to their complex lives lived between two worlds. In the translation, we have noted those moments that were originally spoken in English with bold type, although in performance, one might distinguish between these sections by the use of Persian-American accents to convey the characters' use of English.

By incorporating three generations of Iranian-American women, Khosrowjah's play interrogates the clash between the old guard of Persian cultural purists and the younger generation that attempts to assimilate with Western culture. This debate between tradition and modernity has been central to Persian cultural politics for over a century. Meanwhile, Khosrowjah's attention to specificity in language (both Persian and English) attests to her characters' wistful attachments to their homelands and their sense of shared identity. Interestingly, although *Bird of Dawn* is set in Los Angeles, it presents the most overtly Iranian characters and narrative among the plays in this anthology. Nevertheless, Khosrowjah's play deals with themes that reach far beyond Iran—exploring diasporic identities and longing, probing generational conflicts, and examining the shifting roles of women as both personal and systemic forms of misogyny come under growing scrutiny.

BIRD OF DAWN

Sepideh Khosrowjah

A laundromat in Los Angeles with several washers and dryers, a table for folding clothes, a payphone with a chair next to it, and a table in the middle, scattered with a few old magazines and surrounded by a few chairs. A large clock on the wall reads 3 a.m., which is when the play takes place.

Lights up. Ms. Arjumand, a woman in her seventies, enters. She holds a basket filled with clothes, with a cassette player on top. With deep sadness on her face, she sets the basket on the table, takes out the cassette player, and turns it on. The song "Bird of Dawn" begins to play.[1] *She takes some men's clothes out of the basket and smells them, then carries the basket to a washer. She chooses a machine carefully, but lingers before throwing the clothes in. Very slowly she puts the clothes in the machine, as if she is participating in a mourning ritual, or scattering someone's ashes in the sea. She adds laundry detergent and turns on the washer. She stares at it for a while before sitting down. The cassette player is still playing "Bird of Dawn," but the song gets cut off for a moment, with someone calling "Parvin," and then resumes. Ms. Arjumand rewinds the cassette to hear the voice again. She smiles. Then she takes a deck of playing cards out of her purse and starts a game of fortune telling. She is not yet done with laying the cards on the table before Sima enters.*

Sima is about thirty-five years old. She doesn't expect to see anyone at the laundromat at this hour, so she is shocked to see Ms. Arjumand, who also takes a quick peek at her. Their eyes meet briefly. Sima decides

---

1 The song is a passionate cry for liberty from Iranians who have endured through time. In the form of a dramatic monologue, the poet addresses the bird of dawn, urging it to sing of the ordeals that Iranian people have faced through history.

to leave but then changes her mind. Holding a clothes basket filled with sheets, she tries not to disturb Ms. Arjumand. Sima seems to be a very kind woman but is a bit nervous tonight. She gently puts the basket on the table and approaches a washing machine. All of a sudden, Sima realizes that she has forgotten something and wants to leave. She looks at Ms. Arjumand but hesitates to ask for help. Finally, she decides to do so.

SIMA. **Excuse me!**[2]

(*Ms. Arjumand doesn't feel like answering.*)

(*Louder*) **Excuse me!**

MS. ARJUMAND (*compelled*). **Yes?**

SIMA. **I've forgotten my laundry detergent. Can I borrow some from you?**

MS. ARJUMAND. **Borrow? You mean you'll give it back to me?**

(*Sima is upset.*)

Sure. Help yourself. How many loads do you have?

SIMA (*looking at her basket*). **Only one.**

MS. ARJUMAND. **I'm so sorry. I guess that you either need to wait or come back later.**

SIMA (*surprised*). **How come?**

MS. ARJUMAND. **My machine is the only one that's working. The others eat your coin and they can't do anything.**

SIMA (*distressed and indecisive*). **Well, I don't know. Maybe I'll come back later.**

---

2 **Bold typeface** indicates that the text was written to be spoken in English in the original Persian play.

FIGURE 25. *Bird of Dawn*. Directed by Hamid Ehya in Berkeley, CA, 1997. *Photograph by Hamid Ehya.*

(*Ms. Arjumand is pleased that her lie worked and Sima is leaving, but Sima stays and starts toying with the machines. Ms. Arjumand is nervous that her lie might be discovered. Sima realizes the deception but decides not to make Ms. Arjumand uneasy.*)

I wonder why there is no sign?

MS. ARJUMAND. **They were not working yesterday, maybe they are fixed now.**

SIMA. **Maybe.** (*She decides it is time to reveal that she is Iranian.*) Excuse me, ma'am, are you Iranian?

MS. ARJUMAND (*annoyed at not being left alone*). No dear, I'm African. Of course, miss. Yes, unfortunately, I am Iranian, that's why I'm listening to "Bird of Dawn."

SIMA. I'm sorry, I didn't want to disturb you. That's why I started off with English. I thought you'd say something if you wanted to. Didn't you notice my accent?

MS. ARJUMAND. I notice Iranians from hundreds of miles away, my dear.

SIMA. How so?

MS. ARJUMAND. I don't know, we are all miserable; and somewhat obnoxious.

SIMA (*taking offense*). How are we being obnoxious?

MS. ARJUMAND. I mean we've really been through the wringer; we think we are so special. One more thing we all share is sad eyes.

SIMA. Well, it's 3 a.m.—everyone's tired.

MS. ARJUMAND. No, dear. This has nothing to do with not sleeping tonight or the night before. It is due to centuries-long hardships.

SIMA. How beautiful. You are right. I couldn't have said it any better. (*Pause*) Why didn't you say anything about being Iranian? Why didn't you speak with me in Persian?

MS. ARJUMAND. I don't dare to be that rude. I no longer have the courage to ask my countrymen whether they are Iranians. I swear I've been let down so many times that I don't dare to take that kind of risk anymore. Besides, between the two of us, you were certain that I was Iranian, but you started talking in English. And now I should have humiliated myself and asked whether you were Iranian? I was humming along to "Bird of Dawn."

SIMA. I'm sorry. I didn't mean ill when I spoke in English. Rest assured I am not that kind of Iranian. (*Silence. She sits; and as it appears, she has no intention of leaving.*) Do you live around here?

MS. ARJUMAND. Yes.

SIMA. I am Sima.

MS. ARJUMAND. Nice to meet you. (*Pause; she hesitates to introduce herself, but finally*) I am Arjumand.

SIMA. I'll wait until you are done with the machine, because it's too hard for me to go back and forth.

MS. ARJUMAND (*not particularly pleased*). Suit yourself.

SIMA. I won't be disturbing you. Please keep playing.

(*Ms. Arjumand continues her card game of fortune telling; she doesn't seem to be interested in Sima's interruptions.*)

Are you reading your fortune? (*Silence.*) I used to do it all the time. I was so addicted to it that it had turned into a crazy obsession. I mean, I was getting to a dangerous point. Like going as far as using the cards to see if the tea was steeped or not.

MS. ARJUMAND (*raises her head after a while*). Maybe you should try other machines to see if they've been fixed or not.

SIMA (*not wanting to move*). When did you say they were broken? Yesterday? It's impossible that they're already fixed. Doesn't matter, I'll read a magazine, or write a letter. I won't be disturbing you. Why did you turn off the cassette player? I love "Bird of Dawn." I love the old *Irooni* songs.

MS. ARJUMAND. "Irani." Irani, not "Irooni."[3]

SIMA (*shocked*). I'm sorry, Irani.

---

3 "Irani" is a formal adjective akin to "Iranian," which is commonly used by the people of Iran to refer to their nationality. "Irooni" is a more informal and common term used by some in the diaspora to describe their origin. Ms. Arjumand's disdain for "Irooni" is rooted in this cultural tension. She believes that those who use "Irooni" to describe themselves have been away from Iran for too long.

MS. ARJUMAND. This new generation, they haven't even set foot in Iran, or have never returned after moving away, completely clueless—but they keep saying "Irooni," acting like they're natives.

SIMA. I am not from this new generation. I came here after high school. But you're right, we should say "Irani."

(*Silence. Ms. Arjumand is surprised by Sima's friendliness, but still continues to be grumpy. Sima starts reading a magazine.*)

Do you go to . . . (*careful not to say "Irooni"*) Iranian concerts?

MS. ARJUMAND. No. I have nothing to do with the Iranians here, or, as you say, "Iroonis."

SIMA. I mean traditional music,[4] not these new untalented singers who pop up every day. Traditional music like Alizadeh,[5] Nazeri,[6] and the like.

MS. ARJUMAND. No, unfortunately, I haven't been able to see them. (*Gentler*) You must know how difficult life is outside of one's country. You need to be in the mood to go to concerts. And more importantly, you need money. These people are ruthless. Twenty-five dollars for a ticket! As if we are printing money here!

SIMA. Yeah, you are right! The reason I asked—I don't exactly remember which one, but one of these traditional music groups who came here gave a fantastic rendition of "Bird of Dawn." It was so beautiful that I cried. I got up to clap as my tears rolled down. People applauded for a long time until they came back and performed the song again.

---

4 *Dastgāhi* is the Persian name for Iranian classical music, consisting of seven modal systems (or *dastgāh*) that form the basis for improvisation.

5 Hossein Alizadeh (b. 1951) is an eminent Iranian musician and composer famous for his tār and setār performances.

6 Shahram Nazeri (b. 1950) is a revered Iranian tenor, well known for his traditional Kurdish and Persian songs.

I wish they hadn't. The second time was not as good as the first. We just wanted to stand there and clap.

MS. ARJUMAND (*having forgotten her initial bitterness*). Really? Everybody liked it? Even the younger people?

SIMA. Yes, ma'am. Young and old.

Sima continues to browse the magazine.

MS. ARJUMAND. That's great. I always say these kids don't know what kind of culture we had back home; had they known, they would have liked it.

SIMA (*pausing; looking at her magazine*). Oh my God, have you heard that in Afghanistan they have fired all women from their jobs, and they've closed the girls' schools?

MS. ARJUMAND. We always thought things couldn't be worse than they were for us.

SIMA. It says here that Googoosh is traveling abroad in a month.[7]

MS. ARJUMAND. They've been saying that for a long time. But that's something exceptional! If she comes, I will go to her concert. (*Pause*) Well, if I can manage to make it work.

SIMA. You like Googoosh?

MS. ARJUMAND. I have fond memories of some of her songs. I'm just saying!

---

7 Fa'eqeh Atashin (b. 1950), whose stage name is Googoosh, is a prominent Iranian pop singer and actress who rose to fame before the 1979 Revolution. After the revolution, women singers were banned from the stage, prompting many of them to leave Iran. Googoosh, however, remained in the country for many years, before eventually emigrating in 2000. Her return to the stage marked a powerful comeback, stirring deep nostalgia among many Iranians who remembered her pre-revolutionary hits.

Sima suspects that Ms. Arjumand has financial difficulties or something along those lines.

SIMA. I don't have anyone to go with. If you'd like, we can go together . . . I'd come and pick you up. My treat. I insist.

MS. ARJUMAND. You are kind. No offense I hope, but I don't think you really mean it. I've learned not to count on anyone. When you leave this laundromat, you're not gonna even remember me.

SIMA. Ms. Arjumand, you're wrong about me. I am not one of those people. I stand by my word.

MS. ARJUMAND. Well, I should see how it works with my husband's schedule.

SIMA. Oh, your husband is here too?

MS. ARJUMAND. Yeah, why?

SIMA. Nothing. It's just that many Iranian women live here with their children, while their husbands are back in Iran. I mean—not that they are divorced or anything. You know. Because of life's circumstances. It's very good that you're not alone. This is exactly why people get married.

(*Ms. Arjumand looks at her but says nothing.*)

I mean . . . for when the kids are grown up and gone.

MS. ARJUMAND (*very gently*). No, I'm not alone.

SIMA. Where is he?

MS. ARJUMAND. Who?

SIMA. Mr. Arjumand?

MS. ARJUMAND. Mr. Arjumand? Uh, my husband's name is not Arjumand. It's Tavakkoli. He's in Las Vegas. He went there with his friends. He really likes it there. He says, "Parvin, when I pull the crank on these slot machines, I don't think about anything but the machine. Nothing!" (*She contemplates*) Yeah, he is in Vegas.

SIMA. My husband really likes it there too, but he goes there only once in a while. He can't find anyone to go with. I'm not into gambling or drinking or smoking. But he likes them all.

MS. ARJUMAND. Oh, you're married? Where is your husband?

SIMA. He's working. He works at night.

MS. ARJUMAND. How sad! What does he do?

SIMA. He works at a store. He studied agricultural engineering back in Iran, but didn't try to find a job in his field here. And now we are both suffering. He has to go to work at night. So I work during the day. I ask him what kind of life this is—we don't see each other at all. He says we see each other just enough. I took a few days off so that we could be together. You have no idea what he did. He came back from work at nine in the morning and went straight to bed until five in the afternoon. Then he took a shower, had something to eat, and went back to work. He did that for several days. A few weeks later he took some days off and went to San Francisco with his friends.

MS. ARJUMAND. Wow! How about the weekends?

SIMA. His days off are during the week, Tuesday and Thursday.

MS. ARJUMAND. That's awful. You don't see each other at all.

SIMA. As he says, we see each other just enough. I went to a gynecologist, and she asked, "What kind of protection do you use?" I said, "The natural one! We don't touch each other!" It had been nine months since the last time we made love. (*Pause*) I am sorry, I know I shouldn't discuss these kinds of matters.

MS. ARJUMAND. No, dear. This is America, now we let it all hang out. Doesn't matter, dear! Unburden yourself!

SIMA. Anyway, after nine months I complained. But let's move on, I don't wanna talk about him. This is probably why you can't tolerate Iranians. Each of us has a tragic backstory.

MS. ARJUMAND. Ms. Sima, everyone is a tragedy. Doesn't matter if they are Iranians or Americans. We all have the same stories—one's husband is bad, the other's son, one is bankrupt, the other, I don't know, can't sleep at night because of all the injustice in the world. Don't blame yourself! Do you have kids?

SIMA (*avoids answering the question*). You are done with the washer; it's my turn now. I'll use your detergent if you don't mind.

MS. ARJUMAND. Of course, no problem! Take one of these sheets too, whaddya-call-it—the dryer sheets. They are very good.

SIMA. Thanks.

Sima goes to a washing machine and starts dumping her linens in it.

MS. ARJUMAND. Do you know how to play *pasur*?

SIMA. Yes, the Jack game! My mother's uncle used to say it is a game for prostitutes! Sorry.

MS. ARJUMAND. Ms. Sima!

They both laugh.

Camille, a girl in her twenties, wearing a punk outfit and with heavy makeup, enters and heads for the payphone. Nervously, she combs through her big bag, and keeps muttering curse words in English. Finally, she finds a coin and starts dialing.

CAMILLE. Hello. (*Begging*) **Don't hang up . . . Don't. I can't go home. My mom is going to get angry. Where am I supposed to go? Wait a minute.**

(*Silence*)

Please, sweetheart, why, why are you doing this to me? I love you! . . . Shut up shitface, goddamn you! You are an asshole? Yes, I am too, but at least, I am decent enough to admit it.

No, for God's sake, don't hang up the phone.

(*Ms. Arjumand and Sima realize that she is Iranian.*)

Only tonight. I promise to leave tomorrow morning before the **bitch** arrives. I call her whatever I want. **I hate her . . .** No, no, don't hang

FIGURE 26. *Bird of Dawn*. Directed by Hamid Ehya in Berkeley, CA, 1997. *Photograph by Hamid Ehya.*

up. Hello? Hello? (*Forcefully hangs up and screams while crying*) **DAMN! Do you hear me, damn you! . . . God! Help me.**

She digs in her bag again, finds another coin, and dials a number. This time, though, nobody answers. She hangs up, gently sits down, and cries. Ms. Arjumand and Sima look at each other. For Ms. Arjumand, Camille's behavior is inexcusable, but Sima feels sympathy and approaches her.

SIMA. Don't cry, miss! Can I do anything for you?

CAMILLE (*looking at Sima curiously*). **No Thanks.** No one can do anything. I am an idiot.

SIMA. Come on, cheer up! Do you want some water?

CAMILLE. No, thanks. Do you have a cigarette?

SIMA. No, I don't smoke. (*To Ms. Arjumand*) Do you?

MS. ARJUMAND. No, I hate smoking. Although my husband smokes like a chimney.

CAMILLE. **Cool!** You're both Iranians. Is that your mom?

SIMA. No, we've just met.

CAMILLE. Of course. If she was your mom, you would know if she smoked. How **stupid of me! . . . This is weird! Three Iranian women, 3 a.m., in a laundromat!**

SIMA. Let me know if you need anything.

CAMILLE. No thanks. I need to go buy cigarettes.

(*She starts to leave, but thinks of something. Sima and Ms. Arjumand go back to playing card, but keep an eye on Camille, who now approaches Sima.*)

Now that you offered—I mean—could you come with me and knock on someone's door? I mean—how do I say it—my boyfriend doesn't open the door. Maybe he'll open it for you, and then if he does . . .

Silence.

SIMA. Then what? You'll force yourself in? He'll kick you out again.

CAMILLE. Maybe he won't in front of you?

SIMA. Why? Is he trying to keep face with me?

CAMILLE. Well, ask him to open the door and let me in.

SIMA. Why do you think he would listen to me?

CAMILLE. Because he listens to elders.

SIMA. Oh dear, I understand your feelings, but let's say he opened the door and you went in. Then what?

CAMILLE. **OK It seems you are not comfortable—that's cool.**

SIMA. Of course I'm not comfortable with knocking on a stranger's door at 3 a.m. and then the two of us barging in! Besides, I'm sure he doesn't respect elders that much.

CAMILLE. **Cool, cool! Don't do it.**—You just asked if there was anything you could do for me.

SIMA. I meant for you. Like if you want, you can stay the night with me. Something like that.

CAMILLE. No, thanks. I don't need anyone's help. I just want to get into that house. (*Goes toward the payphone; finds another coin in her bag and dials a number*) Hello? Don't hang up . . . Wait . . .

SIMA. Why don't you wait till tomorrow? By then, you'll be less angry.

CAMILLE. **I just can't. I love him.**

(*Ms. Arjumand turns on the cassette player at a lower volume than before.*)

Oh shit, tonight is not my night. Excuse me, could you turn that down?

(*Ms. Arjumand doesn't respond.*)

SIMA. The volume is very low. Besides, if you listen, it will calm you down.

CAMILLE. **No way. I hate it. It makes me gag!**

(*Ms. Arjumand gets angry but doesn't say anything. She takes knitting needles out of her purse and starts knitting. Camille looks at Ms. Arjumand; it seems she is ashamed of her behavior.*)

No hard feeling, OK? It's cool.

MS. ARJUMAND. I don't even understand your language. Please leave me alone. If the music bothers you, I will turn it off.

She turns off the cassette player.

CAMILLE. **Don't take it too hard!**—Don't take it strong![8] I mean . . . Take it easy! Please turn it back on!

Camille goes toward the cassette player to turn it on, but Ms. Arjumand takes it away.

MS. ARJUMAND. Please don't touch it! Leave me alone! As you say, don't **invade** my **space.**

CAMILLE (*goes back.*) **OK, OK**—I did apologize, didn't I?

SIMA. Forgive her, Ms. Arjumand. She is "javan o jahel."

CAMILLE. What do you mean?[9]

---

8 Camille is trying to translate a Persian idiom word for word into English. Realizing that it does not make sense, in her second attempt, she wrongly translates the idiom back to Persian, using an incorrect synonym for the word *sakht*, which means difficult, strong, or hard.

9 Sima uses a common idiom, *javān-o jāhel* [young and ignorant], to explain what she believes to be Camille's misbehavior. *Jāhel* is an old-fashioned word that Camille is not familiar with.

SIMA. "Javan o jahel"—young and naive. (*She laughs; to Camille*) Don't take offense! Naive is not that bad after all; it only means inexperienced.

CAMILLE. **Naive**—yeah, I am very **naive.**

SIMA. It is indeed very strange, three Iranian women, at 3 a.m., on this side of the world in a **laundromat.**

MS. ARJUMAND. There are many Iranians in this area.

CAMILLE. **Ya, we're all lonely!**

MS. ARJUMAND (*now upset*). Ma'am, could you please leave me out of this and stop counting me in? I am not **lonely.**

CAMILLE. Whoever is here at 3 a.m. is **lonely, otherwise** they wouldn't have been here.

SIMA. Ms. Arjumand likes to be by herself. Leave her alone!

CAMILLE (*doubtful*). **Oh ya?! . . . Fine with me.**

MS. ARJUMAND (*begins to gather her belongings*). What a miserable life!

SIMA. Where are you going, Ms. Arjumand? Your clothes are not dry yet. Don't get upset.

CAMILLE. **Hey, cool it!**—I said I was fucking sorry.

MS. ARJUMAND. Please watch your language!

CAMILLE. That's all I needed! What's wrong with you? I am upset enough. Leave me alone, for God's sake!

SIMA. Well, it's late. We're all tired. It's 3:30.

CAMILLE. By the way, what did you say you were doing here at this time of the night?

SIMA. You mean this time of the morning.

MS. ARJUMAND (*sarcastic*) No one has kicked *us* out of our homes!

CAMILLE (*distressed*). This is cruel! **You are so cruel! What's your problem?**

MS. ARJUMAND. My problem is none of your business.

SIMA (*changing the subject*). Please, enough. (*To Camille*) My name is Sima, and this is Ms. Arjumand. What's your name?

MS. ARJUMAND. There is no reason to introduce me to her.

CAMILLE (*looks at Ms. Arjumand with indifference*). My name is Camelia. They call me Camille.

SIMA. Are you mixed?

CAMILLE. Mixed? (*At first she doesn't understand*) Oh, no, my parents are both Iranian. But they named me Camelia.

SIMA. What an interesting name! Your personality also reminds me of the movie, *Camille Claudel*. Have you seen it?

CAMILLE. Yeah, good film.

SIMA. How about you, Ms. Arjumand? Have you seen the film?

MS. ARJUMAND. No.

SIMA. It's the story of a woman sculptor who is very talented. She gets to know Rodin, the famous French sculptor, and they fall in love. Long story short: after an unforgettable experience, Camille Claudel wants Rodin to come and live with her, but Rodin, who was with another woman before—I don't know if she was his wife or not—anyway he had lived with her for years, and he doesn't accept Camille's offer to live together.

(*Ms. Arjumand's knitting yarn falls from the table. Camille rises, picks it up, and gives it to Ms. Arjumand. Sima and Ms. Arjumand look at each other. Ms. Arjumand smiles.*)

The other woman wasn't an artist or anything. Rodin says, I have been with this woman for years and I'm not gonna leave her. He says very beautifully to Camille Claudel that this woman only has him in the world. But Camille Claudel goes mad. The poor thing goes to Rodin's place at night, begging and cursing him. She was deeply in love—it was a tear-jerker. I cried the whole film—in the end, she dies of a broken heart.

MS. ARJUMAND (*while knitting, calmly*). Her own damn fault!

SIMA. Whose?

MS. ARJUMAND. This lady *Coude* you mentioned. She shouldn't have had a relationship with a married man. Why didn't you feel bad for the wife who wasn't an artist? I really like this guy Rodin. It shows that you can find decent men even in France!

CAMILLE. It's love, ma'am!

MS. ARJUMAND. Come on, what the hell is love?! These are excuses for selfishness. Ms. Sima, did this Ms. Coude know about Mr. Rodin's wife or not?

SIMA. Claudel. Yes, the wife even came after her one time and they had a good fight over Rodin. But you know, the heart wants what the heart wants!

MS. ARJUMAND. What do you mean "what the heart wants"? Come on, people do all sorts of filthy things and then say what the heart wants! How about character? Humanity? Decency and loyalty? Has the statute of limitations passed on those? No, you see, if a man does something bad, we all say men are bastards. But for each bastard man, there is an indecent woman co-conspirator, right? You see, we women are to blame as well.

SIMA. You are right! Believe me, no one understands what you say more than me. But sometimes, it is the heart's work, especially with this poor thing who went mad.

MS. ARJUMAND. No, this woman would have gone mad anyway, if not for this, then perhaps from something else. I should also say, how dare Mr. Rodin pursue her in the first place? But God bless him for not leaving his wife!

SIMA. I am not sure if it is a good idea to stay together only out of pity.

CAMILLE. That's why I hate marriage. It is always by force! Being together by force is wrong.

MS. ARJUMAND. Well, well, well, you are so good at prescribing! Why don't you diagnose yourself? Right now you wanna go to your Mr. Boyfriend's house, or whoever you called, by force! Yet you say that forcing things is wrong? Marriage is wrong? And so forth?

CAMILLE. Yeah, but this is different. I am in love with him.

MS. ARJUMAND. Ms. Camille, who says there is no love in marriage? In the fifty years of my married life, I've always been in love with my husband. And the same goes for him. We'd die for each other. We've always respected each other. I remember when my daughter was disrespectful to me, he yelled at her, "Don't you remember how we went through thick and thin to send you to America? You forced us to come here. We came over here because you guys insisted that the entire family should be together. You invited us to live with you." My daughter didn't even raise her head. I swear to God I was worried that he was going to have a heart attack. But he was very strong. As tough as nails! And then he told her, "Don't you dare think that we are your slaves or that we need you! We can stand on our feet here too. We are as good here as we were there. I swear to God I will never forgive you." And then he looked at me and said, "Parvin, we will get our own apartment this week. You are in safe hands." At the age of sixty-five, he went to an Iranian supermarket, and started working in the produce section, for five dollars an hour!

FIGURE 27. *Bird of Dawn*. Directed by Hamid Ehya in Berkeley, CA, 1997. *Photograph by Hamid Ehya.*

(*Softly to herself*) So that he could take care of me . . . I told him, "My dear, after all those years of living decently, I don't want to see you weighing people's potatoes and onions." You know what he said, Ms. Camille? He said, "Parvin, I'd do anything for you!! Even one strand of your hair makes it worth it to me. There is no shame in earning an honest living. Work is work!"

CAMILLE. So now your husband—I mean—**he passed away?**

Ms. Arjumand looks at Camille. Sima, worrying that they might pick a fight again, interferes.

SIMA. Her husband is on a trip.

CAMILLE. Oh, **sorry.** I am, well, young and, as Ms. Sima said, *jakel.*[10]

Sima laughs. Ms. Arjumand can't help smiling either; she is now nicer to Camille.

MS. ARJUMAND. No dear, it's *jāhel*—comes from *jahl*, meaning ignorance. But Ms. Sima didn't mean it that way. She meant naivety.

CAMILLE. Naivety, yes like **inexperienced.** But I mean ignorance is more suited to me than naivety. Unfortunately, I've had a lot of experience in relationships. But I am very **naive**. Whenever I see someone, I wanna stay with him and marry him. But I don't know why they leave me after a while. They say it was all **physical**, and then go with somebody else!

MS. ARJUMAND. Because you should have more respect for yourself. Mashallah,[11] there is nothing wrong with you. You're such a beautiful girl. When you walked in, I thought you were one of those spoiled and misbehaved kids, but even within these few minutes that I saw you, I realized that you're very kind-hearted. Dear, don't beg! It's not befitting. To hell with him if he doesn't want you! He doesn't deserve you! Look dear, if you want people to respect you, the first step is for you to respect yourself. It doesn't matter if it's your child, your husband, or whoever, they'd only respect you when you gain their respect.

SIMA. Yeah, why do you belittle yourself for no reason?

CAMILLE. I know, you're right—how about you? Are you married too?

---

10 Having just learned the word *jāhel*, Camille mispronounces it.

11 An Arabic phrase that literally means "whatever God wills." In Persian, it is used as a blessing to protect someone from the evil eye.

SIMA. Yes, but my experience is completely different from that of Ms. Arjumand. It's more like your idea of marriage.

CAMILLE. How so?

SIMA. Well, it's a long story.

CAMILLE (*ashamed that she can't control herself*). I know both of you think I am stupid and lack character, but I have to go to him tonight to explain something. **I have to tell him, one more time!** (*Goes to the payphone and dials the number*) Typically, he eventually answers and lets me go see him. (*Waiting for him to answer*) No matter who he goes with, he always comes back to me. It's been three years that we have been together. He knows very well no woman takes his **shit** as much as I do.

(*Sima and Ms. Arjumand look at each other and shake their heads.*)

Answer! For God's sake, answer!

Pause; Camille hangs up.

SIMA. Maybe he turned off his phone and went to bed. It's 4 a.m. Wait till the morning and call him again.

CAMILLE (*anxious and impatient like an addict*). No, he's waiting for a phone call from that **bitch.** I think they have a mutual arrangement—like, call two times, then hang up, and call again. Shit like that. She even calls when I'm at his place. **Oh my God! You should see the bitch!** You don't believe me, this woman was my friend. They met each other through me. I opened my heart to her and told her about my miseries. She **pretended** that she was my friend. I should have known when she said, "Oh, your boyfriend is so **cute**!"

SIMA. That's usually how it happens. It's less common for some stranger off the street to be the home-wrecker. It's usually those people closest to you.

CAMILLE. Do you have children?

SIMA. No, unfortunately. Or fortunately!

CAMILLE. Ms. Arjumand, how about you?

MS. ARJUMAND. Yes, a daughter and a son.

CAMILLE. How old? I mean, are they younger than me or older?

MS. ARJUMAND. Much older than you. They are about the same age as Ms. Sima. Thirty-five and forty.

CAMILLE. Are you close to them?

MS. ARJUMAND. No. They are busy with their own lives. I don't expect anything either. I've learned over the years not to expect anything from anyone.

SIMA. That's so sad. One works hard to bring up children. It'd be so bad if they don't attend to their parents. Are they in the same city?

MS. ARJUMAND. Yes, in the same area. But their financial situations are much better than ours, so they live in upscale neighborhoods.

SIMA. How strange! But you should be grateful that your husband is a decent person. (*To Camille*) Before you walked in, I was telling the story of my husband. He works at night, and I work during the day. Anyway, we don't see much of each other. Some time ago, he had a night **off, and** I told him, "Let's go out for dinner tonight." He said, "I have one night **off** and I wanna have fun, I'm going out with my friends." Then he put on his clothes and left. In the morning, I found a match box in his pocket from one of these Iranian cabarets. He went there to see one of these trashy singers.

CAMILLE. What a jerk! . . . oops, I'm sorry.

SIMA. Exactly. A **jerk** in the true sense of the word. But that's not even the whole story. I told him, "How about our relationship?" He said, "What? What do you mean?" I said, "But we never see each other."

He said, "How is it my fault that you have no kids to keep you busy? All women are busy bringing up kids, and they don't get on their husbands' nerves. You make me antsy. Go to the movies, find some friends! Find a way to keep yourself busy!" Stupid me, I thought, well, he is right, it is my fault that I don't know how to keep myself busy. It had been nine months that we hadn't touched each other. When I complained, he said, "This is a phase and it will pass. Give me some time, you have become something sacred for me, like my mother and sister." I was so furious . . . ! A few weeks after that conversation, I realized where the mother and sister business came from. We were having dinner, he was home, and I had set such a lovely table! I had been working for four days to prepare for that and wanted to **impress** him. Out of the blue, he said, "Sima, what do you think about an open relationship?" I just burst into tears.

CAMILLE. **I've heard that before!**—Open relationship—**Shit!**

SIMA. I wiped away my tears and said, "You mean we see different people?" He said, "Yes." I said, "How come? Do you have someone in mind?" He said, "No—just saying." I said, "I am not that type of person—if you want a divorce, just be honest." Then, crying my eyes out, I said, "After nine months of not having any relationship, how dare you say such a thing?" He got upset, grabbed his coat, and said, "You don't even let me eat in peace here. Why are you being so hysterical? I just made a suggestion—you're fucking with my mind!" He then slammed the door and left. I realized he is after his "open relationship." I put on my clothes and went to the same cabaret that I found the matches from in his pocket—he was sitting there with a woman. I went closer and realized that I know the woman. My eyes went blank. I was about to faint. It was my own friend, Laleh. It had been a while since I saw her. I felt such hatred for both of them. I had opened my heart to that bitch. No wonder she used to call every minute asking, "Sima dear, what else is new?" I went to them and said hi. They both froze. I said, "You're really a pair of assholes, how dare you?" Laleh kept silent. My husband got up and said, "What are you doing here? Go home, I'll come back and we'll talk." I couldn't hear anything anymore. I slapped him hard right in the face, and knocked over their table like in the movies. And then I ran out of the cabaret, crying. I came home, packed all of his stuff into two suitcases, and put them by the door. Then I sat on the bed, staring at the wall. After two hours, he came home. He said "Sima, I . . . " and I didn't let him finish. I said, "Your suitcases are by the door. Laleh's house is large and has enough room." He said "I . . . " but I said, "Please go and never have anything to do with me anymore." It was the first time I saw him crying. He picked up his suitcases and came to kiss me. I didn't even look at him. He turned away to leave when he saw our wedding picture. Can you believe that? He reached to take the picture with him and I jumped and grabbed it from his hands. I said, "No, no, this is not yours." And then I hugged the picture and sat down right there. When he was leaving, he said, "Forgive me, Sima. I love you." It was so strange—it had been years since I was that emotional. Later I heard that he broke up with Laleh too. She sent a card and apologized. You should have seen the card. (*She breaks down in tears*) It's been four months since then. I hadn't washed the sheets all these four months so that his scent would stay with me. But tonight, at 1 a.m., I got up and decided to wash them. To wash his memory off my mind. It's about time. Everything is over and I should accept things. That's why I am here at this time of the night.

She wipes off her tears, overwhelmed with sadness.

FIGURE 28. *Bird of Dawn*. Directed by Hamid Ehya in Berkeley, CA, 1997. *Photograph by Hamid Ehya.*

MS. ARJUMAND. Don't cry, dear! It's not worth it for such a nice girl like you. They will get what they deserve.

CAMILLE. No, Ms. Arjumand. **I don't think so.**

MS. ARJUMAND. Yes dear, **think so.** They will. They have already. Come, let's play a game of *pasur*! Fortune-telling with cards is for when you're alone. Thank God I am not alone tonight. (*To Sima*) Come, don't think about it! You're still young and beautiful. You'll move on. There are lots of men for you. Good men. That bastard didn't deserve you.

CAMILLE. Where are these good men? I have not met even one!

MS. ARJUMAND. You will find them. Come now, let's play *pasur*!

CAMILLE. What's *pasur*?

SIMA. The game where the cards have to add up to eleven.

CAMILLE. Oh yeah—**cool,** the one where **clubs** are important and the Jack beats them all?

SIMA. Yes, so you know how to play.

CAMILLE. Yeah, my grandmother taught me. By the way, Ms. Arjumand, you remind me of her. She always told fortunes with cards too, but you are so **cool**.

MS. ARJUMAND. I'll shuffle.

They all sit around the table.

CAMILLE. Ms. Arjumand, why are you here at this time of the night?

SIMA. Her husband is traveling . . .

MS. ARJUMAND (*cutting Sima off*). No Ms. Sima, he's not traveling . . . (*To Camille*) You're very smart, why do you think I came here?

CAMILLE. Honestly, I thought . . . your husband . . . (*She pauses.*)

MS. ARJUMAND. Yes dear, you are right . . . I am also alone . . . My husband has gone on a trip—the final trip—tonight is his anniversary. I had kept his clothes and I used to smell them. But tonight I decided to accept reality. I wanted to come here, listen to the song we both loved, and in silence, make plans for my future (which is not that long after all). All this time, I wanted God to take me where he is. But tonight, I decided to live the rest of my life. I was still doubtful, but after seeing you two, I am certain now. Yes, I want to live out the rest of my life. I think this is what he wanted too—to take care of me.

SIMA. I'm so sorry, I didn't know at all. I'm sorry that I kept asking questions and disturbed you. I'm so sorry, I don't know what to say!

CAMILLE. Me neither.

MS. ARJUMAND. You didn't disturb me at all. I am so happy to have met you. I think it was kind of *ghesmat* to meet each other here.

CAMILLE. It was what?

SIMA. *Ghesmat*, it means **destiny.**[12]

CAMILLE. **Maybe!** You remind me of Iran. Of my grandmother who used to play cards with me and eat nuts.

MS. ARJUMAND. How old were you when you came here?

CAMILLE. Seven. I was a kid.

SIMA. Good for you! I was twenty-something when I came here. I left a lot of things back there—memories—I wish I could wash them off with these sheets!

MS. ARJUMAND. Ms. Sima, when you say stuff like that, what should I say then? Are your families here?

---

12 *Ghesmat* or *qesmat*, a common belief among Iranians, refers to the idea that one's fate is pre-ordained and unavoidable.

CAMILLE. Aha. All my family is **practically** here.

SIMA. My parents and my siblings are in Iran. I wish they were all here.

MS. ARJUMAND. Don't wish for those things! Leave them alone! Let them live their lives. Since my husband passed, my kids were around for only two weeks. But since then, my son calls once in a while, and my daughter keeps saying, "Mom, I'm busy—I will come and see you as soon as I can." I don't complain. People are busy here!

SIMA. I'm not like that, Ms. Arjumand. I love my parents. If they come to America, they should definitely live with me. Just imagine how things would be different if they were here.

CAMILLE. My mom and dad are here, but they are only **trouble. You see, you never know!** I am so sorry, I know you think I am so stupid, but I should call him again.

MS. ARJUMAND. Yeah, he might answer your call now!

SIMA. When I'm done here, I can come with you if you want.

MS. ARJUMAND. I might come too. Maybe he'll see my gray hair and open the door out of respect.

CAMILLE. He doesn't understand respect and things like that. He even curses his own mother. (*She approaches the payphone but hesitates.*) But you were kidding, right?! Are you really willing to come with me?

MS. ARJUMAND. Yes, it's like an adventure. It will keep me busy. I really want to see the face of this guy who you'd die for.

CAMILLE. I'm sure you'd be **disappointed.** He's not handsome.

MS. ARJUMAND. He's not handsome, or well-mannered. Then what do you see in him?

SIMA. Ms. Arjumand, the heart wants what the heart wants.

MS. ARJUMAND. What does that even mean? I don't understand, why can't the heart want someone decent?!

CAMILLE. I have yet to meet someone decent.

MS. ARJUMAND. You're very young now. Know your worth.

Camille goes to the phone. She waits a bit, but doesn't dial a number, and comes back to the table. Sima and Ms. Arjumand look at her with surprise and admiration.

SIMA. Let's all go to my house. No one's there. We'll make breakfast and take a nap—Let's just be together!

MS. ARJUMAND. You are so kind. For now, we are already together!

SIMA. Such a great night! I didn't expect it to turn out this way.

MS. ARJUMAND. Me neither.

CAMILLE. Me neither. I thought I'd go buy cigarettes somewhere, then I would sit in the car, smoke, listen to music, and cry. By the way, Ms. Arjumand, could you please turn on your music? **I mean it**—I really liked it. Also, you speak very good English.

MS. ARJUMAND. I was an English teacher in a high school in Iran.

She turns on the cassette player.

CAMILLE. Is this old?

SIMA. Yeah, very old.

CAMILLE. I kind of like it.—To be honest, I really don't like Persian music, I mean this—(*She imitates traditional Persian vocal forms*)[13]

SIMA. But this "Bird of Dawn" is something else!

MS. ARJUMAND. This is a song for all of us!

---

13 *Tahrir*, a stylized use of vibrato, is a form of oscillation in pitch common in Persian vocal music.

Camille calls again. This time someone answers.

CAMILLE. Hello? Are you home? Aha, me, no, I'm at the **laundromat—It's OK I know . . .** —Yeah I'm fine—**OK—OK—Bye**

She hangs up. Sima and Ms. Arjumand look at her with curiosity.

SIMA. Well, what did he say?

CAMILLE. He said "**I'm sorry.**" He then said, "**Nobody can replace you.**"—He said, "Hurry up and come back home."

MS. ARJUMAND. What are you waiting for then?

Camille pauses, then takes off her coat.

CAMILLE. Do you guys still have time to play a few hands of *pasur*?

Ms. Arjumand looks at Sima and Sima at Camille; they all exchange smiles.

MS. ARJUMAND. Yes, we do—don't we, Ms. Sima?

SIMA. Of course!

CAMILLE. **This is so cool!**

They all sit around the table. Ms. Arjumand shuffles and deals the cards. "Bird of Dawn" gets louder and lights fade.